THE FEMINIST READER

The Feminist Reader

Essays in Gender and the Politics of Literary Criticism

EDITED BY CATHERINE BELSEY and
JANE MOORE

First published 1989

Published in the USA by
Basil Blackwell, New York

Printed in Hong Kong

Library of Congress Cataloging in Publication Data
The Feminist reader.
   Bibliography: p.
   Includes index.
   1. Feminist literary criticism.   2. Feminism and
literature.   I. Belsey, Catherine.   II. Moore, Jane,
1962–
PN98.W64F46   1989   809   88–7756
ISBN 1–55786–045–9
ISBN 1–55786–046–7 (pbk.)

TO OUR PARENTS

Contents

viii   *Contents*

Preface

The aim of this anthology is to make available to the feminist reader a collection of essays which does justice to the range and diversity, as well as to the eloquence and the challenge of recent feminist critical theory and practice. The idea of the book arose directly from our experience of teaching feminist criticism. Existing anthologies, though excellent in many ways, seemed to us to be composed on too narrow a basis to display the difference within feminism and the debates which are the evidence of its continuing vitality. But we felt that we could not reasonably ask our students, with their shrinking resources, to buy several collections. This book is offered as a solution to that problem.

The anthology begins, therefore, at the point a great many feminist readers start from, a feeling of outrage at the patriarchal nature of the canon and the relative exclusion of women from literary history. It goes on to consider the implications of this. Is writing by women necessarily feminist? What kind of literary history would serve the needs of feminism? Is there a women's language?

The essays, in other words, either implicitly or explicitly, enter into a kind of dialogue with each other, enlisting the reader in a developing debate. The diversity of feminism thus appears as the effect of a continuing discussion, and not simply as a range of distinct and static points of view.

Some of the available positions are difficult to grasp, at least in the first instance, because of their unfamiliarity. We have done our best to make them accessible without intruding between the reader and the essays themselves. The Introduction offers a very general map of the field of feminist critical theory. In addition, before the author's Notes on each essay we have offered a Summary of the essay's main propositions. We have also added a Glossary of terms which may be unfamiliar to readers not already acquainted with poststructuralist varieties of feminism. And finally, we offer annotated Suggestions for Further Reading, in a bibliography which sets out to be selective rather than comprehensive. The project of all this is to facilitate discussion of the questions the essays raise, the issues which seem to us to matter to the feminist reader.

No feminist critic ever works alone. We are grateful to friends, colleagues and students who have shared our feminist commitment and discussed questions of criticism with us. The contributors have been a pleasure to work with. And we should like to thank in particular Andrew Belsey, Moira Eminton, Chris Evans, Kate McGowan, Susan Moore, Beverley Tarquini and Chris Weedon for their help and support.

Catherine Belsey
Jane Moore

Acknowledgements

We are grateful to the publishers for permission to reprint the following material: Associated Book Publishers (UK) Ltd. for extracts from Dale Spender, *Mothers of the Novel*. Grafton Books for an extract from Rosalind Coward, *Female Desire: Women's Sexuality Today*. Croom Helm Ltd for Mary Jacobus's essay from *Women Writing and Writing about Women*. Johns Hopkins University Press for Sandra M. Gilbert and Susan Gubar, 'Sexual Linguistics: Gender, Language, Sexuality'; and Shoshana Felman, 'Women and Madness: the Critical Phallacy'. University of Minnesota Press and Manchester University Press for Hélène Cixous, extracts from *The Newly Born Woman*. Batsford, and Littlefield, Adams and Co. for extracts from Toril Moi's essay in *Modern Literary Theory*. The University of Chicago Press for extracts from Gayatri Chakravorty Spivak, 'Three Women's Texts and a Critique of Imperialism'; and Julia Kristeva, 'Women's Time.' Full bibliographical details of each essay are given in the Notes.

1 Introduction: The Story So Far

Catherine Belsey and Jane Moore

The feminist reader is enlisted in the process of changing the gender relations which prevail in our society, and she regards the practice of reading as one of the sites in the struggle for change.

For the feminist reader there is no innocent or neutral approach to literature: all interpretation is political. Specific ways of reading inevitably militate for or against the process of change. To interpret a work is always to address, whether explicitly or implicitly, certain kinds of issues about what it says. The feminist reader might ask, among other questions, how the text represents women, what it says about gender relations, how it defines sexual difference. (A few texts, of course, do not depict any women at all, and say nothing about gender relations, and from a feminist point of view that too signifies.) A criticism which ignores these issues implies that they do not matter.

A feminist does not necessarily read in order to praise or to blame, to judge or to censor. More commonly she sets out to assess how the text invites its readers, as members of a specific culture, to understand what it means to be a woman or a man, and so encourages them to reaffirm or to challenge existing cultural norms.

Feminist criticism has in a sense no beginnings. When in the seventeenth century Esther Sowernam and Bathsua Makin pointed out that many classical texts identified powerful deities and influential muses as women, they were reading from a feminist perspective. When Mary Wollstonecraft at the end of the eighteenth century argued that sentimental novels encouraged women to see themselves as helpless and silly, she was practising a form of feminist criticism. Indeed, Wollstonecraft contributed to a feminist anthology of sorts called *The Female Reader*.[1] Two of the most distinguished feminist readers of the twentieth century were Virginia Woolf in *A Room of One's Own* and Simone de Beauvoir in *The Second Sex*.

Nevertheless, the politics of gender entered a new phase in the late 1960s, and since that time feminist criticism has been developed, debated, institutionalised and diversified as never before. In 1970 three revolutionary books appeared within a few months of each other. Germaine Greer's *The Female Eunuch*, Kate Millett's *Sexual Politics* and *Patriarchal Attitudes* by Eva Figes were all bestsellers. They were witty, eloquent, wide-ranging and polemical, and they caught and crystallised a moment when the challenges of the sixties to a range of existing authorities had given a new impetus to the politics of liberation. These three works, and others like them, did much to define an agenda for a new, self-conscious phase of feminist reading.

It is a striking feature of all three books that when they discuss literature they refuse to isolate it from the culture of which it forms a part. Indeed, they are not primarily works of literary criticism at all in the conventional sense of that term. Figes considers the Brontës and George Eliot in the context of the restricted range of possibilities for women in the nineteenth century. Greer analyses Shakespeare's plays to find in them a depiction of love and marriage new in the sixteenth century, when romantic love became the basis of marriage as partnership, and the nuclear family emerged as the main unit of a developing consumerism. Millett's denunciation of the Lawrentian idealisation of the phallus – unforgettably entertaining, and probably unsurpassed, however much more complex feminist criticism has since become – is part of a generalised analysis of sexual power relations in a range of texts, not all of them fictional. Millett herself draws attention to the nature of her book as 'something of an anomaly, a hybrid, possibly a new mutation altogether'.[2] Greer makes no apology for discussing literature alongside popular culture: she simply points to the parallels between

D. H. Lawrence and Barbara Cartland, and leaves it at that.

The challenge to traditional literary criticism was in this respect extremely radical. 'Art' was no longer a cover for politics; 'literature' ceased to be a special category, a repository of timeless truths concerning an eternal human nature; and 'great authors' could get it wrong. The works on the syllabus, it appeared, were not necessarily neutral, not simply depictions of reality, but interpretations of the world, and some of them presented women in trivialising or degrading ways. Writing was a cultural rather than a purely individual phenomenon, and the social context of literature was more than an explanatory 'background'. Fiction, it seemed, both manifested and influenced the ways in which societies understood themselves and the world. Literature was in this sense profoundly historical.

History itself has always been important to feminism, because it is history which provides us with evidence that things have changed. And if they have changed in the past, they do not have to stay as they are now. 'Nature', on the other hand, has long been one of the most powerful weapons in the war against change. If women are passive, helpless and subservient by nature, then feminism is already a lost cause: we shall inevitably revert to type as soon as the present moment of rebellion comes to an end. If men have always been more rational, more judicious, more authoritative, patriarchy is a fact of nature, and women might as well lie back and enjoy it. But feminist history shows some cultures as more patriarchal than others. Greer traces the emerging tyranny of the nuclear family; Figes sees male domination increasing from the Middle Ages onwards, reaching its highest point in the Victorian period, when women were most enthusiastically idealised and most thoroughly subordinated.

And feminism too has its history. Millett traces the development of women's resistance to patriarchy during the epoch of their deepest oppression. The official inauguration of the Women's Movement in America took place in 1848. The degree and the effectiveness of patriarchal control seem to have varied from one historical moment to another.

It follows that gender relations have more to do with custom than with nature. 'Women', as Eva Figes puts it, 'have been largely man-made'.[3] Feminist cultural history emphasises the ways in which social convention has tended to operate on behalf of the dominant group, and norms of femininity have worked in the interests of men.

It comes as something of a shock to encounter 'he' as the generalised pronoun in these books published in 1970, though even at that stage a certain unease was beginning to be evident about what feminists have since called he-man language. Germaine Greer drew attention to the wide range of abusive terms applicable solely to women. Figes exploited the ambiguity of 'man'. But when, ten years later, Dale Spender published *Man Made Language*, the title drew explicit attention to the patriarchal implications of the supposedly gender–neutral term. The human race, it implied, was male, and if women were included, it was on condition that, linguistically at least, they were neither seen nor heard.

By this time a good deal of work had been done on language from a feminist point of view, and feminists were becoming aware that it was only women who were likely to chatter, gossip, tittle-tattle, whine, nag or bitch. On the other hand, only men could be virile and potent: there were no female equivalents for these terms of praise. Powerful creatures that they are, men conventionally perform the sexual act, while women are merely involved in sexual relationships. Men, but not women, are entitled to be aggressive or, better, abrasive, and women who protest about it are inclined to be shrill or, worse, strident. But then none of this should surprise us, in view of the asymmetries that have developed between masters and mistresses, wizards and witches, governors and governesses, knights and dames. In each case the word for women has negative meanings or connotations, while the male term consistently implies authority.

As Spender points out, these binary oppositions, in which one pole is privileged over the other, are 'fundamental premises in an order based on the supremacy of one group over another'.[4] Language does not merely name male superiority: it produces it. The tendency of words to seem transparent, to appear simply to label a pre-existing reality, indicated to feminists the crucial role of language in the construction of a world picture which legitimates the existing patriarchal order.

Meanings, it became clear, are cultural, and are learned, though we learn them so young that they seem to be there by nature.

It was a common theme of feminists of the early seventies that the patriarchy they denounced was reinforced by psychoanalysis. Freud, they maintained, was an arch-misogynist, and the role of the psychoanalytic institution was to reinstate within the patriarchal order women whose symptoms showed evidence of rebellion against it. Kate Millett's account is the most detailed, and probably the hardest to resist. In her analysis Freud, who evidently felt threatened by them, set out to disarm the feminists by invoking the concept of penis-envy. The little girl, he argued, glimpsing the penis of the little boy, instantly recognises her own inadequacy. As she matures, she becomes reconciled to her inevitable condition of inferiority, and learns to replace the desire for a penis with the wish for a baby. Motherhood is thus 'really' a manifestation of the desire to be a man. If, on the other hand, the little girl fails to mature adequately, she continues to pursue masculine aims: she seeks independence, competes with men and becomes a feminist – or a neurotic. In either case, it is well known that women in general are prone to feelings of insecurity and jealousy; they have a reduced sense of justice, a less developed commitment to moral principles than men; and they are more commonly motivated by feelings than by reason. In his early work Freud made some allowances for the role of culture in what he observed, but as time went on he attributed it increasingly to nature.

Millett engagingly ridicules all this and, temporarily at least, renders Freud quite as unreadable, as impossible for feminists as Lawrence. But the position did not long go uncontested. In 1974 Juliet Mitchell published *Psychoanalysis and Feminism*, arguing that Freud's pessimistic account of women was indeed a description of a particular culture, and not an interpretation of a universal human nature. Only the structures psychoanalysis identifies, and not their content, are in Mitchell's reading universal. What is radical for feminism in Freud is the theory of undifferentiated infant sexuality: the initial object of desire for little girls as well as little boys is the mother. The Oedipus complex represents the entry into a specific culture and thus into the gender roles defined by that culture. Psychoanalysis, Mitchell urges, explains how we acquire sexual identity by repressing desires which are culturally unacceptable; it does not require us to believe that sexual identity is synonymous with anatomy.

Mitchell's reading of Freud owes something to the work of Jacques Lacan, who reread Freud in the light of Saussure's account of the nature of language. Jacqueline Rose, who has worked with Juliet Mitchell, also draws on Lacan to take Mitchell's position a stage further. Rose argues that psychoanalysis is indispensable to feminism, on the basis that it provides a theory of sexual identity as culturally enjoined and constantly resisted. The complexity of undifferentiated sexual desire is repressed when the child learns to identify itself as either masculine or feminine. Anatomy is not the source of sexual difference, but its reductive *figure*, its representation. But for these reasons the identification required by culture can never be complete. What is radical in Freud is the concept of the unconscious, that 'other scene', as Lacan calls it, which challenges and resists the cultural norms imposed on it. Femininity is never achieved; the unconscious refuses to submit to what Lacan calls the symbolic order, the discipline of language and culture. At this ultimate level, in other words, we reject the Law of the Father, the symbolic order of a patriarchal society.

> Feminism's affinity with psychoanalysis rests above all, I would argue, with this recognition that there is a resistance to identity at the very heart of psychic life. Viewed in this way, psychoanalysis . . . becomes one of the few places in our culture where it is recognised as more than a fact of individual pathology that most women do not painlessly slip into their roles as women, if indeed they do at all.[5]

And Rose goes on in the same volume to bring psychoanalysis and feminism to bear on George Eliot and *Hamlet*.

The disagreement about psychoanalysis within feminism has tended to be perceived as a conflict over the *truth* of Freud's texts. One side or the other, it was assumed, must have got it wrong, failed to grasp the key meanings of his writings or distorted his views. But there is no need to understand the debate in this way. Even in this very simplified summary of representative positions, it is possible to see that Millett on the one hand, and Mitchell and Rose on the other, are implicitly asking different questions about psychoanalysis. Millett asks, 'how has psychoanalysis contributed to the oppression of women?' Mitchell and Rose ask, 'how could psychoanalysis be read as an explanation of the oppression of women?' The different questions elicit different answers. Millett looks for evidence of patriarchal assumptions, and finds penis-envy. Mitchell and Rose look for explanatory terms, and find undifferentiated infant sexuality and unconscious resistance.

Freud's texts are increasingly misogynistic; psychoanalysis can be appropriated in the interests of feminism. These statements are not contradictory. The debate throws into relief something that feminists had known all along in practice, if not in theory. The texts of psychoanalysis, like all writings, and like culture itself, are plural: different approaches produce different readings. The practice of interpretation is not neutral, but takes place from a specific perspective. In this instance, one approach is not more feminist than the other. The difference is that Millett is concerned with the way patriarchy victimises women, while Mitchell and Rose are concerned with evidence that the victims of patriarchy are in a position to strike back.

In a similar way, a second current of feminist literary criticism grew up alongside and in response to the analysis of patriarchal culture. This was concerned with women's writing, and specifically with writing as a mode of resistance. Kate Millett, denouncing patriarchy, necessarily attended most carefully to writing by men. In what Elaine Showalter inventively terms 'gynocritics', the study of woman as writer, women are invited to speak for themselves, even if they continue to do so from within a patriarchal culture.[6] Showalter's eminently readable and excellently documented book, *A Literature of Their Own*, published in 1977, is perhaps the most influential of the accounts of women's writing in its difference from men's. Showalter identifies a female subculture in which fiction by women constitutes a record of their experience. She defines three separate but overlapping phases, 'feminine', 'feminist' and 'female'. In the first of these, from the 1840s to 1880, women wrote mainly in imitation of masculine models, but with distinctively feminine concerns; in the second phase, which lasted until 1920, they formulated specifically feminist protests and demands; and in the third, from 1920 to the present, women's writing moves increasingly towards self-discovery, the exploration of an inner space of female experience.

Though she takes Freud for granted, Showalter explicitly repudiates literary theory. In *The Madwoman in the Attic* (1979), their expansive analysis of Victorian women's writing, Sandra Gilbert and Susan Gubar present women's resistance to social and literary constraint in terms of a theory of the anxiety of patriarchal influence. Appropriating for feminism Harold Bloom's model of the writer struggling to overthrow the domination of a strong literary father, Gilbert and Gubar trace in women's writing the inscription of tension, self-doubt, renunciation and, above all, rage against the society which confines them.

Paradoxically, however, it was Ellen Moers's *Literary Women*, published in 1976, apparently less scholarly and more popular than either Showalter's book or Gilbert and Gubar's, which in the event broke most radically with the assumptions of conventional criticism. Moers reinstates the by now traditional feminist interest in literature as an aspect of the whole culture. *Literary Women* is a contribution to cultural history in its analysis of the way that the exclusion of women from so many aspects of social and political life was precisely what propelled them into a form of utterance requiring no formal professional training and no special equipment. It was possible for women to write – in the middle of the night if necessary – and by this means to make money, especially to make the capital sums which would render them marriageable. Not simply a lonely struggle against patriarchy, women's writing in the eighteenth and nineteenth centuries also appears in *Literary Women* as one of patriarchy's unintended consequences. The evidence is presented in snatches of biography, but the mode of reading in *Literary Women*, though sometimes artlessly biographical, is often compelled by the nature of the material it confronts to break with the assumption that writing is a simple transcription of experience. In discussing the love poetry of so many nineteenth-century virgin poets, Moers takes into account the degree to which poetry is a form of fiction. And her analysis of Ann Radcliffe's Gothic fantasies, travel stories about capable heroines, and thus feminine equivalents of the contemporary picaresque tradition, implicitly acknowledges the degree to which fiction is the effect not only of experience but of other fiction. Perhaps inadvertently, but none the less effectively, *Literary Women* throws into relief the limited explanatory power of traditional literary history.[7]

Gynocritics also has the effect of challenging conventional critical value judgments. It has drawn attention to the work of a great many women writers whose work has been forgotten or suppressed, among them Mary Brunton, who made Jane Austen nervous because she was so clever. 'Who,' asks Ellen Moers ironically, 'wants to associate the great Jane Austen, companion of Shakespeare, with someone named Mary Brunton? Who wants to read or indeed can find a copy of *Self-Control* (1810) by that lady . . .?'[8] Within ten years of the question, however, Mary Brunton and a number of her contemporaries were to become available in paperback in the series *Mothers of the Novel*, edited by Dale Spender.

These different modes of feminist criticism, the denunciation of patriarchy on the one hand, and the study of women's writing on the other, have often been presented as rival approaches, each competing to be more politically correct than the other. It is not necessary to see them in this way, but it might be helpful to point out that each has (inevitably) its limitations, and that these limitations have specific political implications. The early denunciations of patriarchy, for instance, tended to retreat from the most radical aspects of their own analysis into an insistence that the patriarchal account of life was false, a distortion of the truth about women. Of course, in some instances this has been the case: motherhood is not inevitably a serene experience; housework is not necessarily fulfilling; clitoral orgasm is not immature. But in general the insistence that a political practice, the subordination of women, is based on falsehood, seems to imply that there is a truth about women which is outside culture, outside language and meaning, a question of nature. What was radical, however, about the work of Millett, Greer and Figes was precisely their break with the myth of a known and knowable nature that could be invoked in defence of specific political practices. Meanwhile, the construction of a feminine subculture, a form of writing which is essentially different from men's, paradoxically shares something of the same difficulty. It too takes culture for nature. The danger here is that the emphasis on difference tends either to have the effect of leaving things exactly as they are, with women eternally confined to a separate sphere, or to lead to a politics of separatism, which despairs of changing patriarchy and settles instead for an alternative space on the edges of it.

If feminist analysis was to continue to develop, therefore, it was necessary to confront in theory the implications of the radical discoveries that had been made in practice. In *Feminist Practice and Poststructuralist Theory* Chris Weedon makes a lucid and persuasive case for the feminist appropriation of recent (mainly French) theories of language and culture. These theories enable us to analyse both the injustices of patriarchy and women's resistance to them, while at the same time identifying specific pressure points for change.

In poststructuralist theory meanings are cultural and learned, but they are also unfixed, sliding, plural. They are in consequence a matter for political debate. Culture itself is the limit of our knowledge: there is no available truth outside culture with which we can challenge injustice. But culture is also contradictory, the location of resistances as well as oppression, and it is therefore ultimately unstable. It too is in consequence a site of political struggle.

In Britain developments within poststructuralist theory have given a new direction to the forms of cultural history practised by Millett, Figes, and Greer. Rosalind Coward's *Female Desire*, Rachel Bowlby's *Just Looking* and Stephen Heath's *The Sexual Fix* are accessible, witty, compelling poststructuralist books which analyse a range of cultural practices, products and knowledges. In many respects, these books stand in a direct line of descent from earlier feminist cultural history: they refuse either to isolate literature from its cultural context, or to privilege it above other cultural signifying practices. Fiction is identified as only one site, albeit an influential one, of shifts in the different modes of subjectivity and sexuality available to women in history. Thus, Rosalind Coward explores contemporary constructions of female desire 'across a multitude of different cultural phenomena, from food to family snapshots, from royalty to nature programmes' and from fiction to fashion.[9] Rachel Bowlby looks at the construction of modes of femininity and female desire by the 'specularisation' of commodities which accompanied the growth of department stores, advertising and photography in late nineteenth-century consumer capitalism; and Stephen Heath employs the work of Michel Foucault in his analysis of the construction of sexual norms by the discourses of sexology and psychoanalysis.

As well as building upon and extending earlier forms of cultural analysis, these theorists offer a radically new approach. Not only do they identify representations of sexuality and female desire, they also demonstrate how meanings work and how they can be challenged. This is done by seeking out uncertainties – the problems, ambiguities and, above all, contradictions, which the representations reveal.

In *Female Desire* Rosalind Coward consistently and cleverly uncovers the gap between what patriarchal society claims women enjoy and what women actually enjoy, or don't. She begins by noting that under patriarchy female 'dissatisfaction is constantly recast as desire, as desire for something more . . . for the ideal'.[10] But this ideal is contradictory: it depends on women experiencing a relentless lack, with the result that the ideal can never be attained. She shows in consequence that it is possible for feminists to question the adequacy of patriarchal representations of female pleasure, and to counter them with female pleasures which offer women positive modes of being that are not based on lack.

Rachel Bowlby also analyses the construction of desire. She locates the implications for women of the forms of female desire constructed by patriarchy. One of these is the constitution of women as the victims of a limitless 'longing and lacking'.[11] Another is the maintenance of the status quo. This is because, as Stephen Heath argues, the function of the desire/pleasure axis in capitalist patriarchal cultures is to 'propose and confirm' a 'sexuality to which we are then referred and held in our lives, a whole *sexual fix* precisely'.[12] The 'sexual fix' is at work even in the pre-Aids atmosphere of so-called sexual liberation. Here Heath uncovers a major contradiction which has implications for how women read fiction which claims to be liberating and feminist. This is the contradiction that the 'much-vaunted "liberation" of sexuality' is not a liberation but a myth.[13] For it is no more than a new mode of conformity, a new sexual fix.

An important and contentious issue raised by *The Sexual Fix* is the question of the relationship between author, sex and text. More specifically, the question is whether the sex of an author determines the sexuality of a text. Heath's reading of passages from novels which describe the sexual act suggests that it does not, since his examples show no qualitative difference: stereotypical codes and patriarchal images are used by men and women authors alike. Following on from this, Heath concludes that it is the inscription of feminist subject positions in texts, which can be penned by men as well as women, that determines their potential radicalness, and not the author's biological sex.

While Heath usefully offers the feminist reader a non-essentialist way of theorising the relationship between sexuality and textuality, it may be the case that the question of authorship poses different problems in the context of the debate on the issue of 'men in feminism', which is the title of an anthology of poststructuralist essays on sexual difference.[14] Two different but related questions are raised here: first, should feminists willingly use poststructuralist theories whose chief proponents have been men? Second, how should feminist theorists react politically to men who write about issues pertinent to feminism from a sympathetic vantage point, when this, given the male privileges they enjoy within an academic system that has historically marginalised women, is also a point of advantage?

In answer to the first question, Rosalind Coward has shown in practice and Chris Weedon has argued in theory that it is possible as well as politically fruitful to appropriate poststructuralist theories of language, sexuality and subjectivity for feminism, even if those theories' founding fathers have no declared feminist interests. The second question is perhaps more problematic and, while there can be no 'right' answer, it may be useful to recognise the political implications of our replies. To insist that men should not be involved 'in' feminism maintains a crucial political distinction: feminism is a politics of struggle by women on behalf of women. But it also carries essentialist implications: 'only women can theorise their oppression, because only women *experience* it.' A way out of this seeming impasse may be to change the terms of the debate, so that the question is not whether men should be allowed in feminism, but whether work by men on patriarchal constructions of masculinity and sexual difference can illuminate and be illuminated by feminist theory. This approach would stress that feminist subject positions are not given but are constructed in discourse: not all women are feminists.

One of the issues which feminists placed on their political agenda during the 1970s was language. After Spender's influential *Man Made Language* it was no longer possible to treat language as gender–neutral. Poststructuralist theory, particularly the French feminist variety, has also addressed and developed questions raised implicitly by Spender's book. Perhaps the most urgent, if not the most widely discussed, question French feminists have raised is the possibility of a specifically 'feminine' discourse.

Luce Irigaray and Hélène Cixous have identified a difference between men and women in their use of and abuse by language. Extending the Lacanian psychoanalytic concept of a symbolic phallocentric order of language, from which women are excluded on account of their lack of a penis, Irigaray and Cixous have suggested that one of the ways in which women are able to challenge the effects of a patriarchal symbolic order is by writing a language of their own. Luce Irigaray argues for the liberating effects of a mode of speech and writing she calls 'womanspeak'; Hélène Cixous suggests that by writing herself in the discourse of *écriture féminine*, 'woman will return to the body which has been more than confiscated from her' by patriarchy.[15]

In both Irigaray's and Cixous's theories, then, language is closely bound to sexuality. Luce Irigaray argues that womanspeak is produced from women's libido. This is fundamentally different from men's and so too, therefore, is their language. Where female sexuality is unfixed and decentred, since *'woman has sex organs just about everywhere'*, male sexuality is fixed and centred on the penis.[16] His language is rational, linear, comprehensible; hers is irrational, non-linear and incomprehensible – to men. Unlike womanspeak, however, *écriture féminine* is a feminine discourse, not a female language, and can therefore be written by both men and women. Consequently, Cixous is less inclined than Irigaray to ground language in an essential sexuality, although her claim that under patriarchy women have a more immediate relation to *écriture féminine* than men leads her ultimately towards essentialism.

In a similar way to Dale Spender, Cixous locates in the symbolic order of language a series of binary oppositions which privilege the masculine pole over the feminine. Where Cixous moves beyond Spender is in her appropriation of Derrida's notion of the supplement, which Cixous uses to theorise the position of the feminine in the symbolic order. Conceptualised as supplementary to the patriarchal symbolic, the feminine is seen both to exceed and to threaten patriarchy.

Although both Cixous and Irigaray draw on Jacques Lacan's work on psychoanalysis and language, they do not do so uncritically. Irigaray modifies Lacan's theory of desire in language by arguing that female desire and sexuality are constituted not by a lack, in relation to the male symbolic order, but by their total otherness to male sexuality. This reworking of Lacanian theory offers feminists a way of appropriating psychoanalysis to affirm a positive mode of female desire. Whereas feminists like Rosalind Coward argue that the forms of female desire constructed by patriarchy support the status quo, Irigaray seeks to demonstrate that female desire, inscribed in writing, is a force capable of rupturing the patriarchal symbolic order. By reformulating a psychoanalytic theory of sexual difference in the light of the deconstructive theory of the supplement, Cixous, too, offers the feminist reader a positive version of femininity.

Common to both theorists is the absence of any sustained attention to history and culture. Language is viewed by implication as a universal structure that oppresses all women in the same way. It is difficult, therefore, to see how woman-speak and *écriture féminine*, which are theories of language based on sex, are able to escape their separatist implications and, correspondingly, provide feminism with a theory of social change.

But this does not mean that it is necessary for the feminist reader to face the dilemma of accepting or rejecting psycho-analytic theories of language and subjectivity, and of seeing this choice as one for or against essentialism. Rather it is possible, as feminists such as Mary Jacobus have shown, to use psychoanalytic theory within a historical framework. Jacobus does not argue the case for or against psychoanalysis: she simply uses it, and does so to great effect. In her readings of nineteenth-century women's novels Jacobus employs Freud's theory of the unconscious as a way of uncovering a series of textual omissions, contradictions and uncertainties. She shows how these uncertainties 'return' at various moments in the text, and argues that their effect is to render the text's official discourses fundamentally unstable. The return of a text's repressed 'unconscious' meanings also calls into question the possibility of a unified omnipotent authorial self.

It is evident here that Jacobus shares French feminism's concern with how the female subject inscribes herself in writing. Her more recent work, however, suggests a new way of approaching the relation of sex to text. This involves a shift of emphasis from the feminist writer to the feminist reader, which Jacobus effects by posing the 'double question of reading woman (reading) or woman reading (woman)'.[17] 'Reading woman (reading)' shifts attention from author to text and from woman's biological make-up to the way in which language makes her up, or constructs her, so that it is possible to read 'woman' as a metaphor of her sex rather than as the transparent signifier of a biological self. Correspondingly, Jacobus urges feminists to stop seeking out woman as if she were something *in* a text and to start seeing her as something which is eminently textual: 'Perhaps the question that feminist critics should ask themselves is not "Is there a woman in this text?" but rather: "*Is there a text in this woman?*"'[18]

Not all feminist critics would agree that the shift Jacobus proposes from writer to reader is in their interests. For some lesbian and black feminist critics, especially, the role of the author/writer as the source of textual meaning is of crucial political importance. The title of Bonnie Zimmerman's essay, 'What Has Never Been: An Overview of Lesbian Feminist Criticism', hints at why this is so. Given the marginalisation of lesbian feminism within patriarchal as well as mainstream feminist literary canons, Zimmerman argues that the primary task for lesbian critics today is to make their *distinct* voices heard by developing 'a unique lesbian feminist perspective' and establishing a canon of past and present lesbian texts.[19] How lesbian texts are defined is problematic: we cannot always establish an author's sexual orientation. Nevertheless, Zimmerman suggests that we should not rule out the author in this process, because to do so is to risk losing the specificity of an essential lesbian sexuality.

Black feminist critics have also perceived an integral relationship between author and text. In an early essay, published in 1977, Barbara Smith calls on the black woman writer 'to think and write out of her own identity and not to try to graft the ideas or methodology of white/male literary thought upon the precious materials of Black women's art.'[20] But in the same essay Smith also argues against trying to establish lesbian texts on the basis of what is known of the author's life, and she proposes instead to identify lesbian writing by the textual strategies employed. Although these statements appear to contradict one another, and have been accused of being politically reactionary by later black critics, Smith's proposals can be interpreted in a way which renders them both consistent and non-essentialist. For Smith's call to black women to write their own identity is arguably premised not on essentialism, but on the need to recognise cultural difference. If black authors write differently from white, that is not because of their biological skin colour, but because of the different subject positions that being black in a white society constructs. It is in consequence perfectly consistent for Smith to propose reading lesbian texts in terms of the subject positions their language constructs.

Common to both Smith's and Zimmerman's essays is the confidence that they inspire in the feminist reader who seeks to challenge the assumptions of white/patriarchal culture.

Rather than only positioning black and lesbian women as victims of the coercive power of white/male critical norms, Zimmerman and Smith offer positive black and lesbian subjectivities that counter and resist them. Thus, they show how change is possible.

More recently, black feminists have suggested that in order to envisage strategies for change, black feminism needs to break more conclusively with separatist and ahistorical essentialist theories of language and subjectivity. Deborah E. McDowell argues for a 'contextual' approach to black literature which 'exposes the conditions under which literature is produced, published, and reviewed.'[21] And Susan Willis insists: 'Black women's writing is not a mere collection of motifs and strategies, but a mode of discourse which enables a critical perspective upon the past, the present and sometimes into an emerging future.'[22]

Nevertheless, both of these theorists acknowledge the importance, in the first instance, of specifying the difference of black from white literature, and of establishing a separate literary canon. Only in this way, they suggest, can black feminists make themselves visible in white culture. It may come as something of a shock to white feminist poststructuralists, who insist on the autonomy of texts from their authors, to encounter such a determined refusal by black and lesbian feminists to efface the author from their textual readings. Perhaps this is the point at which black feminism challenges the presuppositions of a critical apparatus which is predominantly Western and motivated by white interests. If white Western feminists do not acknowledge the specificity of their theoretical aims and objectives, it may well be that they implicitly affirm the imperialist values and re-enact the colonial practices that have structured the history of Western patriarchal cultures.

It is precisely with the cultural blindness which results when white Western critics assume that their theories have universal application that Gayatri Spivak takes issue. Spivak's challenge to this blindness is not to reject Western poststructuralism (she is one of the best-known practitioners of deconstruction), but to show how 'First-World' theories can illuminate readings of 'Third-World' texts, while at the same time demonstrating the ways in which those texts question and throw into relief the presuppositions of culturally-specific modes of textual analysis.[23]

One such assumption is a belief in the universal primacy of the need to establish individual, usually Western, identity in fiction and in theory – a point which Spivak brings out here in her reading of *Jane Eyre*. As an antidote to the importance that the establishment of individuality has assumed in Western feminist criticism, Spivak proposes 'a simultaneous other focus', which asks 'not merely who am I? but who is the other woman? How am I naming her? How does she name me?'[24] By asking these questions, which stress position over essence, the 'First-World' feminist reader is less likely to reproduce unthinkingly the theoretical concerns of Western critical discourses in her reading of 'Third-World' as well as 'First-World' texts.

One of the most potentially liberating effects of poststructuralism for feminism is that it enables the feminist reader to uncover the discursive production of all meanings, to pinpoint whose interests they support, and to locate the contradictions which render them fundamentally unstable and open to change. Some meanings may be more familiar than others, but they are no more fixed, natural or true for that. By the same token, poststructuralist theory is no less unstable or more true than other ways of reading – although it does have different political implications which feminists may agree with or not. Certainly feminists have found it necessary to reformulate aspects of poststructuralist theory in order to appropriate it for feminism. This process of reworking and reformulating theories is potentially infinite: feminism is a politics in progress. It is not surprising, therefore, that a new current is already being identified within feminist criticism.

This fourth current is, arguably, what is called postmodernism in America, and modernism in France.

In her book *Gynesis*, Alice Jardine argues that an extensive process of requestioning and rethinking the foundations of Western critical thought is taking place in France. This process has arisen out of the collapse of the West's master-narratives. These accounts of the world, which claim to explain it, centre on 'Man, the Subject, Truth, History, Meaning.'[25] Jardine calls the process of requestioning and destructuring 'gynesis'.

Gynesis is 'the putting into discourse of woman'; it is the manifestation in discourse of the uncertainty and unfixity that have traditionally connoted femininity, which Jardine defines as the excess of a patriarchal history, not as biological woman. Gynesis, therefore, is not necessarily concerned with woman; on the contrary, it refuses all essentialist, fixed modes of thought; it goes beyond the history of sexual identity:

> Gynesis has taken place in France within a movement away from a concern with identity to a concern with difference, from wholeness to that which is incomplete, from representation to modes of presentation, metadiscourse to fiction.[26]

Language thus no longer guarantees identity, or meaning: all figuration is chaotic, disorganised and non-transparent. (And this collapse of simple referentiality renders it impossible to formulate a feminist politics based on experience.) Out of the chaos resulting from the collapse of the master-narratives a new space is produced. This space is of particular interest to feminism, not least because of its feminine connotations. It is the space of the unknown and of 'the master narratives' own "nonknowledge", what has eluded them, what has engulfed them', 'a "space" over which the narrative has lost control'.[27]

It is, perhaps, also the utopian space identified here by the French feminist, Julia Kristeva, as the conceptual territory occupied by her 'third generation' of women. Like the space where gynesis works, this is a terrain on which the sexual opposition man/woman is undone; for, asks Kristeva, 'what can "identity", even "sexual identity", mean in a new theoretical . . . space where the very notion of identity is challenged?'[28]

Kristeva's and Jardine's non-essentialist theories of subjectivity and sexuality as unfixed and 'in process' pose a radical challenge to the common-sense belief in the unified subject who issues, controls and fixes meaning. The space they conceptualise is not yet fully known or inhabited; in this sense it is available for further exploration. And while other feminists may well insist that we need to pay more attention than do Jardine and Kristeva to the determination by history and culture of this space and its subjects, its potentially liberating implications for feminism are great. This is because the opportunity is here for the feminist reader to peruse a different narrative from 'the male stories women – and men – have been forced to live'.[29]

Now read on . . .

2 Women and Literary History

Dale Spender

I have no reason to suspect that my own university education was peculiarly biased or limited. On the contrary, it appears to have been fairly representative. Yet in the guise of presenting me with an overview of the literary heritage of the English-speaking world, my education provided me with a grossly inaccurate and distorted view of the history of letters. For my introduction to the 'greats' was (with the exception of the famous five women novelists) an introduction to the great men. Even in the study of the novel where women were conceded to have a place, I was led to believe that all the initial formative writing had been the province of men. So along with other graduates of 'Eng. Lit.' departments I left university with the well-cultivated impression that men had created the novel and that there were no women novelists (or none of note) before Jane Austen.[1]

There was no reason for me to be suspicious about what I was being taught. I was a student in a reputable university being tutored by experts who referred me to the literary scholars who, without qualification, asserted the ascendancy of men. For example, the authoritative treatise on the early novel was by Ian Watt and was entitled *The Rise of the Novel: Studies in Defoe, Richardson and Fielding* (1957) and it opened with the bald statement that the novel was begun by Defoe, Richardson and Fielding, and that it was the genius of these three men that had created the new form. Had it even occurred to me to be dubious about the frequency with which I was asked to accept men's good opinion of men, by what right could I have questioned the scholarship and authority of such established and sanctioned critics?

Besides, what contrary evidence was available? No matter where I looked around me, I encountered almost exclusively the publications of men. Like Virginia Woolf in the British Museum (*A Room of One's Own*, 1928) I too found that the library catalogue and shelves were filled with books predominantly authored by men. And in the bookshops a steady stream of new and attractively packaged editions of early male novelists helped to reinforce the belief that it was only men who had participated in the initial production of this genre. I neither stumbled across fascinating 'old' editions of women's novels on the library shelves nor found interesting republications when browsing through bookshops. As far as I knew both the old and the new were representative of the books that had been published, and as there were virtually no women among them, it had to be because women had not written books.

So I had no difficulty accepting the statements of Ian Watt: men were to be congratulated for the birth of the novel. Women – or more precisely, one woman – entered only *after* men had ushered the novel into the world: Jane Austen, writes Ian Watt in 'A Note' at the end of *The Rise of the Novel*, provided a steady and guiding influence for this new form but neither she, nor any other woman, had helped to bring it into existence. In this book in which Fanny Burney is mentioned on only three occasions (and in less than three lines) he does say that 'Jane Austen was the heir of Fanny Burney',[2] but as this is the only cursory reference, the impression remains that when it comes to women novelists there was no one to speak of, before Jane Austen.

It does not, of course, strain the limits of credibility to believe that for women, Jane Austen started it all. Her novels reveal such a great talent that it is possible to accept that she was capable of bringing forth – in fully fledged form and without benefit of female 'models' – those superb novels which to my mind still stand as one of the high points of achievement in English fiction. But if it is possible to accept this version of women's literary history, I have discovered since that it is exceedingly unwise. For to see Jane Austen as a starting point is to be dreadfully deceived. Any portrayal of her which represents her as an *originator* and not as an *inheritor* of women's literary traditions is one which has strayed far from the facts of women's fiction writing. And when Jane Austen is seen to *inherit* a literary tradition this has ramifications not just for the history of women novelists but for the history of novelists in general.

For more than a century before Jane Austen surreptitiously took up her pen, women, in ever increasing numbers and with spectacular success, had been trying their hand at fiction. And not just the few women already referred to either, although obviously the Duchess of Newcastle, Aphra Behn and Delarivière Manley had played an important part, and Eliza Haywood, 'a woman of genius', had helped to conceive the possibilities and realities of fiction. And not just the 'refreshing' Fanny Burney or the 'worthy' Maria Edgeworth who are sometimes briefly acknowledged in passing for their 'historic interest'. (Maria Edgeworth is not mentioned in Ian Watt's *The Rise of the Novel*.) But a whole gallery of women: women from different backgrounds, different regions, and with different concerns, who all published well-acclaimed novels by the end of the 1700s.

That such women and their writing exist raises numerous questions about the traditions of women: this also raises questions about the traditions of men!

Without doubt the novel came into its own during the eighteenth century; the publication figures in themselves tell a story of sure and steady growth: 'The annual production of works of fiction, which had averaged only about seven in the years between 1700 to 1740, rose to an average of about twenty in the three decades following 1740 and this output was doubled in the period from 1770 to 1800', writes Ian Watt.[3] About two thousand novels in all, by the end of the century. And the distinct impression that they were written mainly by men.

Now, it's not possible to make definitive statements about how many of these two thousand novels were written by women, and how many by men. In quite a few cases, the sex of the author remains unknown – particularly because of the penchant for anonymous publications, a practice, it must be noted which was more likely to tempt (particularly modest) women rather than men. But even if the 'sex unknown' authors are subtracted from the list of novelists of the 1700s, the number of women novelists and their works which remain is little short of astonishing, given that we have been led to believe that women played no part in these productions. As a result of a little detective work and a great deal of perseverance, I have been able to find one hundred good women novelists of the eighteenth century and together they were responsible for almost six hundred novels.

This means that even by the most conservative standards women would have to be granted a half-share in the production of fiction in the 1700s. And yet they have *all* 'disappeared'. In must be noted that this is not a reference to the occasional obscure woman writer who has slipped through the net of literary standards, not the 'one-off' achievement that has unfortunately been lost, not the eclipsing of one woman of genius like Eliza Haywood. This is at least half the literary output in fiction over a century; it is six hundred novels which in their own time were accorded merit.

And if since the eighteenth century it has become a well-established fact that women did not write novels during the 1700s, or that women did not write good novels, this was a fact which was *not* known at the time. For it was then widely appreciated that women wrote novels, and wrote them well. So firmly entrenched was this belief that it affords a most unusual and interesting chapter in the history of letters. While ever since it has been men who have been seen as the more significant and better novelists – to the extent that on occasion women have tried to increase their chances of publication by pretending to be men – it was not unknown during the eighteenth century for men to masquerade as female authors in the attempt to obtain some of the higher status (and greater chances of publication) which went with being a woman writer.

So frequent had this practice become that as early as June 1770 the *Gentleman's Magazine* thought it proper to conduct its own investigations as to the sex of authors, in the interest of being able to provide its readers with information on whether the latest production from a supposedly female pen was indeed genuine. For as the reviewer commented, 'among other literary frauds it has long been common for authors to affect the stile and character of ladies' (page 273). Which means that eighteenth-century readers knew something that twentieth-century ones do not: namely that in the beginning, and for quite a long time thereafter, the novel was seen as the female forte.

In 1773 the *Monthly Review* stated that when it came to fiction the field was filled by ladies, and well into the nineteenth century it was conceded that not only were women novelists plentiful, but that they were good.

Yet by the twentieth century when Ian Watt comes to outline the rise of the novel, women are no longer held in high esteem. He does – in passing – acknowledge that *the majority of eighteenth-century novels were written by women*, but how very damning is this faint and only praise.

How is it that we have come to lose this knowledge about many good women novelists? How have we come to lose it so completely that its one-time existence does not even register, so we are blissfully unaware of what has been lost? So that we do not even appreciate the significance of the single sentence that once women wrote (and published) reams? For so thoroughly have early women novelists been edited out of the literary records and removed from consciousness, their absence does not even ordinarily prompt comment, let alone concern.

And it is not because they were all no good that these hundred women novelists and their six hundred novels have been consigned to oblivion. For when the pronouncements of the literary establishment are perused for the case against the worth of these women writers, a curious omission comes to light. *There is no case against them.* If these many novels have been evaluated, the findings are not contained in the official literary records. And when the worth of women writers is not being based on any consideration of their writing, the only conclusion which can be drawn is that their worth is being determined by their sex.

That the writing of women does not count because it is written by women is the distinct impression given by Ian Watt. While his assertions about the quality of male novelists are based on a detailed examination of their writing, it is clear that he thinks the stand he takes on the absence of quality in women's writing does not even call for substantiation. He devotes three hundred pages to his assessment of male novelists and restricts his assessment of females to a single sentence: 'The majority of eighteenth-century novels were actually written by women.'[4] With no further discussion of the women, no entry to them in the index, and no explanation for his failure to discuss 'the majority' of novels of the eighteenth century, Ian Watt indicates that it is not necessary to examine the writing of women to know it is of no account.

Perhaps Ian Watt offers no evidence for the simple reason that it does not support his beliefs.

In the eighteenth century it was not known that women writers did not count. Quite the reverse. Charlotte Lennox, Mary Wollstonecraft, Fanny Burney, Elizabeth Inchbald, Mary Hays, Amelia Opie and Maria Edgeworth were not just 'actually' the majority, they were the *esteemed* majority. They were highly praised by readers and reviewers alike. They were valued by some of the best educated and most distinguished persons – of both sexes. And if today they do not count among the scholars and critics this was not how it was in their own day, when their writing was read and studied, when their efforts were consistently applauded, when they enjoyed extensive and positive reviews, when they were congratulated on their contribution to literature. (One way of rediscovering these women novelists is to go through the review sections of the literary periodicals of the day.)

Strange that those who read the novels then should have found them so good when today the verdict is that they are so bad they do not warrant examination. This is a most interesting additional insight. Now when we are presented with an exclusively male literary tradition – and this is how the early novel *is* presented – we must bear in mind that this is not because women did not write, could not get published, or went unacclaimed. Women qualified on all these counts. It was only later that they were disqualified.

How do we explain this transition from prominence to negation? What does it mean when women who were esteemed in their own lifetime are later denied and dismissed? It could be the rationale of an 'individual case' when earlier this century attempts were made to prove that Aphra Behn did not even exist, but such an explanation will not suffice when we are confronted with one hundred women whose work appears to have been systematically denied. Could it be that there is pattern and purpose in this treatment of women?

Germaine Greer certainly thinks so. She has referred to the 'phenomenon of the transience of female literary fame, and not just in relation to the novel. It is her contention that there have always been good women writers, in every area and every era, and that they always disappear. Since the days of Aphra Behn, she states, there have been 'women who have enjoyed dazzling literary prestige during their own lifetimes, only to vanish without trace from the records of posterity'.[5]

Once acclaimed, but now denied. This is the problem of women writers and it is one which almost every woman critic of the past few decades has addressed. Although in some circles it may be in order to 'accept' the disappearance of women writers as just a strange and random quirk of literary history, such an explanation has no place among women critics who have noted that the same fate does not await men. Of course many male writers have fallen by the wayside with the passage of time – but not *all* of them, not one hundred of them over a century. And not those who were widely acclaimed in their own day. Enough men are retained to allow for an uninterrupted tradition of men writers. The same is not true for women.

In the eighteenth century women wrote in much the same (if not greater) numbers than men, with much the same (if not more) success than men, and attained much the same (if not more) status than men. Yet not only has this achievement of women been edited out of literary history, but a false version has been substituted in its place. A distorted version which makes no mention of women's former greatness, but which presents the birth of the novel solely in terms of men. So Daniel Defoe's *Robinson Crusoe* (1720) is transformed into the first novel; Samuel Richardson's *Pamela* (1740) becomes a turning point in the development of the novel and is celebrated; Henry Fielding, Lawrence Sterne and Tobias Smollett are accorded the status of proud parents of this new form. And all this with little or no regard for 'the facts of life'.

How is such a falsified version of events to be explained? And is it a practice of the past or one that persists in the present? For if the denial of women's literary achievement continues to this day, what fate awaits some of the current women writers who enjoy considerable literary acclaim? They too could be consigned to oblivion so that future generations would neither know nor suspect that there has been an 'explosion' in women's writing over the last few years. To those who are yet to come could be bequeathed the legacy of Norman Mailer, Anthony Burgess, Graham Greene and it could be as though Fay Weldon, Alison Lurie, Edna O'Brien, Erica Jong, Marilyn French, Anita Brookner, Mary Gordon, Margaret Drabble and so many more – never existed.

A range of explanations has been offered for the transience of female literary fame. At one end of the spectrum are rationalisations that as literature became increasingly institutionalised during the eighteenth and nineteenth centuries, the decision-making powers were concentrated in the hands of men who not surprisingly found the good and the great among their fellow men. While the novel was in a state of flux – as it was in the earlier part of the eighteenth century – while there was much new activity and little form to follow, women had been able to find a place in literature – as had Aphra Behn in the ferment which accompanied an earlier literary upheaval during the Restoration; but once things settled down, once patterns and experts and credentials were established, the traditional relationship of the sexed reasserted itself, and the dominance of men as critics and writers soon became the reality of the literary world.

Such an account is plausible. It posits a male-dominated society and presumes a male-dominated literary tradition as a result. It is based on the premise that when women and men are equal, they will have literary traditions in which women and men are equally represented.

But there are women critics, past and present, who have gone further than this explanation of men finding in favour of their own sex; further even than arguing that men find fault with women. They have introduced the argument that in a male-dominated society, women are denied the right to their own creative resources and that these resources are *taken* by men to augment their own. And such a conceptualisation provides a very different framework for interpretations of the treatment of women writers.

It suggests that the men of letters are not blind to the achievements of women but instead of according them validity in their own right, men take from women what they want and leave the rest – which they determine to be of no value – to fade from view. So men writers and critics can deny women's creativity and appropriate women's efforts, claiming women's achievement as their own. So Eliza Haywood can be reduced in stature to a mere copier, her contributions appropriated by her male colleagues, and in the eyes of the critics her achievement is denied and becomes the property of the men.

This explanation is plausible when applied not just to Eliza Haywood, but to all the women novelists of the eighteenth century. It is not just that Walter Allen or Ian Watt neglect to include the women writers, but that they deny the way the men profited from the women's work. The end result is that the reputation of men is built at the expense of women and, in the words of Matilda Joslyn Gage, this is nothing other than the *theft* of women's creativity.

Men 'steal the fruits of women's creative labour,' declared Matilda Joslyn Gage,[6] and according to some contemporary women critics men continue to engage in such illicit literary practice. Hilary Simpson has pointed to the extent to which D. H. Lawrence, for example, appropriated the creative resources of women and passed them off as his own: and she has also noted that within the literary establishment there has been no accusation of foul play.

Without acknowledgement of his sources, D. H. Lawrence 'solicited notes and reminiscences from Jessie (Burrows), from his wife Frieda, from Mabel Dodge Luhan and others . . . he also took over women's manuscripts and rewrote them, as in the cases of Helen Corke and Mollie Skinner . . .'.[7] If one such distinguished man of letters could feel that it was in order to take these creative contributions to enhance his own achievement, then the possibility can be admitted that a collective of men of letters could act in the same way, and

take the contributions of the early women novelists to enhance
their own claims.

If F. Scott Fitzgerald could take the creative resources of
Zelda Fitzgerald's diaries as his own property and build his
novels upon them, if he could see *her* creativity as the raw
material for *his* work – and if the law upheld his right to do
this and prevented Zelda from publishing her own work
(which it did) – then the practice of men stealing women's
creativity is hardly outrageous or unknown. It is accepted
practice and as such its widespread presence should be
expected.[8]

Were these but isolated examples, the evidence in support
of Matilda Joslyn Gage's thesis of theft would not be so
strong: but Samuel Richardson, Thomas Hardy and William
Wordsworth are among other great writers known to have
similar propensities for taking the writing of women and using
it for their own ends. Further investigations in this area might
even yield more examples of men at this work. Perhaps behind
the dedications or ritual brief acknowledgements to 'the skills
of the wife' there lie more examples of women's intellectual
and creative resources being appropriated by men to lend
substance to their own claims to fame. Marion Glastonbury
certainly thinks so.[9] With these examples in mind – and more
to follow – it seems reasonable to suggest that it could have
become routine for literary men to perceive women's work as
available for their own use. And unless challenged why should
they not continue with this arrangement?

However, whether the men of letters have overlooked
women's writing, or whether they have exploited it, what can
be stated unequivocally is that they have in effect suppressed
the traditions of writing women. And the question that arises
is – does this matter? Does it really matter to past, present,
future generations of women – and men – that the early
women writers have been removed from the literary heritage
so it is as if they never existed? Is it not a little short of
fanatical to dig up all these lost women and to confront the
seemingly benign men of letters with an accusation which
borders on being a charge of malign conspiracy? What possible
difference can it make to writers, readers, or the world in
general to know that contrary to what we've been led to

believe, women as well as men (and even more significantly than men) participated in the conception and development of the new genre, the novel?

The answer depends on the role and importance that is attached to tradition. On the one hand it won't make an immediate and tangible difference to insist on the acknowledgement of women's literary contributions – or to challenge the massive censoring exercise that has been undertaken by men. It won't lead to direct improvements in women's poverty or bring a dramatic end to world wars. But on the other hand, the reinstatement of women's meanings and achievements within the culture could make a very big difference: Virginia Woolf thought that in the long run it would even make a difference to women's poverty and to the prospects of war.

No one can quantify but few would want to totally repudiate the influence that the cultural heritage of the past has on the attitudes and values of the present. And when that heritage of the past blatantly mistreats and devalues half of humanity why should it not be assumed that this predisposes the society which possesses such a heritage to mistreat and devalue human beings?

When, for example, the literary traditions represent the views and values of one small select group of men who agree that those who are not in their own image are not worthy of recognition – or that they are available for exploitation – then the divisions of good and bad, rich and poor, dominant and subordinate, are readily constructed. And the implications of such divisions extend far beyond the confines of the woman writer; they affect women, men, the whole society. This was the stand taken by Virginia Woolf in *A Room of One's Own* (1928) where she made the connections between women's cultural poverty and women's material poverty; it was the stand she took in *Three Guineas* (1938) where she linked the male domination of the cultural heritage with exploitation, violence and war.

She associated the injustice of the suppression of women's meanings with social injustice on a grand scale and she insisted that it was imperative – for the sake of society and the survival of the species – that women's *different* meanings should be reinstated in literary (and other cultural) traditions. Part of

Virginia Woolf's argument was based on the premise that *one* world view – the view of men who exercised power – was simply not enough to provide full understanding about the way the world worked. It was too limited: too much was left out. It was the very perspective of those who did *not* exercise power, over whom power was exercised, and who were defined as alien, other, and unworthy of recognition, that was needed for a full view of the world, she insisted. It was her fundamentally simple assertion that women could see much that men – because of their position – could not; that women could see in men precisely what men could not see in themselves; it was this that led her to argue that the meanings forged by women, and represented in their writing, should be included in the cultural heritage. Only then would it provide a fair and reliable basis for making sense of the world.

This is the argument of many women: that in the broadest possible sense, the knowledge of women's contribution could make a significant difference to the judgments and practices of the whole society. Women, whose philosophies are as far apart as Dora Russell's, Elizabeth Robins's, Kate Millett's and Adrienne Rich's have nonetheless agreed on the central point that male dominance means women's silence and that society can no longer afford to neither hear nor heed the voice of half of humanity.[10] These women – and many others as well – have insisted that while women are kept out of the cultural traditions we have a heritage which is comprised of nothing other than political propaganda, in which the powerful decree their world view as the *only* world view, and in which those who differ from the powerful are censored, suppressed, outlawed. To reclaim and revalue the women writers men have removed is, in this framework, to do more than challenge a biased version of literary history: it is to take a political stand and to challenge the propaganda of a dictatorship.

Whether or not one subscribes to the theory that women should seize and control their own creative resources, or concedes the sweeping claim that the reinstatement of women in the literary traditions will lead to a better society, it seems safe to assert that the establishment of the existence and extent of the cultural heritage of women could make a big difference to women. A big difference to the image of women and to the reality of female achievements. While the catalogues, the library shelves, the bookshops, the reviews, the courses of study, all help to suggest that women are without a literary tradition, the belief in female inferiority is surely sustained. And it erodes women's confidence; it undermines the woman writer; it produces doubts. If women were indeed without a great literary tradition, much could be said for the advisability of inventing one, for the positive influence it could provide for women and women's literary endeavours. Such is the power of a tradition.

3 The True Story of How I Became My Own Person

Rosalind Coward

Fiction is a passionate pleasure in many women's lives, far more so than it appears to be for men. Women, it seems, are addicted to fiction. As novelist Rachel Billington put it, 'Women read fiction. Women need fiction. Men do too but only the discerning. They read good novels. Women, even those with brains like razors, never lose that longing for the Big One, the big emotional high' (*Guardian*, 5 October 1981). And not only do women consume fiction, but novel writing is one of the few areas of the arts where women are recognised as equal to men.

It is not just novels in general that women consume. Recently a new genre of novel has appeared aimed at a specifically female audience and usually written by women. These are not just the novels of a publishing house like Mills and Boon specialising in romantic fiction for women; there are also more recent publishing ventures like Virago, committed to printing and reprinting books by women which are aimed at a female audience. Virago director Carmen Callil explained the commercial success of Virago as satisfying women's demand for women-centred fiction: 'We have shown there is a real public demand. We are looking for things in books which are central to women's experience' (*Guardian*, 26 January 1981).

The production of such novels where women's experiences are at the forefront and which are aimed at a specifically female readership is not, however, confined to the feminist press. The success for commercial publishers of novels like *Kinflicks*, *Original Sins*, *The Women's Room*, *The Bleeding Heart*,

Fear of Flying and *The Woman Warrior* can hardly be overlooked. They have all at one time or another been hailed as 'the number one international best-seller'. And the success of women writers, appealing with their women-orientated fiction to women, means that commercial publishers are looking out for more. Women *are* the fiction market. 'An English male writer in America was recently asked to use only his initials in order to disguise his unfashionable sex' (Billington, *Guardian*, op. cit.). What then is the history of these women-centred novels? What form of pleasure do they offer women and why have they become so popular now?

Women-centred novels are by no means a new phenomenon. Indeed, novels like *Pamela* and *Clarissa* are usually seen as the precursors of the modern novel and they had the lives of individual women at the centre of the narrative.[1] The novel as we know it today emerged as a distinct form of entertainment in the eighteenth century. It was to be enjoyed in private, and at its heart was a narrative following the life of one individual. The novel, as an entertainment form, almost certainly emerged because the pleasures and interests which it offered corresponded to distinct historical conditions. Some think that the life and experiences of individuals came to the fore-front in these stories at the same time as the values of the new bourgeoisie came to dominate social beliefs. The values of economic competitiveness and individualism, for instance – both crucial to the early novel – came into their own in this period.[2]

In the cases where a heroine occupied the position of central consciousness, the novel was invariably preoccupied with questions of sexual morality, and especially marriage. In fact novels increasingly featured the movement towards marriage as the centrally significant event of the narrative. Marriage was the point where the narrative was resolved and often concluded. *How* that point was reached, of course, was all-important and varied enormously between writers. For Jane Austen, the movement towards marriage was invariably also a movement towards an intellectual apprehension of social values. For all the women protagonists in Jane Austen's novels, marriage represents the establishment of certain social values. In *Emma*, the sentimental lesson in the protagonist's appreciation of her love for Mr Knightley is also an intellectual lesson where her impulsive behaviour is criticised. In *Mansfield Park*, the marriage of Fanny represents the triumph of the established order of the house Mansfield Park, upheld in the face of disintegration through new sexual, moral and economic forces.

Even though the progress and forms of the novels are quite different, it is still worth making some general points about marriage as a central narrative device. In most novels of this early period there is a crucial moment for the individual, embodied in the choices around marriage. For the individual heroine, it is a moment where *significant events may happen*, after which her choices and identity are lost for ever.

By the nineteenth century this narrative had become quite rigid, even though this is, of course, remembered as the period where the novel reached its greatest expression. In *Shirley*, Charlotte Brontë can write of her protagonist: 'Caroline was just eighteen years old and at eighteen the true narrative of life has yet to be commenced' – more accurate would be, 'the true narrative of the novel of this period'. For what is implicit is that the novel can justify this concentration on the consciousness of the heroine only around these moments of social and sexual decision. It is interesting to reflect that the consciousness of the heroine and her eventual marriage are dominant themes in the popular literature of the nineteenth century.

In retrospect, it is not so difficult to see why the 'heroine', her particular qualities and the decisions she took about marriage were so important for that period. One aspect shows this clearly. The female protagonists of the nineteenth-century novel are profoundly silent. Their characters express sensitivity and inner feelings. Their looks, as the saying goes, 'speak volumes'. Thus the same Caroline in *Shirley* speaks only through her appearance: 'her face expressive and gentle; her eyes were handsome, gifted at times with a winning beam that stole into the heart with a language that spoke to the affection.'

The female protagonists invariably hold the position of understanding; silently feeling, they naturally perceive and uphold what is truly valuable. As in Elizabeth Gaskell's *North and South*, the female protagonist in *Shirley* represents the soft and understanding aspects of humanity.

Women, then, were represented as somehow outside social relations. In both *Shirley* and *North and South*, the women are in some way untainted by the harsh world of economic competition which their lovers inhabit; they represent the realm of pure feeling. Indeed the heroines of this period do not even speak their desire and their love; they blush and their eyes are downcast. Theirs is a silent sexuality expressed again from the body, physically but without a voice.

Small wonder that women writers of this period had such difficulty with their female protagonists. Silent and subdued heroines didn't always suit the aspirations of women writers, who sometimes produced 'strange' atypical heroines such as Lucy in Charlotte Brontë's *Villette*. Lucy clearly experiences violent, if not pressing, sexual desire but cannot express it. The novel, for that matter, cannot speak it explicitly either, except in terms of what would now be taken to be a nervous breakdown, and through the strange identification Lucy feels with a neurotic, religious and sexually repressed teacher. *Villette*'s themes of derangement, fantasy and hallucination are typical and recur in other women's novels of the period. Derangement and hallucination are responses to the burden of interiority placed on the heroine by the novel form, responses to the speaking silence of the female figure. Nor is it surprising to find women writers who followed this route and expressed this burden through their writings now rediscovered as the precursors of contemporary feminist writers.

In the nineteenth century, then, the consciousness of the heroine was treated in a recognisable format. Her choices were for a brief moment before marriage of crucial importance, socially and sexually. Yet she is the silent woman, necessarily so because she is outside the cruelty and viciousness of the economic order. In retrospect we can now see how this novel form in fact corresponded to certain definite social ideologies. The marriage of this heroine whose sentiment and sensibilities put her above the economy provided a sort of validation of the social structure. Her love was somehow untainted and contributed very forcefully to the ideology which was able to separate the public, economic realm from the domestic. The domestic sphere could then be represented as the realm of pure feeling – borne by the woman – where men's true identity could be expressed. Novelistic conventions contributed to the rigid separation between the public economic sphere and the private domestic sphere. The ideology promoted within the novels allowed individuals to live at ease with their consciences; it enabled them to believe that in loving a woman, a man expressed his true goodness. The ideology of the domestic sphere and the love of a good woman allowed people to treat their homes as if the economic world did not exist and as if individuals were not implicated in the injustice of this world.

This narrative structure dealing centrally with the heroine's marriage arose at a definite historical period and had distinct social reasons for existing. But in spite of historical changes, this kind of narrative still exists. Interestingly, though, it has moved to the margins, and is dismissed by the critics as pulp fiction. Pleasurable though this form of novel may be, it is a frozen and repetitive form, unable to lay claim to being serious literature because it no longer deals with the main problems of contemporary life. Contemporary romantic fiction is repetitive and predictable – speechless and pure heroine with a masterful and cruel lover whose better self is expressed in his love of the heroine. But it is no longer a form able to explore central social problems.

The *mainstream* of popular fiction, however, appears to have completely inverted the values of the Victorian novel. If Victorian heroines spoke only through their eyes and their central nervous systems, contemporary women protagonists are positively garrulous about their intimate personal histories. Everything must and can be told. ' "You must not tell anyone," my mother said, "what I am about to tell you," ' opens *The Woman Warrior*, and then proceeds to tell it all.[3] Contemporary woman-centred fiction is characterised by this; above all, the female protagonist has become the speaking sex.

If sexual desire rendered the Victorian heroine mad, it now appears to be a vital component of 'the number one international best-seller'. So much so, that 'women-centred' novels have become almost synonymous with the so-called sexual revolution. More than anything, the sexual revolution is presented as the transformation of women's relation to sex:

Liberating the libido. Getting sex straight was an essential
first step along the noisy road to liberation; writing about
it could be the next leap forward. Books by women surveying
sex, and novels by women whose heroines savour sex, are
selling like hotdogs in America – beating men into second
place and turning authoresses into millionairesses at the
drop of a hardsell dust-jacket.

Sunday Times Colour Supplement

These novels are often seen by the writers themselves as
relating to feminism, although many feminists have received
them with suspicion. Sometimes consciousness-raising is used
as a narrative device, as in *Loose Change* and *The Women's Room*;
often the encounter with feminism and the discovery of how
general the individual's experience as a woman actually is, is
a vital element of the narrative. But regardless of this political
commitment, the commercial world has recognised these
novels as a genre of sexual writing, showing that women can
write about sex as well as if not better than men.

What then are we to think about these novels? What needs
do they appear to satisfy? How did they arise and can they,
as is sometimes claimed, 'change lives' and contribute to a
more progressive understanding of women's sexuality?

One point which is immediately striking is that these novels
have followed the general pattern in fiction towards sexual
confession. The confessional novel has become more and more
dominant in contemporary fiction, both male and female.
Increasingly the novel's structure has been based on the voice
of the protagonist describing the significant events in his or her
life. Since the turn of the century this stream of consciousness
writing has been widespread. But recently, the consciousness
has been more and more preoccupied with talking about sex.
Sexual confessions moved to the mainstream in the 1950s and
60s with writers like J. D. Salinger, Kingsley Amis, Henry
Miller and Philip Roth. These novels exhibit interesting
similarities with Victorian pornography which took the form
of detailed pseudo-autobiographical accounts of sexual encounters.[4] But it wasn't until the late 1960s that this kind of writing
became virtually synonymous with women writers and sexual
revolution.

Where the sexual confessions – both male and female – differ from their pornographic and romantic precedents is in the fact that the narrative has expanded to encompass a much wider span of significant moments. If the narrative of life was just beginning at eighteen for Charlotte Brontë's heroines, the contemporary heroine has met the crucial determinants of her life in the 'formative' encounters of childhood and adolescence. Childhood has become a period permeated with sexual meanings, foretastes and crucial moments in the development of sexual identity.

It is appropriate, too, that with this concentration on childhood should have come a peculiarly regressive form of writing. This form is the written equivalent of the family album. It has generated a convention where humorous sketches are delivered. 'Here's Aunt Emily. She married Uncle Morgan who ran off with the post-lady. They lived down White Bay Creek, and used to take in drifters.' Then follows the anecdote, the vignette to show just what type of person Uncle Morgan was. This often has the effect of reducing the characters to the bare bones of their particular eccentricity. And this form of writing is one of the reasons why many reviewers can't make up their minds whether they are dealing with a 'riproaring, hilarious' novel or something actually quite serious. Lisa Alther's *Kinflicks* is a novel which has met this fate. *Kinflicks* embodies a real tension in trying to make serious points about women's experience in a form which is basically 'playing for laughs'. I call this style of writing regressive because it arises from an ideology of how children are supposed to see the world. The central protagonist is shown making sense of the world as a child makes sense of its world: children, it is believed, work out their world slowly, only through enquiry, eavesdropping, prying and looking into the closets of their immediate family. The child in this ideology is a sort of miniature detective, working out its genealogy, with a quick eye for the missing links.

This ideology also postulates that the child sees its world as essentially eccentric. All children, after all, believe that their family is more bizarre than the next one. And the ideology assumes that the child's view of its parents is extended to the whole world. The world is bizarre and eccentric, full of haphazard events, and occurrences which have no apparent causal connection. These novels about women's lives frequently attempt a re-creation of this childish world of eccentricities, anecdotes, and the sense of haphazard happenings.

Of course, this view of the world is a version of how reality is to the child. The lack of causal explanations, the haphazard events and inexplicable eccentricities are visions which, if they ever existed, are rarely carried into the adult world. In the adult world, a sense of the causal connection between things has been profoundly and irreversibly formed by that early history. In the adult world, strong feelings about how things happened are usually present. The adult blames and feels guilt, feels dependent on some people and rejects others, in short has taken up a place. This place is conditioned no doubt by infantile experiences, but these experiences are now interpreted in the light of the adult personality. How indeed could a writer produce a 'true' narrative, in the sense of an objective account of events, not yet coloured by emotional dramas?

Yet these novels make their claim to a 'higher degree of realism' than their romantic predecessors precisely by attempting to produce an objective sequence of events and re-create a childish consciousness which does not see and does not evaluate the connections between people's actions. When it comes down to it, of course, even within this ideology the novels are making clear choices about what events are picked out as the most significant. In these novels where women's experience is highlighted, it has become a standing joke that we are to expect the first period, first kiss, first (fumbled) intercourse, first (disastrous) marriage, lesbian affair and usually lonely resolution. The end product is normally that the protagonist feels she has 'become her own person'. This disingenuous construction of an adolescent world derives precisely from the novel's attempt to create a higher realism. The complex family history and interrelations, the anecdotes presented as if passed from generation to generation, the eccentric view of the world, are all practices aimed at creating the sense of the autobiographical. This is something which is often reinforced by the way in which the central characters, as in *The Women's Room* (Marilyn French) or *Sita* (Kate Millett), are themselves writers or novelists.

It is no coincidence that high on the best-seller lists alongside these 'novels that change lives' are the sexual autobiographies of so-called personalities – Mandy Rice Davies, Joan Collins and Fiona Richmond – who also employ these confessional tactics: family genealogy, school days, first sexual encounters, then the hard stuff of adult sexual experience. Women-centred novels represent a fictionalised version of our culture's contemporary obsession with autobiography and with intimate revelations.

Certain points can be made about the confessional forms of writing and their preoccupation with sexuality. I have hinted that this telling all does not in fact bear witness to a radical break with our 'repressed' past. What used to be the structure of written pornography has now appeared in the mainsteam merged with the traditions of the novelistic, derived from the heyday of the Victorian novel. In fact, it has been suggested elsewhere that this obsessive talking about sexuality represents a continuation of certain practices relating to the control of sexuality. Sexuality in fact has never been repressed as the vision of the Victorians would have it. For several centuries now, sexuality has been at the heart of a number of discourses, and since the last century has been made more and more important. In the Victorian period, these discourses were directed towards the prohibition of certain sexual practices, such as masturbation or female 'promiscuity'. We can see this negative aim in the educational and medical writings of the Victorian era. But however negative and controlling these discourses were, they all had sexuality as the central object of concern. In contemporary society there has been a shift rather than a liberation in the treatment of sexuality; now the discourses are directed at making sex explicit rather than denying it.

In countries where the Catholic Church had a powerful presence the confessional seems to have influenced the form taken by these social and scientific discourses on sex. Like church confessionals, they simultaneously enquire into sexuality and command that all be revealed in its most minute and detailed ramifications. This detailed pursuit of the tiniest pleasures in sexuality was, of course, a method of control. Owning up to the pleasures of the flesh, the subject accepted the control of the Church, which was seen as having the key to the soul, bestowing forgiveness and absolution. Scientific discourses also 'listen' to sexuality *and* take sexuality to be the true expression of innermost identity. Hence pseudo-medical disciplines like sexology developed, classifying individuals according to their constitutional and sexual predisposition, anxious to fix and describe a whole classificatory system of sexualities. Michel Foucault, in *The History of Sexuality*, described the way in which power can be exercised through concern with sexuality. The identity of the subject is found within these discourses, which multiply the areas and possibilities for sexual pleasure only to control, classify and subject.

These ideas are useful because they indicate how the centrality of sexuality in novels, either coyly in romantic fiction or explicitly in confession of sexual experiences, has definite correspondences with the wider social organisation of sexuality. We have to treat with suspicion the whole notion of sexual revolution which these novels are said to represent because there has been no such violent change from repression to freedom. Even the most apparently open and explicit detailing of sex can be an expression of sex in a way which means it is structured by very definite social movements and relates to the structures of power in society at large.

Within the novel, the 'confession' has appeared overdetermined by traditions specific to the novel. In particular it has been influenced by the importance of narrative which organises a series of events or experiences as significant and progressing towards a meaningful conclusion. This space of time, or narrative, is one in which the central character or characters undergo a series of experiences which radically affect their lives or transform their attitudes. The effect of this structure is to create a distinct ideology of knowledge and indeed life – that experience brings knowledge and possibly wisdom.

But where novels focusing on women's lives are concerned, a distinctive variant has occurred. Knowledge or understanding has been focused exclusively on sexual experience – love, marriage, divorce or just sexual encounters. This has the effect of reproducing the ideology where (albeit now disillusioned) women are viewed in relation to their sexual history. Women again defined through their sexuality, are the sex to be interrogated and understood. Becoming my own person or woman is in the grain of the sexual; it is how a woman deals with her sexuality. Novels with male characters may well also concentrate obsessively on sex. But what the sex means is different. For men, sexual encounters represent access to power, a series of encounters and experiences which build up a sense of the individual's power in having control over women's bodies. Sexual experience in women's novels represents access to knowledge, rather than power. Sexual experience becomes the way in which a woman finds out about herself.

There's a danger that such structures reproduce the Victorian ideology that sexuality is somehow outside social relations. The idea that a woman could become her own person just through sexual experience and the discovery of sexual needs and dislikes again establishes sexual relations as somehow separate from social structures. The emphasis on sex as knowledge may well obscure the fact that sex is implicated in society as a whole, that sex has consequences and that there are always other people to consider in a sexual experience. Questions of social responsibility and not hurting other people are no less important to women critical of conventional morality. Yet there's a danger that sexual experience has been represented as an end in itself, as if other social decisions and work experiences didn't affect us as much.

It is hardly surprising that women have been represented as having a crucial role in the 'sexual revolution'. Sexology, psychology, psychoanalysis, films, pornography all ask the question, 'What is women's sexuality?' At a period when a society represents itself as shaking off the mysteries of our repressed past it is women who are represented as being at the centre of this transformation.

This society chooses to represent women as responsible for the sexual revolution: sexual repression was overthrown as soon as women were clear about wanting and needing sex as much as men. In fact, women have realised that greater freedom of opportunity for sexual intercourse does not of itself bring about changes in men's attitudes towards women, or changes in how the sexes relate to one another. Men, in short, have remained in their position of privilege, often contemptuous of women, who therefore did not gain from a discovery of their sexual personalities in the ways represented.

But does this invalidate these novels and their spoken commitment to changing the position of women? I think not. Because like feminism itself, these novels probably transcend their origins in wider social movements. It is not sufficient to suggest that because women have been shot to the fore as the speaking sex they simply reproduce the values which have made women the group whose sexuality is interrogated. For as with the Victorian heroine, the current preoccupation with women's sexual experiences corresponds to a general social concern with women's social position and how it will be resolved. Women's social position and possibilities have changed radically in the last fifty years; conceptions of what is possible and what is desirable have been greatly changed and such changes represent upheavals to some of the most dearly held ideologies and beliefs of this society. It would suit society to reduce women to being *the* sex – the talking, the experiencing sex – because again this would pose little threat to the idea of the experiential individual at the heart of this society. But because women have always been confined to this realm, albeit in different ways over different historical periods, any investigation of this construction has the potential for exposing it *as construction*. Thus even those novels which appear to correspond to most widely held sexual ideologies often attempt more interesting things. For the autobiographical voice of these contemporary women-centred novels often appeals to a collectivity. I am, but I am a representative of all women. The history of my oppression is the history of all women's oppression.

And beyond the format are those writers who have begun to deconstruct the whole notion of identity, at the same time challenging the conventions of the novel. Writers like Doris Lessing or Fay Weldon both occasionally disrupt the conventions of a central narrative voice or character, and their writing becomes a myriad of historical, social and sexual concerns which do not belong to any individual subjectivity. And both Doris Lessing and Angela Carter explore the fantastic and the erotic in ways that do not appeal to any realistic identification with a self-discovering heroine on the way to her own personhood. Nor is it surprising to find reinstated other earlier novelists who also stretch the reader's understanding beyond the conventions of a sexual self-discovery. Some of Rosamond Lehmann's novels, for instance, appear to explore the whole basis of fiction, creating a narrative which can never be validated, where the hopes and fantasies of the individual protagonists are validated and the objective narrative rendered fictional.

The term 'women-centred' novels covers a multitude of sins. But at the heart of this multi-faceted phenomenon is one dominant convention, a type of narrative which corresponds to existing (and therefore problematic) ways of defining women through their sexual personhood. Because the whole issue of women's sexuality and changes in structures of living are crucial to our experiences now, these novels are sometimes able to explore the question of how female identity has been constructed and how this relates to society as a whole. Often, though, the convention itself pulls the novels back into banal repetitions, asserting a world without fantasy where women struggle on, often grim, brutalised and victimised. I'm not sure that becoming my own person is sufficient compensation for such a world.

4 The Difference of View
Mary Jacobus

For George Eliot, as for her heroines (wrote Virginia Woolf),

> the burden and the complexity of womanhood were not
> enough; she must reach beyond the sanctuary and pluck
> for herself the strange bright fruits of art and knowledge.
> Clasping them as few women have ever clasped them, she
> would not renounce her own inheritance – *the difference of
> view, the difference of standard . . .*[1]

The terms here are worth lingering on; they bring to light a
hidden problem as well as articulating an obvious one. The
problem explicitly located is, in one way or another, the theme
of many of the essays included in this book – or rather, their
question: that is, the nature of women's access to culture and
their entry into literary discourse. The demand for education
('the strange bright fruits of art and knowledge') provides the
emancipatory thrust of much nineteenth- and twentieth-
century feminism, and goes back to Mary Wollstonecraft's
attempt to appropriate the language of Enlightenment Reason
for her own sex in *The Rights of Woman*. But this access to a
male-dominated culture may equally be felt to bring with it
alienation, repression, division – a silencing of the 'feminine',
a loss of women's inheritance. The problem, then, is not
George Eliot's alone; it is that of women's writing (and of
feminist literary criticism) itself. To propose a difference of
view, a difference of standard – to begin to ask what the
difference might be – is to call in question the very terms
which constitute that difference.

The terms used by Virginia Woolf, therefore, also uncover
something of the rift experienced by women writers in a

patriarchal society, where language itself may re-inscribe the structures by which they are oppressed. Reaching beyond the sanctuary, transgressing the boundaries of womanhood (*womanhood*: the sacred hearth, at once home, womb and tomb; something is being stilled into silence, for the burden of womanhood is also the burden of the mystery) – the movement becomes an exit from the sacred into the profane. In this scheme, woman as silent bearer of ideology (virgin, wife, mother) is the *necessary* sacrifice to male secularity, worldliness, and tampering with forbidden knowledge. She is the term by which patriarchy creates a reserve of purity and silence in the materiality of its traffic with the world and its noisy discourse. Feminised, the Faustian hero becomes a militant adventuress, Eve, plucking 'the strange bright fruits' that bring both knowledge and unhappiness. The archetypal gesture installs George Eliot in a specifically Judaeo-Christian drama, that of sin and death; the fall is from innocence (mindlessness?) into mortality. It's not surprising, therefore, that Virginia Woolf should end her essay with what amounts to a funeral oration. For her, George Eliot was literally worn into the grave by the battle with 'sex and health and convention' which attended her quest for 'more knowledge and more freedom'.

In this traditional drama, a lively sense of sin is matched with a weighty sense of ancient female suffering and hopeless desire; but George Eliot's heroines, Virginia Woolf tells us, no longer suffer in silence:

> The ancient consciousness of woman, charged with suffering and sensibility, and for so many ages dumb, seems in them to have brimmed and overflowed and uttered a demand for something – they scarcely know what – for something that is perhaps incompatible with the facts of human existence.[2]

(That notion of dumbness and utterance, of demand for an impossible desire, forms a recurrent motif in both women's writing and feminist literary criticism.) What is striking here is the association of ancient suffering and modern desire with women's inheritance, as if they were almost synonymous. This is elegy, not affirmation. Elegy which, in Virginia Woolf's case, one might justifiably link with the death of a mother or mothering step-sister. Our mothers were killed by the burden and the complexity of womanhood; or, like George Eliot, died in giving birth to their writing (as Dorothea rests in an unvisited tomb in order that 'George Eliot' may write her epitaph). Such, at any rate, seems to be the melancholy inference. It's surely significant that for at least one woman looking back at another, the price of combining womanhood and writing seemed so high – that the transgression of writing seemed to bring with it mortal consequences; the sacrifice not only of happiness, but of life itself.

Contemporary feminist criticism is more likely to stress pleasure than suffering – the freeing of repressed female desire; *jouissance* and '*la mère qui jouit*' (no longer barred from sexual pleasure) as against the burden of womanhood. Recent French writing about women and literature, marked as it is by the conjunction of neo-Freudian psychoanalysis and structuralism, has particularly tended to diagnose the repression of women's desire by representation itself, and by the order of language as instated by the Law of the Father: the symbolic order, predicated on lack and castration.[3] In this theoretical scheme, femininity itself – heterogeneity, otherness – becomes the repressed term by which discourse is made possible. The feminine takes its place with the absence, silence, or incoherence that discourse represses; in what Julia Kristeva would call the *semiotic*, the pre-Oedipal phase of rhythmic, onomatopoeic babble which precedes the symbolic but remains inscribed in those pleasurable and rupturing aspects of language identified particularly with *avant-garde* literary practice. But here again, there's a problem for feminist criticism. Women's access to discourse involves submission to phallocentricity, to the masculine and the symbolic: refusal, on the other hand, risks re-inscribing the feminine as a yet more marginal madness or nonsense. When we speak (as feminist writers and theorists often do) of the need for a special language for women, what then do we mean?

Not, surely, a refusal of language itself; nor a return to a specifically feminine linguistic domain which in fact marks the place of women's oppression and confinement. Rather, a process that is played out within language, across boundaries. The dream of a language freed from the Freudian notion of castration, by which female difference is defined as lack rather than otherness, is at first sight essentially theoretical, millennial and Utopian. Its usefulness lies in allying feminism and the *avant-garde* in a common political challenge to the very discourse which makes them possible; the terms of language itself, as well as the terms of psychoanalysis and of literary criticism, are called in question – subverted from within. Woman and artist, the feminine and the *avant-garde*, are elided in the privileged zone of contemporary intellectual and aesthetic concern: writing. Such a move has the advantage of freeing off the 'feminine' from the religion-bound, ultimately conservative and doom-ridden concept of difference-as-opposition which underlies Virginia Woolf's reading of the 'case' of George Eliot. *Difference* is redefined, not as male *versus* female – not as biologically constituted – but as a multiplicity, joyousness and heterogeneity which is that of textuality itself. Writing, the production of meaning, becomes the site both of challenge and otherness; rather than (as in more traditional approaches) simply yielding the themes and representation of female oppression. *Difference*, in fact, becomes a traversal of the boundaries inscribed in Virginia Woolf's terms, but a traversal that exposes these very boundaries for what they are – the product of phallocentric discourse and of women's relation to patriarchal culture. Though necessarily working within 'male' discourse, women's writing (in this scheme) would work ceaselessly to deconstruct it: to write what cannot be written.

So much for one formulation of the question: what is the nature (the difference) of women's writing? Another way to pose the question is to explore the extent to which patriarchal representation, by contrast, 'silences' women – the extent to which *woman* or *womanhood*, considered not as an image but as a sign, becomes the site of both contradiction and repression. For D. H. Lawrence, woman is 'the unutterable which man must forever continue to try to utter'; she achieves womanhood at the point where she is silenced (like Sue Bridehead) and installed within the sanctuary.[4] If writing is a transgression punishable by death, being written about, by however loving a Father, can also prove fatal. Take the disquieting way in which Hardy, in a famous scene from *Tess of the D'Urbervilles*, reveals the sign *woman* to be a rich source of mythic confusion, ideological contradiction, and erotic fascination:

> She was yawning, and he saw the red interior of her mouth as if it had been a snake's. She had stretched one arm so high above her coiled-up cable of hair that he could see its satin delicacy above the sunburn; her face was flushed with sleep, and her eyelids hung heavy over their pupils. The brim-fulness of her nature breathed from her. It was a moment when a woman's soul is more incarnate than at any other time; when the most spiritual beauty bespeaks itself flesh; and sex takes the outside place in the presentation. (XXVII)

Sex having taken the outside place in the presentation, it's not surprising that within a short space Tess should become, first feline, and then Eve. The language of incarnation (body and soul, presence and absence) signals an underlying structure which comes near to collapse before the threat of female sexuality. Though Hardy seems to be salvaging Tess's body for spirituality (the vessel is brim-full), the yawning mouth opens up a split in the very terms he uses. The incarnate state of Tess's soul appears to be as close to sleep – to unconsciousness – as is compatible with going about her work. At the same time, the snake-mouth marks the point of (desired) entry to an interior which is offered to us as simply yet more body (she is all red inside, *not* all soul). Fascination with this unknown, unrepresentable, interiorised sexuality is surely at the centre of male fantasies of seduction and engulfment. No wonder that Hardy goes on to make Tess, not the object of male gaze, but the mirror in which the male is reflected ('*she* regarded *him* as Eve at her second waking might have regarded Adam'; my italics): otherness is domesticated, made safe, through narcissism – the female mouth can't utter, only receive and confirm the male.

Tess's silence, like her purity, makes female desire dumb; places her on the side of unconsciousness and, finally, death. 'Shut up already' might be the hidden message which a feminist critique uncovers. But to stop at such readings (or at exposing the reproduction of sexist ideology by male critics) is to take only the first step towards uttering an alternative. Utterance, though, brings the problem home for women writers (as for feminist critics). The options polarise along familiar lines: appropriation or separatism. Can women adapt traditionally male-dominated modes of writing and analysis to the articulation of female oppression and desire? Or should we rather reject tools that may simply re-inscribe our marginality and deny the specificity of our experience, instead forging others of our own? – reverting, perhaps, to the traditionally feminine in order to revalidate its forms (formlessness?) and preoccupations – rediscovering subjectivity; the language of feeling; ourselves. The risks on either side are illuminatingly played out in the writing of feminism's founding mother herself: Mary Wollstonecraft. *The Rights of Woman*, in claiming sense for women rather than sensibility, pays a price that is reflected in its own prose. Putting herself outside the confines of a despised femininity, aligning herself with 'sense', Mary Wollstonecraft also eschews 'pretty feminine phrases' as a male conspiracy designed to soften female slavery. Linguistic pleasure (literary language) is placed on the side of the feminine; banned, like female desire:

> I shall disdain to cull my phrases or polish my style. I aim at being useful, and sincerity will render me unaffected; for, wishing rather to persuade by the force of my arguments than dazzle by the elegance of my language, I shall not waste my time in rounding periods, or in fabricating the turgid bombast of artificial feelings, which, coming from the head, never reach the heart. I shall be employed about things, not words! and, anxious to render my sex more respectable members of society, I shall try to avoid that flowery diction which has slided from essays into novels, and from novels into familiar letters and conversations. ('Author's Introduction')

A swagger of busy self-presentation makes this as much the creation of an alienated persona as it is a feminist preface to *Lyrical Ballads*. A plain-speaking utilitarian speaks not so much *for* women, or *as* a woman, but *against* them – over their dead bodies, and over (having attempted to cast it out) the body of the text too: 'I shall be employed about things, not words!'

Speaking both for and as a woman (rather than 'like' a woman): this is the problem of women's writing. For the feminist critic, the problem may resolve itself as one of style. For Mary Wollstonecraft, the solution lay in fiction that gave her access not only (paradoxically) to her own situation as a woman, but to literarity. *The Wrongs of Woman* inverts both the title and the assumptions of her earlier essay in order to show how, if 'sense' excludes women, 'sensibility' confines them – yet offers a radical challenge to patriarchy; a challenge which it must repress. (When the heroine pleads her own case in a court of law, the judge alludes to 'the fallacy of letting women plead their feelings . . . What virtuous woman thought of her feelings?', thereby exposing the double-bind.) The prison of sensibility is created by patriarchy to contain women; thus they experience desire without Law, language without power. Marginalised, the language of feeling can only ally itself with insanity – an insanity which, displaced into writing, produces a moment of imaginative and linguistic excess over-brimming the container of fiction, and swamping the distinction between author and character:

> What is the view of the fallen column, the mouldering arch, of the most exquisite workmanship, when compared with this living memento of the fragility, the instability, of reason, and the wild luxuriancy of noxious passions? Enthusiasm turned adrift, like some rich stream overflowing its banks, rushes forward with destructive velocity, inspiring a sublime concentration of thought. *Thus thought Maria* – These are the ravages over which humanity must ever mournfully ponder . . . It is not over the decaying productions of the mind, embodied with the happiest art, we grieve most bitterly. The view of what has been done by man, produces a melancholy, yet aggrandizing, sense of what remains to be achieved by human intellect; but a mental convulsion, which, like the devastation of an earthquake, throws all the elements of thought and imagination into confusion, makes contemplation giddy, and we fearfully ask on what ground we ourselves stand.[5]

This is what it means for women to be on the side of madness as well as silence. Like the rich stream overflowing its banks, a wash of desire throws all the elements of thought and imagination into confusion. By contrast with the ruins of (male) cultural imperialism, the earthquake is feminised; demands 'on what ground we ourselves stand'; opens on to a feminist sublime where all foundations are called in question.

Mary Wollstonecraft's concern in this passage for 'words', not 'things', makes it a crucial moment for both women's writing and feminist literary criticism. A mental convulsion breaches the impasse between undifferentiated disappearance into a 'male' text and the prison of sensibility. Rejecting the essentialism that keeps women subjected as well as subjective, it also rejects mastery and dominance. Madness imagined as revolution, or the articulation of Utopian desire ('a demand for something – they scarcely know what'), represent gestures past the impasse played out by Mary Wollstonecraft's prose. In writing, such gestures may release possibilities repressed by a dominant ideology or its discourse. The transgression of literary boundaries – moments when structures are shaken, when language refuses to lie down meekly, or the marginal is brought into sudden focus, or intelligibility itself refused – reveal not only the conditions of possibility within which women's writing exists, but what it would be like to revolution-ise them. In the same way, the moment of desire (the moment when the writer most clearly installs herself in her writing) becomes a refusal of mastery, an opting for openness and possibility, which can in itself make women's writing a challenge to the literary structures it must necessarily inhabit.

'Thus thought Maria' – the container overflowed by autho-rial Enthusiasm – has its analogue in a famous 'awkward break' noticed by Virginia Woolf. Her example is Charlotte Brontë's intrusion into *Jane Eyre* with what *A Room of One's Own* rightly identifies as a protest against the confinement of the nineteenth-century woman writer:

It is in vain to say human beings ought to be satisfied with tranquillity: they must have action; and they will make it if they cannot find it . . . Women are supposed to be very calm generally: but women feel just as men feel; they need exercise for their faculties, and a field for their efforts as much as their brothers do; they suffer from too rigid a restraint, too absolute a stagnation, precisely as men would suffer . . . It is thoughtless to condemn them, or laugh at them, if they seek to do more or learn more than custom has pronounced necessary for their sex.

When thus alone, I not unfrequently heard Grace Poole's laugh . . .[6]

('That is an awkward break, I thought', comments Virginia Woolf.) The author herself has burst the bounds of 'too rigid a restraint' – making action if she cannot find it. By a breach of fictional decorum, writing enacts protest as well as articulating it. It is not simply that the excess of energy disrupts the text; it is that the disruption reveals what the novel cannot say within its legitimate confines, and hence reveals its fictionality. The unacceptable text gets the blue pencil from Virginia Woolf ('the woman who wrote those pages . . . will write in a rage where she should write calmly . . . She will write of herself where she should write of her characters. She is at war with her lot'); but it also opens up a rift in her own seamless web. What she herself cannot say without loss of calmness (rage has been banned in the interests of literature) is uttered instead by another woman writer. The overflow in *Jane Eyre* washes into *A Room of One's Own*. This oblique recuperation of feminist energy has implications for feminist criticism as well as for fiction; might, in fact, be said to characterise the practice of the feminist critic, for whom the relation between author and text (her own text) is equally charged. Editing into her writing the outburst edited out of Charlotte Brontë's, Virginia Woolf creates a point of instability which unsettles her own urbane and polished decorum. The rift exposes the fiction of authorial control and objectivity, revealing other possible fictions, other kinds of writing; exposes, for a moment, its own terms.

The slippage here is both seductive and threatening. Seductive, because passion is involved; threatening, because the structures on which both fiction and criticism depend are seen to be built on words alone. And perhaps the correction of authorial transgression – the domestication of authorial desire – may be necessary in the interests of writing itself.

Take a significant moment of self-censorship like that which closes the 'Finale' of *Middlemarch*. George Eliot's compassionately magisterial verdict on the 'determining acts' of Dorothea's life ('the mixed result of young and noble impulse struggling amidst the conditions of an imperfect social state, in which great feelings will often take the aspect of error, and great faith the aspect of illusion') cancels what had originally been 'an awkward break' in the final pages of the first edition:

> They were the mixed results of young and noble impulse struggling under prosaic conditions. Among the many remarks passed on her mistakes, it was never said in the neighbourhood of Middlemarch that such mistakes could not have happened if the society into which she was born had not smiled on . . . modes of education which make a woman's knowledge another name for motley ignorance – on rules of conduct which are in flat contradiction with its own loudly-asserted beliefs. While this is the social air in which mortals begin to breathe, there will be collisions such as those in Dorothea's life, where great feelings will take the aspect of error, and great faith the aspect of illusion.[7]

Authorial indignation risks turning the neighbourhood of Middlemarch into 'social air', uncovering fiction as polemic. Whether the cancellation springs from loss of nerve or aesthetic judgement, it makes George Eliot (so to speak) the heir of Virginia Woolf as well as Charlotte Brontë. In doing so, it opens up the possibility of the author's dissolution into her own text; the closing sentences of the novel point beyond the 'Finale' to their own writing – to the full nature that has its strength broken by being diverted into channels whose effect is incalculably diffusive:

> Her finely-touched spirit had still its fine issues, though they were not widely visible. Her full nature, like that river of which Cyrus broke the strength, spent itself in channels which had no great name on the earth. But the effect of her being on those around her was incalculably diffusive: for the growing good of the world is partly dependent on unhistoric acts; and that things are not so ill with you and

me as they might have been, is half owing to the number who lived faithfully a hidden life, and rest in unvisited tombs. ('Finale')

Earlier, George Eliot has referred to Casaubon's turgid scholarship as 'minor monumental productions'; monuments to dead languages. By contrast with this sterile imperialism (Casaubon *versus* the world), we have the unhistoric acts that make for growing good. Though a new St Theresa will find no conventual life to reform, a new Antigone no Creon to oppose with self-immolation ('the medium in which their ardent deeds took shape is forever gone'), still, the writer may find another 'medium' of her own for ardent deeds. Dorothea's hidden life and entombment make her a silent reformer, an unremembered protester; but her silence and anonymity are the sacrifice which allows 'George Eliot' speech and name.

If the gain seems marginal, this may be because writing is itself marginal, unhistoric; if diffusive, incalculably so. But the possibility glimpsed at the end of *Middlemarch* – that of Enthusiasm overflowing into ink – points to the quietly subversive power of writing, its power to destabilise the ground on which we stand. In *A Room of One's Own*, Virginia Woolf dissolves 'truth' (the withheld 'nugget of truth') into 'the lies that flow from my pen'; the subject of women and writing becomes a fiction: 'I propose, making use of all the liberties and licences of a novelist, to tell you the story . . .'[8] As hard fact dissolves into fluid fiction, so the authorial 'I' becomes 'only a convenient term for somebody who has no real being'; many 'I's', many Marys, ('Mary Beton, Mary Seton, Mary Carmichael' and I) – a plurality contrasted to the unified 'I' which falls as a dominating phallic shadow across the male page, like Casaubon's monumental egotism. And as the subject ('I') is dissolved into writing, so boundaries themselves are called into question; rendered, not *terra firma*, but fiction too. Once returned to its proper medium (the Cam), the thought-fish which swims through *A Room of One's Own* 'as it darted and sank, and flashed hither and thither, set up such a wash and tumult of ideas that it was impossible to sit still'. The story becomes the narrative of its own inception, then of the arrest of verbal energy – this darting, flashing, linguistic play –

by the figure of a man, representative of the Law, of the phallic 'I' that bars and bounds:

> It was thus that I found myself walking with extreme rapidity across a grass plot. Instantly a man's figure rose to intercept me. Nor did I at first understand that the gesticulations of a curious-looking object, in a cut-away coat and evening shirt, were aimed at me. His face expressed horror and indignation. Instinct rather than reason came to my help; he was a Beadle; I was a woman. This was the turf; there was the path. Only the Fellows and Scholars are allowed here; the gravel is the place for me. Such thoughts are the work of a moment. As I regained the path the arms of the Beadle sank, his face assumed its usual repose . . .[9]

The protest against male exclusiveness is obvious enough; so is the comical reduction of an educational institution to a grass plot and a clockwork beadle. Acquiescing in the terms of her trespass, Virginia Woolf yet shows, with pleasurable obliqueness (via her short cut), that these terms are arbitrary – a matter of cut-away coats and gravel paths.

Virginia Woolf's satire, in delineating the confines within which women must walk ('This was the turf; there was the path') traverses and exposes them. The story she tells is in fact that of her own oblique relation, as a woman writer, to the dominant culture and to patriarchal institutions (she labels them Oxbridge, the educational system which inscribes her marginality). At once within this culture and outside it, the woman writer experiences not only exclusion, but an internalised split. Elsewhere in *A Room of One's Own* she puts it like this:

> if one is a woman one is often surprised by a sudden splitting off of consciousness, say in walking down Whitehall, when from being the natural inheritor of that civilisation, she becomes, on the contrary, outside of it, alien and critical.[10]

'Alien and critical' – the stance glimpsed behind the urbane and playful style of *A Room of One's Own*. Though Virginia Woolf never fails to remind us that the matter of inheritance is absolutely a matter of access to power, property and education, an experienced division forms part of that inheritance too. To recognise both the split and the means by which it is constituted, to challenge its terms while necessarily working within them – that is the hidden narrative of the trespass on the grass. But what about that elusive thought-fish? For Virginia Woolf, rage drove it into hiding; the rage that for her distorts Charlotte Brontë's fiction ('She will write in a rage where she should write calmly'). It is in this light, perhaps, that we should re-read her famous remarks about androgyny – not as a naïve attempt to transcend the determinants of gender and culture (though it is that), not as a Romantic enshrining of Shakespearian creativity (though it is that too), but rather as a harmonising gesture, a simultaneous enactment of desire and repression by which the split is closed with an essentially Utopian vision of undivided consciousness. The repressive male/female opposition which 'interferes with the unity of the mind' gives way to a mind paradoxically conceived of not as one, but as heterogeneous, open to the play of difference: 'resonant and porous . . . it transmits emotion without impediment . . . it is naturally creative, incandescent, and undivided.'[11] That's as good a description as one could wish, not of the mind, but of Virginia Woolf's own prose – and of the play of difference perpetually enacted within writing.

The gesture towards androgyny is millennial, like all dreams of another language or mode of being; but its effect is to remove the area of debate (and the trespass) from biological determination to the field of signs; from gender to representation ('words' not 'things'). And in holding open other possibilities – otherness itself – such writing posits 'the difference of view' as a matter of rewriting. 'A woman writing thinks back through her mother'; thinking back through the mother becomes at once recuperation and revision. The rediscovery of a female literary tradition need not mean a return to specifically 'female' (that is, potentially confining) domains, any more than the feminist colonising of Marxist, psychoanalytic, or poststructuralist modes of thought necessarily means a loss of that alien and critical relation which is one aspect of women's inheritance. Rather, they involve a recognition that all attempts to inscribe female difference within writing are a matter of inscribing women within fictions of one kind or another (whether literary, critical, or psychoanalytic); and hence, that what is at stake for both women writing and writing about women is the rewriting of these fictions – the work of revision which makes 'the difference of view' a question rather than an answer, and a question to be asked not simply of women, but of writing too.

5 Representing Women: Re-presenting the Past

Gillian Beer

This essay was originally a lecture addressed to a group whose views and assumptions I largely share; its function was to make us look critically at some of those assumptions. In preparing it as an essay I have not tried to erase the traces of its first form, since much of the energy of my counter-assertions works out from this communal starting point. Our shared position affirms the value of women's studies, the importance of theory in giving us a purchase on literary and political practice, and the need to recognise ways in which the past is appropriated and re-written to justify the present. In the argument of the essay itself my emphasis falls on literary history, on the need to recognise the *difference* of past writing and past concerns instead of converting them into our current categories. Rather than seeking always the 'relevance' of past writing to our present reading, we may need to learn lost reading skills which bring to light elements in the text not apparent to our current training. I argue also the necessity within women's studies to analyse writing by men alongside that by women. All these elements are concentrated on bringing to our notice the 'presentism' and the fixed gender assumptions that may lurk still in some of our critical practice. In giving the paper, I was, of course, *there*: in my body, as a woman, with a woman's voice. The absence of any but a nominal presence of writer in writing must shift some of the balances within the argument, and I have tried to take account of that in my presentation. Though I'm still sorry I can't be there to argue with the reader.

We favour currently the word 'representation' because it

sustains a needed distance between experience and formulation. It recognises the fictive in our understanding. It allows
a gap between how we see things and how, potentially, they
might be. It acknowledges the extent to which ideologies
harden into objects and so sustain themselves as real presences
in the world. The objects may be books, pictures, films,
advertisements, fashion. Their encoding of assumptions and
desires re-inforces as natural and permanent what may be
temporary and learnt. So representations rapidly shift from
being secondary to being primary in their truth-claims. This
speedy shift to claiming authority we can all observe, in
others' practice and our own. Representations rapidly become
representatives – those empowered to speak on behalf of their
constituency: the authentic voices of a group. That is where
the trouble starts when the claim is representing women:
speaking on behalf of women – speaking on behalf of who?
Are we offering and receiving formulations of an abiding
group; offering accounts of a person, or a group of people,
conceived as stable?

One thing needs to be clear, then, as I start to de-stabilise
my title. *I* am not a representative woman representing all
women: I am not speaking on behalf of all of us, or occupying
the space of those who differ from me. The demand that as
women we claim women as our constituency may rapidly
move from desirable solidarity to tokenism. So the woman
finds herself there *in place of* a wide range of other women,
uttering wise saws on their behalf, creating the uniformity of
universals all over again. As Gayatri Spivak puts it, woman
is not one instrument added to the orchestra. But, the refusal
that I am offering also takes us into a contradiction that persists
in representation. Though I resist the role of representative, to
others I may represent women – or a particular type of
woman – and certainly I *am* a woman, at home in my body,
liking much of the condition, and closely sharing with other
women, concerned with the theoretical consequences – and
the practical ones – of my gender. We women are a body of
people and share bodily features. Go too far along that
road and we find biologism, with its emphasis on bodily
characteristics, particularly those of reproduction, as the
essential characterisation of all women. We need to prevent

metaphor settling into assumption, the fate of Cixous's famous 'writing in milk'.[1] As much recent gender theory (Chodorow, Dinnerstein, etc.) has emphasised, that body, those bodies, have been produced culturally as well as physiologically.[2] They are then *recognised* culturally and those recognitions are further internalised. These embodied recognitions have ricocheted back and forth as description between men and women, forming psychic conditions over time within which we live, write, and expect.[3]

If we are to understand the processes of gender formation within a culture, and if we are to understand the shiftiness with which cultures have laid claim to the formulations of their predecessors in order to naturalise their own perceptions, we need to study how things have changed. This requires the reading of men's and women's writing side by side. *How* things have changed is likely to challenge any notion of a sustained arc of progress in representing women; it will challenge also the notion of a stable archetypal order. Clutter, inertia, scurry: the hoped for and longed for, long delayed but informing the present – these are more often the motions we shall discover in reading through the writing of past periods.

To assert in our theory that men have dominated discourse and yet to pretend in our practice as students and teachers that women's writing is autonomous, by studying only genetically female authors, becomes sentimental. Moreover, it leads to theoretical confusion because it expunges economic, epistemic, shared historical conditions of writing and makes it impossible to *measure* difference. To read Joyce, and Lawrence, and Woolf alongside, for example, does not collapse difference: it specifies it; it takes us some way into understanding the complex relationships between modernism and feminism, as well as between male and female non-combatants' experience of the First World War (all were non-combatants, of course). Moreover, if gender is a largely cultural product it is risky to read women's representations of women, even, as if the gender of the writer makes them thereby automatically authoritative. Such an assumption is to simplify our understanding both of the writing and of our own internalisation of past gender constructions.

In the eighteenth century, particularly, the mere naming of

authors as female may in any case lead us into a crasser kind
of error. Many men then wrote as women. John Cleland
commented, as Halsband reminds us, 'in reviewing a novel
entitled *The School for Husbands. Written by a Lady*:

> "As ladies are generally acknowledged to be superior to our
> sex in all works of imagination and fancy, we doubt not
> this is deemed a sufficient reason for placing their names
> in the title-page of many a dull, lifeless story which contains
> not one single female idea, but has been hammered out of
> the brainless head of a Grubstreet hireling."

In this novel, he continues, many of the scenes convince him
of 'the *femality* of its Author.'[4]

The crux here is that what has made the fraud desirable is
the ascription of *imagination* to women as a specifically female,
rather than a human power – and then thereby its peripheralis-
ation on to the edge of power patterns. Qualities, however
fine, which are prescribed exclusively to one gender become
falsified. Evelyn Fox Keller has recently shown how the
metaphoric representation of men's activities in science has
narrowed the methodological range of scientific practice. As
women we may like many qualities exclusively prescribed for
us in the past (insight, nurturing, empathy) and prefer them
to those exclusively represented as men's (dominance, go-
getting, genius), but we should cast an extremely sceptical
eye on the grounds of that preference, and not naturalise it.
As Mary Hays pointed out towards the end of the eighteenth
century, men have valued 'women's' virtues, such as prudence,
patience, wisdom, when they prove convenient to themselves.

> Prudence being one of those rare medicines which affect by
> sympathy, and this being likewise one of those cases, where
> the husbands have no objections to the wives acting as
> principals, nor to their receiving all the honors and emol-
> uments of office; even if death should crown their martyr-
> dom, as has been sometimes known to happen. Dear,
> generous creatures![5]

Literary history will always be an expression of now: current needs, dreads, preoccupations. The cultural conditions within which we receive the texts will shape the attention we first bring to them. We shall read as readers in 1987 or 1988, or, with luck, 1998, but we need not do so helplessly, merely hauling, without noticing, our own cultural baggage. That is likely to happen if we read past texts solely for their grateful 'relevance' to our expectations and to those of our circumstances that we happen to have noticed. The encounter with the otherness of earlier literature can allow us also to recognise and challenge our own assumptions, and those of the society in which we live.[6] To do so we must take care not to fall into the trap of assuming the evolutionist model of literary development, so often taken for granted, in which texts are praised for their 'almost modern awareness' or for 'being ahead of their time'. This presentist mode of argument takes *now* as the source of authority, the only real place.

We can nudge and de-stabilise the word 'representation' in another usable way. It can mean also re-presenting: making past writing a part of our present, making present what is absent. Not bringing it up to date, with the suggestion of the past aspiring to become our present – improved, refurbished, in the hoteliers' discourse – but re-presenting. This means engaging with the *difference* of the past in our present and so making us aware of the trajectory of our arrival and of the insouciance of the past – their neglectfulness of our prized positions and our assumptions. We can use this awareness, if we will, to reinforce and gratify our sense of our own correctness, 'an almost modern understanding' – but that won't get us far. Rather, the study of past writing within the conditions of its production disturbs that autocratic emphasis on the self and the present, as if they were stable entities. It makes us aware too of how far that view continues despite postmodernism.

The problem with the concept of relevance is that it assumes an autonomous and coherent subject. The present, the self, is conceived as absolute; all else as yielding relativistically to it – and unacceptable unless it yields (in both senses). The incorrectness of this once fashionable position has become dramatically manifest with its adoption by the present government: 'relevance' now requires that everything be honed to a meagre utilitarianism. Applied science is to be advantaged over fundamental enquiry with the absurd assumption that applications can be reliably foreseen and that usefulness alone justifies enquiry. Relevance assumes fixity – it is not self-questioning and does not incorporate change.

The connection with the representation of women is not far to seek. Unless we believe in fixed entities – man and woman – we need to be alert to the processes of gender formation and gender change. We cannot construe this in isolation from other elements within a culture, and, moreover, we shall better discover our own fixing assumptions if we value the *unlikeness* of the past. For 'relevance' is not the same as the analysis of internalised history.

The formation of gender, and its condensation in the literature of the time, is not cut loose from economics, or architecture, or class, or, come to that, animal care. No one of these is the single source of authority either: there is no sole source of oppression, though there are dominant forms of it in class, race, and gender power-structures. In the literature of the past we are presented with immensely detailed interconnecting systems: power and pleasure caught into representations so particular as to be irreplaceable. So the informing of the text with our learnt awareness of historical conditions is not a matter simply of providing 'context' or 'background'. Instead it is more exactly in-forming, instantiation – a coming to know again those beliefs, dreads, unscrutinised expectations which may differ from our own but which may also bear upon them.

The task of the literary historian is to receive the same fullness of resource from past texts as from present: to respect their difference, to revive those shifty significations which do not pay court to our concerns but are full of the meaning of that past present. The text fights back: but it can do so with meaning for us only if we read it with enough awareness of the submerged controversies and desires which are *not* concerned with us. The past is past only to us. When it was present, it was/is the present. So, re-presenting literature representing women in a way that is concerned with something other than our own design and story is a challenge which 'relevance' bypasses. We are not at work on a supine or docile text which we can colonise with our meaning or meanings. Instead we have difficult inter-action. Symptomatic reading should not be concerned only to read *through* texts. Why do we so value gaps and contradiction? Is it because it allows us to exercise a kind of social control, to represent ourselves as outside history, like those late nineteenth-century doctors who described their patients and yet exempted themselves from the processes of disease and decay they described? Our necessary search for gaps, lacunae, as analytical tools may have the effect of privileging and defending us. The inquisitorial reading of past literature for correctness and error casts *us* as the inquisitors: we identify with authority and externality.

We can never become past readers: learning the conditions of the past brings them to light. It dramatises what could remain unscrutinised for first readers. We can re-learn lost skills, though. Readers have not all become cleverer since Henry James – only cleverer at reading Henry James. We need different skills for reading Richardson and Wollstonecraft, and different ones again for reading Chrétien de Troyes and Christine de Pisan. We need, always, double reading; or perhaps multiple reading is a better expression – since binarism is another of the hidden metaphors within which we function. The numerology of the culture has replaced the magic of seven, and of three, with the magic of two, with its fixing polarities: what Cixous calls its 'hierarchised oppositions', night/day, law/nature, woman/man, private/public,[7] etc. We need a reading which acknowledges that we start now, from here; but which re-awakens the dormant signification of past literature to its first readers. Such reading seeks intense meaning embedded in semantics, plot, formal and generic properties, conditions of production. These have been overlaid by the sequent pasts and by our present concerns which cannot be obliterated, but we need to explore both likeness and *difference*. Such reading gives room to both scepticism and immersion.

When we were setting up the Cambridge course called 'The Literary Representation of Women' in this area six years ago we wanted to test some of the views then prevalent which seemed close to essentialism and presentism.[8] Among these was the implication that feminism was a product primarily of the past twenty years or so, that there had been a steady arc of progress in women's production and in the recognition of women writers. We wanted to discover whether certain formulations of 'womanhood' persisted irremovably, or whether the cultural inflection of the fourteenth, the seventeenth, the eighteenth centuries would show us real diversity. We wanted, moreover, to understand how men and women construed their gender-identities and their relations in conditions very different from our own. We knew that we would read *now* with all the necessary, and sometimes beloved, baggage of our own cultural responses. But we wanted more than that single reading. So everybody who takes the paper specialises in one or two earlier genre/period complexes: Medieval Poetry; Jacobean Drama; Eighteenth-Century Novel. The second part of the paper concentrates on theoretical issues.

This communal work has made us aware of how sceptically we must survey the virtues and strengths ascribed to women in different periods. In much recent work, such as that of Simon Barker and Patrick Wright, on the re-presentment of past history and literature to justify the present (the Falklands, the Gloriana/Thatcher years, the raising of the Elizabethan ship, the *Mary Rose*) the emphasis has been on the corraling of sixteenth- and seventeenth-century stories.[9] For the representation of women eighteenth-century writing offers a fruitful field, but here it is not so easy to hold a single ideological focus pointed right. Instead, ideas such as the 'natural' powers of women, their enhanced sensibility and imagination, their earth-mother status, are among the myths employed among the left. Our thinking is often at the mercy of our communal metaphors, and though we may develop a sharp eye for those favoured by people with a different ideology from ourselves, we need to remain alert to our own and not allow them to bed down into our consciousness so far that they become determining. This process of persistent recognition involves also an understanding of the changing import of images.

Things mean differently at different historical moments, and different things need to be asserted at different times. This is both obvious and often ignored, so that one may come

across critics accusing George Eliot of capitulating to male
values when she claims the power of generalisation for women,
without noting that the power of generalisation was denied
by men to women at the period when she was writing and
that, typically, she generalises out from the woman's position.
So, Antigone can become the type of the human revolutionary
for her, not only of the female sufferer. She can claim centrality
for the experience of women.[10]

The problem of the relation between the centre and the
periphery has remained in the favoured discourse of feminism
and the left. The danger is that we may begin to welcome
positions ascribed to us, and then find ourselves unable to
move from them. Proper resistance leads to the 'oppositional
mode', to alternative readings and to a celebration of the
periphery. The list of inhabitants of the periphery becomes a
carnivalesque group – the mad, the poor, women and workers –
who are idealised as outside the power centre.[11] Such idealisation of the 'deviant mode' leaves its inhabitants powerless
and may perpetuate exclusion. Even words like imagination
and sensibility may prove synonyms for powerlessness if too
easily invoked. The claimed homology of 'women' and 'nature'
may equally prove a trap, since nature is so socialised a
category.

Just as sociology may be said to be the study of institutionalis-
ation as well as institutions, literary criticism can undertake
the study of naturalisation as well as nature. The identification
of women with nature has sometimes empowered women but
also acts as a restricting metaphor.[12] It has been adopted by
women themselves without always sufficient analysis of its
implications. The words *nature* and *natural* are perhaps the
most artful in the language. They soak up ideology like a
sponge. When we hear the word *naturally* in our own or other's
discourse we should raise our antennae. Argument has already
been prejudged in that word. Communality is being lined up
behind the speaker. The identification of woman with nature
has prolonged the idea of separate spheres and has tended to
figure woman as the object: an object of pursuit, enquiry,
knowing. The pursuit is one which represents man as pursuing,
even, as experimenter, entering and rupturing. In *A Room of
One's Own* Woolf chose as her image for future female friendship

two young women scientists who work in the same lab.[13] She thereby challenged the identification of science as male which she elsewhere identified: 'Science, it would seem, is not sexless; she is a man, a father, and infected too.' The ordinariness of the image of women lab-workers to us is a measure of real change: Woolf's point was that the woman scientist would no longer be exceptional; the lab would become both a humdrum workplace and a site where women could work together. She does not see nature as woman's ally or avatar: 'Nature was called in; Nature it was claimed who is not only omniscient but unchanging, had made the brain of woman of the wrong shape or size.'[14] Woolf here brings out the ideological constituents in the authority of 'Nature', or what George Eliot had her heroine Armgart scornfully describe as 'the theory called Nature'.

One of the most important apparent freedoms that literature offers us is that of crossing gender in our reading experience, disturbing the categories within which society regularises our activities. Is this a specious freedom? In the second part of this paper I want to look at two works which bring into question the reader's and the writer's activity in crossing gender: *Moll Flanders* (1722) and *Orlando* (1928). These works also bring to the surface the problems of historical record – *Moll Flanders* is purported ghosted autobiography, *Orlando* the purported biography of an impossible life. *Moll Flanders*, moreover, is not just a distant eighteenth-century novel by a concealed male author about a mercantile woman prostitute. It is, by means of the social internalisation of literary texts, still partly constitutive of responses – diverse as they may be – to figures like Cynthia Payne. And, in a softened form (Molly instead of Moll), the generic name of the loose woman is incorporated into Joyce's *Ulysses*, shaping our responses by means of half-received reminiscence. *Orlando* is both a response to the exclusion of women from the national records and a joke about the pompous exaggeration of difference within patriarchal society. What's so distinguished about having a penis? Can we give or take a few genitalia and remain much the same? asks the work. Perhaps, if our class position doesn't shift, might be the answer it suggests. Both books – though in very different ways – raise questions about the identification of woman with nature, as well as about the 'nature of woman' argument.

This is not new, entirely. We find Catherine Macaulay, the eighteenth-century historian, heading a chapter in her 'Letters on Education': 'No characteristic Difference in Sex':

> The great difference that is observable in the characters of the sexes, Hortensia, as they display themselves in the scenes of social life, has given rise to much false speculation on the natural qualities of the female mind. – For though the doctrine of innate ideas, and innate affections, are in a great measure exploded by the learned, yet few persons reason so closely and so accurately on abstract subjects as, through a long chain of deductions, to bring forth a conclusion which in no respect militates with their premises.
> . . . It is from such causes that the notion of a sexual difference in the human character has, with a very few exceptions, universally prevailed from the earliest times, and the pride of one sex, and the ignorance and vanity of the other, have helped to support an opinion which a close observation of Nature, and a more accurate way of reasoning, would disprove.
> . . . It must be confessed, that the virtues of the males among the human species, though mixed and blended with a variety of vices and errors, have displayed a bolder and a more consistent picture of excellence than female nature has hitherto done.[15]

She emphasises *correcting women* – but we need to enquire sceptically about 'women's virtues and perfections' as well as 'vices and foibles'.

One thing that became clearer through our joint study is that all strong works can be read along at least two, often contradictory, ideological pathways, and usually more: signs point in more than one direction. With this in mind, it seems useful to compare two works of very different periods of production, both of which tease out issues of gender and its construction: one a pseudo-autobiography written by a male writer in the person of a woman, and with no indication in the early editions of the actual author's name; the other, a rewriting of social history in the form of biography – a biography of the landed classes in England, both male and female. Both works concern themselves with 'history' in the sense of enacted event, and with historiography: the ideological forms within whose patterns we represent events.

Defoe was one of Woolf's most admired writers, though that is not the connection I most wish to discuss. In *Moll Flanders*, and in *Roxana*, Defoe recorded meta-lives which challenged, even while they fawned upon, the ideal possibilities of lives for women imagined by his society. Defoe can be read as a form of soft porn, particularly in *Roxana*, setting up the woman as commodity for the consumption of a male reader. Or he can, with equal justification, be seen as a proto-feminist, disturbing the genre of the rogue's tale to show the woman as capable of her own transactions, engaging in her own trading activities, and surviving.[16] Ideas of 'the natural' are brought under scrutiny and shifted both in Defoe and in Woolf's novels. Luce Irigaray argues in 'When the goods get together' that 'the trade that organises patriarchal society takes place exclusively among men. Women, signs, goods, currency, all pass from one man to another or – so it is said – suffer the penalty of relapsing into the incestuous and exclusively endogamous ties that could paralyse all commerce. The workforce, products, even those of mother-earth, would thus be the object of transactions among men only.'[17] In *Capital* Marx had argued along the same lines: 'Commodities cannot themselves go to market and perform exchanges in their own right.' In this passage, quoted by Irigaray, Marx alludes to women among his list of commodities, though it is not only of women he is speaking when he remarks that 'commodities are things, and therefore lack the power to resist man. If they are unwilling, he can use force; in other words, he can take possession of them.'[18]

In Defoe's writing the women are not merely vessels or mediums. They use their bodies as their capital; they go to market, making men the medium of their survival. Moreover, the first person narrative places Moll at the centre of discourse, as she is the source of trade. She 'utters' in the early as well as in our latter sense: that is, she offers goods for sale as well as speaks. Utterance in trade requires a buyer; utterance in language requires a listener, or reader. The silenced speech of Defoe's book draws our attention to Moll as a source of event and interpretation, and one which the reader finds hard to work against. Moll names everything but herself. The name 'Moll Flanders' is, she insists, not her own. Moll is the generic name for a whore; Flanders a well-known hotbed of venereal disease. Moll has been named by society, but she insists at the outset that this is a fictional name and she keeps her own name secret. The first-person form gives us also a promise throughout our reading of the work that Moll will survive it. Moll is a survivor. At seventy she returns to England, with wealth four pages long, and a husband younger than she by two years. She fulfils more than one kind of fantasy for the reader, and gratifies women and men together and diversely. She is wooed past menopause, always clean (neither she nor any of her associates suffers venereal disease). She is improbably intact at the end of her buffeted life story. She has become, as she wished to be in the book's first scene, 'a gentlewoman', and we have realised the full equivocality of the means she has innocently announced as a child: 'by my fingers' ends.'

Moll is bonny in old age. She is independent and successful. She may seem to be a cheering model for beset female readers. But that sanguine view of her can also be read another way: Moll is an Aunt Sally. She shows that women are tough. The concealed message here is: do what you will to them, they survive. Poverty, sexual ill-usage, depression, imprisonment: they can take it all. So it is not salaciousness which may mislead male readers of this representative woman (there is remarkably little of that in the penning of her adventures). It is *optimism*, the book's licence to conceive women as impermeable.

But there are further ways in which the work constructs its reader. We never read major works of literature simply in our own person, without constraint or re-ordering. The text re-shapes our responses by means of its multiple systems, of genre, of syntax, of semantics, of exclusions, of historical reference. In the case of *Moll Flanders* the genre element is particularly important and has to be re-learnt by present-day readers. This is a deviant text – not in a judgmental but in a generic sense. It is part of an already established tradition of rogue's stories, which allow to the reader the frisson of licensed ill-doing and the safety of the character's bad end. These outlaw tales can bring to the surface the wrongs of society. The characters are also held within an ellipse which allows their views to be voiced but simultaneously disowned. It is one mode in which radical opinions can declare themselves, but it risks a final acquiescence.

The Counterfeit Lady Unveiled (1673), an earlier rogue's story, by Francis Kirkman, explores the theme of women as false traders, able by means of their sexuality to cozen men and to be socially mobile. Kirkman's heroine is disposed of and made to exemplify various follies by the insistent 'I' of the male narrator. One of her first follies was her desire to be a lady, into which she was led by her reading of '*Cassandra, Cleopatra*, and the rest of those romances'. (*Cassandra*, it is worth noting, is La Calprenède's romance from which Defoe drew the name and figure of Roxana). The third-person narrator judges harshly the spirited cozening of society by Mary Carleton, known as 'The German Princess'. The book relishes and dismisses her wit. In a striking passage at the end, one of her female friends, referred to as a 'witty baggage', upbraids men: 'talking of the frailness of human nature, and that these crimes, which men would slip through and make nothing of, were accounted highly criminal with women; but before the great tribunal in heaven, men and women should then have equal justice, adding that it was an unworthy action in men to come only to behold that poor soul there as a wonder, when indeed she was more like a looking glass. "Yes, indeed," replied the prisoner. "I am very like a looking glass wherein you may all see your own frailties." '[19]

Like Mary Carleton, Moll Flanders internalises and reflects the values of her society. She would be a gentlewoman. Defoe, unlike Kirkman, is loyal to and sustains throughout the work her sense of her *self* as valuable. But this value can find expression only in the terms of success offered by her society. She thus becomes a critique of the values of that society, as well as a successful tradeswoman within it. She begins with her body only as her capital and by good husbandry (in both senses) concludes her life, after her transportation, back home

in England with her Lancashire husband. Having earlier in
the book cozened each other, they are thus absolved from the
cheats of marketing into a true affection buoyed up (and
magically verified) by wealth: 'Why, who says I was deceived
when I married a wife in Lancashire? I think I have married
a fortune, and a very good fortune too,' says he. Fortune as
riches and good-fortune and as happiness vouch for each
other, and they end their lives in a comfortable state of 'sincere
penitence for the wicked lives we have lived' – instead of at
Tyburn like the counterfeit lady.[20]

The first-person here allows the reader to participate in
Moll's disasters and triumphs with the confidence of survival.
There is almost no mirroring in this book: inner and outer
are not set sharply off from each other. Moll's inner life is
blandly available to our gaze, not critically distinguished from
the outside 'real' world. This is particularly the case with
Moll's self-justifying fantasies. She peoples the world with
careless, feckless, and thoughtless women who justify her
proceedings, as when she taps on the window of a house in
Greenwich, seeking a possibly careless housewife who has left
her rings unattended, to whom she plans to say that she has
seen two rough-looking men. When the housewife does not
appear, Moll pockets the rings. Likewise, she rebukes the
careless maidservant who has wandered off to talk to her
young man, thus leaving Moll to rob and to be tempted to
murder the little girl left in the nurse's charge. Both maidservant and boyfriend are Moll's fantasies, but as we read we
hardly observe that. The robustness and the lack of challenge
in Moll's address to the reader relies on the absence of doubles,
mirrors, speaking likenesses. Within Moll Flanders we are
presented with a single sign system in which Moll acts out
her needs. Only in Newgate does Defoe introduce images from
without her experience: 'like the waters in the cavities and
hollows of mountains, which petrify and turn into stone
whatever they are suffered to drop upon, so the continual
conversing with such a crew of hell hounds as I was had the
same common operation upon me as upon other people. I
degenerated into stone.'[21]

Of course, in the Preface we have been assured that
this coherence and cleanliness of language (the thing that

establishes Moll Flanders as romance rather than as record is her mealy-mouthedness) is the product of an intervening censorship by a (male) author, 'an author must be hard put to it to wrap it up so clean as not to give room, especially for vicious readers, to turn it to his disadvantage.' He has dressed her fit to be seen, 'no immodest turns in the new dressing up of this story', cleaned up the language, and leaves a tantalising doubt about the degree of her repentance. Like the unknown true name of Moll Flanders her unrecorded natural language lies behind the censored written text, titillating the 'vicious reader'.[22] Here, instead of doubling or mirroring within first-person, there is an obscured further source which gives the reader a lazy and pleasurable licence to imagine that she was *worse* than is here recorded but to enjoy her presence as it is in writing. She is never 'unveiled' in the Kirkman punitive sense, never exposed – and *that* (rather than its cleaned up language) is why *Moll Flanders*, despite its account of whoring and cozening, is not a pornographic text. The reader is not salaciously entangled in the punishing of Moll; she is not there as an object of trade and transaction, but as a tradeswoman, generating barter and exchange and labour. Moll is no 'earth-mother', or, in Irigaray's phrase, 'mother-earth'. She disposes of her children scrupulously but dispassionately. But then trade is for Defoe another form of Nature: 'Nothing obeys the course of Nature more exactly than trade.' Moll turns out to be another, less familiar, representation of nature, here presented as the active principle of interchange, not of nurture.[23]

Moll Flanders may have been received by its first readers as fact, but more probably as in that shameless borderland between event and hope which awakens us, without much pain, to the way things are now: which brings to our notice that they are other than they are represented in the work. Virginia Woolf takes further this shameless and alerting ratification of desire in *Orlando*. Orlando, whose name combines, in throw-away style, gold and land, is the deathless aristocrat. S/he has lived as man and as woman. S/he has by-passed the male-dominated inheritance laws, contriving to preserve her estate in her own right and to bear a son to continue it. In this, s/he is a painfully teasing contrary to Vita

Sackville-West, Woolf's lover and friend, who managed to move freely across gender boundaries, dressing sometimes as man, loving women and her husband, but who could not inherit the family estate, Knole, because she was a woman. Sackville-West suffered intensely the loss of the house in which she had grown up. Woolf re-endows her with it in this fantasy, though at the work's end the house collapses into dust leaving Orlando as a free spirit in the present day of 1928.

Orlando, by being in every way the exception, draws attention to women's disadvantage. Woolf is particularly concerned and angrily amused by their absence from the *historical record*, and in *Orlando* she is responding to the assumption of then new social historians, most notably G. M. Trevelyan's *History of England* (1926), that women can be subsumed under men's concerns.[24] Of Trevelyan's 723 pages, only seven include discussion of the position of women, other than women monarchs. In *A Room of One's Own* (1929) Woolf speaks of the lack of 'facts' about past woman: 'History scarcely mentions her'; and she quotes Trevelyan's chapter headings to show his categorical mis-understanding of 'social' history. In *A Room* she speaks of the possibility of 'a supplement to history', 'calling it, of course, by some inconspicuous name so that women might figure there without impropriety'. But in *Orlando* she offers something bolder: a transformation of history. Instead of her-story, she plays with the interacting power-structures of class, gender, and representation. The pseudo-biographer of Orlando is flummoxed because none of the ordinary narrative categories work for this hero/ine. Woolf herself writes a history of the land as language, parodying with loving *élan* the diversity of writing from the Elizabethans to the present moment. She writes about English landscape in the style of Ruskin, and about Pope in the spirit of Lady Mary Wortley Montague. Her hyperbole is all her own. This blowing up and exploding of the taken-for-granted allows her, through linguistic pleasure, to bring to the surface our false associations. The absurd song-and-dance of reticence and neo-classical personification (Our Lady of Purity, of Chastity and of Modesty)[25] which accompanies the moment when Orlando changes sex makes us have to notice how little embarrassment we ordinarily feel, as readers, in inhabiting the fictional persons of women and of men, how freely we move between them. She de-natures our assumptions about gender, about nature and the natural, and brings to light the collusion that pretends that inheritance through the male line is 'natural law'. All this is possible because she presents the work simultaneously as biography and as fantasy, jarring categories which call attention to masked contradictions.

Both Defoe and Woolf challenge their societies' gender-assumptions, but they challenge also some other assumptions: that autobiography is the space especially inhabited by women writers, that the male writer representing a woman is salacious, that 'nature' has remained a constant concept, and constantly in alliance with women. In order to read them fully we need to respond to their generic shaping and to the different weight they give to apparently familiar concepts, such as trade and the market, class and nurture. Radical reading is not a reading that simply assimilates past texts to our concerns but rather an activity that tests and de-natures our assumptions in the light of the strange languages and desires of past writing.

6 Sexual Linguistics: Gender, Language, Sexuality

Sandra M. Gilbert and Susan Gubar

Pourquoi Pa?
Jacqueline Nacal (1940)

Is anatomy linguistic destiny? Is a womb a metaphorical mouth, a pen a metaphorical penis? From Freud to Lacan to Derrida on the one hand, and from Woolf to Irigaray to Cixous on the other, masculinist and feminist theorists alike have toyed with the idea of a culturally determined body language which translates the articulations of the body into that body of articulated terminology we call language. Lately, in particular, linguistically-minded critics have increasingly called attention to the artificiality and indeterminacy of the terms through which we think we know the world, while psychoanalytic theorists have increasingly emphasised the psychological forces that determine the apparently logical terms in which we think we think. For if language is a process of cultural artifice that both distances and defines nature, then it would seem that its workings might well embody the bodily differences through which each human being first confronts the fundamental sexuality of his or her own nature. It might seem, in other words, that as Julia Kristeva puts it, 'Sexual difference – which is at once biological, physiological, and relative to production – is translated by and translates a difference in the relationship of subjects to the symbolic contract which *is* the social contract: a difference, then, in the relationship to power, language, and meaning.'[1]

In this essay, attempting to integrate the divergent forces of power, language, and meaning, we will examine this relationship between sexual difference and the symbolic contract in an effort to place recent feminist questionings of female linguistic destiny in the larger historical context that has not only produced the questions of feminist desire but has also reproduced the queasinesses of masculinist doubt, dread, and derision. For, as we shall try to show, contemporary female language theorists participate in a long tradition of feminist linguistic fantasy, while male language theorists also inherit a long tradition of masculinist linguistic fantasy. That such traditions demonstrably exist, moreover, implies two points which we will also consider from both a psychological and a historical perspective. First, their content suggests an intuition of the primacy of the mother rather than the father in the process of language acquisition that assimilates the child into what Kristeva calls the 'symbolic contract'. Second, the very existence of a long-neglected tradition of female writing interrogates the widely accepted contemporary assumption that 'the feminine' is what cannot be inscribed in common language. Finally, then, questioning the identification of the symbolic contract with the social contract, we will argue that the female subject is not necessarily alienated from the words she writes and speaks.

There is, of course, a long masculinist tradition that identifies female anatomy with a degrading linguistic destiny. But once the middle-class woman began to write, male defences against female speech became particularly virulent. Among modernists, William Faulkner makes explicit the implicit assumption behind attacks on woman's garrulousness from Spenser to Swift to Dickens when one of his fictional surrogates, celebrating the feminine ideal as 'a virgin with no legs to leave me, no arms to hold me, no head to talk to me,' defines woman generically as 'merely [an] articulated genital organ.'[2] Whether, like Joyce's fluidly fluent Anna Livia Plurabelle, woman ceaselessly burbles and babbles on her way to her 'cold mad feary father,' or whether, like his fluently fluid

Molly Bloom, she dribbles and drivels as she dreams of male jinglings, her artless jingles are secondary and asyntactic. Despite the valorisation of Joyce by feminists like Cixous, it seems that his heroine's scattered logos is a scatologos, for it is at bottom a Swiftian language that issues from the many obscene mouths of the female body. When she speaks as Molly in Joyce's passages, she passes blood and water; when Joyce implores her to write, as he does Nora in 1909, she is begged to express a calligraphy of shit.[3] Furthermore, when like Joyce's Gertie she attempts to etherealise herself, the author wants his readers to realise that she can only ascend to sentimentality. Thus while Gertie's female bloomers titillate Bloom as Nora's did Joyce, her girls' school language simultaneously revolts and titillates her creator, who gets to transcribe not only her voice but the voices of what Hawthorne called 'the damned mob of scribbling women' who produced her prototype in bestsellers like *The Lamplighter*.[4]

Significantly, the contrast between Molly–Nora's mellowy smellowy crapping and the commercial crap of Gertie's genteel Victorian diction symbolises a larger historical phenomenon – namely, the reaction–formation of intensified misogyny with which male writers greeted the entrance of women into the literary marketplace. Like Basil Ransom in James's *The Bostonians*, a number of male modernists react against the voices of evil they associate with a contaminating feminisation of culture, for they fear that 'the whole generation is womanised; the masculine tone is passing out of the world; it's a feminine, a nervous, hysterical, chattering, canting age.'[5] Such an entrance of hysteria into history is even more vividly dramatised by the young T. S. Eliot, James's Bostonian successor. The speaker of the prose poem 'Hysteria', for instance, staring into the deep throat of a laughing woman, surely suffers from a hysteria he has caught from her, a hysteria about her *hyster*, her womb and its mysterious 'hystery'. Contaminated by the female, he has been feminised and paralysed in just the way Eliot's indecisive persona is in the poem called 'Prufrock Among the Women', a draft of the 'Love Song of J. Alfred Prufrock' in which this balding modern Hamlet wanders woefully through what is clearly a red-light district, a sleazy city of women that parallels the equally

sinister city of women from which James's Ransom rescues
his Verena in *The Bostonians*.[6]

'*Blood, mucus, discharge, purulent offensive discharge*': with this
litany of words, underlined on a page torn from *The Midwives'
Gazette*, Eliot responded to Conrad Aiken's praise of an early
volume of his poems, as if to suggest that the letters of literary
men had been permanently polluted by the effusions of the
hyster.[7] It is no wonder, then, that the wastings of *The Waste
Land* are epitomised by the hysterical speech of women who
can 'connect nothing with nothing'. From the querulous
questions of the neurasthenic lady in 'A Game of Chess,' to
the abortion-haunted monologue of toothless Lil's faithless
friend, to the fragmentary complaints of the ruined Thames
daughters in 'The Fire Sermon,' the 'Shakespeherian Rag'
intoned by Mrs Porter and her daughter, and the evil 'whisper-
music' that the vampire woman fiddles on the strings of her
hair in 'What the Thunder Said,' the language of these women
embodies 'the horror, the horror' that the poet spells from an
impotent sibyl's leaves and leavings. Indeed, amid the wasted
No Man's Land of 'a feminine, a nervous, hysterical, chattering, canting age,' the only good woman is a silent woman –
the hyacinth girl whose mute armful of flowers inspires the
speaker to 'look into the heart of light, the silence.' For whether
he celebrates female silence or castigates female cacophony,
Eliot transcribes female language in order to transcend it,
thus justifying Joyce's claim that *The Waste Land* 'ended the
idea of poetry for ladies'.[8]

Even, moreover, when women artists are less obviously
sinister than Eliot's female speakers, modernist males seem to
blame them for the destruction of (male) culture and defens-
ively try to destroy them along with their (female) culture.
Ernest Hemingway, for instance, vilifies the voracious mouths
and wombs of would-be literary ladies in a sardonic poem
called 'The Lady Poets With Foot Notes':[9]

One lady poet was a nymphomaniac and wrote for Vanity
   Fair.[1]
One lady poet's husband was killed in the war.[2]
One lady poet wanted her lover, but was afraid of having a
   baby.

When she finally got married, she found she couldn't have
   a baby.*³*
One lady poet slept with Billy Reedy got fatter and fatter
   and made
half a million dollars writing bum plays.*⁴*
One lady poet never had enough to eat.*⁵*
One lady poet was big and fat and no fool.*⁶*

Similarly, in *Miss Lonelyhearts*, a novel about the feelings that
fuel such satire, Nathanael West helps his newspaper reporters
revenge themselves against their own nihilism by letting them
savour stories about lady writers with three names: 'Mary
Roberts Wilcox, Ella Wheeler Catheter' – 'what they all
needed was a good rape' – and records their special pleasure
in the beating of a 'hard-boiled' woman writer in a bar
frequented by mugs: 'They got her into the back room to
teach her a new word and put the boots to her. They didn't
let her out for three days. On the last day they sold tickets to
niggers.'[10]

   It is against such fantasies as those of West's reporters,
Hemingway, and Eliot that the 'new words' of women's
linguistic fictions had to contend, in a dialectic of the sexes
that centred on the crucial issue of woman's command of
language as against language's command of woman, a dialectic
that now directs our attention to women's historic efforts to
come to terms with the urgent need for female literary
authority through fantasies about the possession of a mother
tongue. As is so often the case, Emily Dickinson is the
foremother who articulates a fantasy about female linguistic
power that empowers not only her verse but – magically – the
voices of both her precursors and her successors. In the poem
about Elizabeth Barrett Browning that begins, 'I think I was
enchanted / When first a sombre Girl— / I read that Foreign
Lady,' Dickinson responds to Romney's charge in *Aurora
Leigh* that his cousin Aurora's poetry is merely 'witchcraft'.[11]
Performing a proto-Derridean *renversement*, this American artist
subversively celebrates the 'Divine Insanity' produced by
Barrett Browning's 'tomes of solid Witchcraft'. In particular,
she valorises such madness as the source of magical incanta-

tions by which 'that Foreign Lady' the woman poet transforms even the most ordinary objects, metamorphosing bees to butterflies and quotidian nature into 'Titanic Opera' (no. 593).

For Dickinson, moreover, such 'Witchcraft has not a Pedigree / 'Tis early as our Breath' (no. 1708), the breath of a new life of female speech that she associates with the life breathed into her by Barrett Browning's enchanting chants. At the same time, significantly, she shows that, even without the authority of a recorded pedigree, such witchcraft establishes a secret ancestry outside the lines of any genealogical tree in 'known' history, so that it serves as an empowering linguistic/literary model through which the woman poet can express a sense of the primacy of her own words and their commonality with the words of other women writers. Thus even while she concedes that 'witchcraft was hung, in History', Dickinson not only emphasises the historical sacrifice of the female associated with (illegitimate) speech and (illicit) sexuality, she also neatly turns the screw by identifying herself with (an implicitly alternative) history as she predicts the continuing triumphs of this underground poetic community dedicated to 'conversions of the Mind'.

That women like Dickinson should feel the need for an alternative speech is not of course surprising in light of the different educational opportunities accorded the two sexes until the late nineteenth century. Specifically, such literary 'daughters of educated men' knew that the education in the classics which their brothers received – that is, education in Latin and Greek – functioned, in the way Walter Ong has shown, as a crucial step in gender demarcation.[12] Just as importantly, as Ong also notes, in boys' schools such a classical education instilled masculinist values through a rhetorical training in 'agonistic' oral competition, which represented a puberty rite that further developed male identity. These men and boys, in other words, had access to a privileged priestly language, what Ong would call a *patrius sermo*, which women could only counter with the vocabulary of witchcraft, the male Mass masked as a female Black Mass. Thus like Virginia Woolf, who fantasised in moments of madness that the birds were speaking Greek to her, women writers from Fanny

Burney to Christina Stead have long been obsessed with the exclusiveness of a (masculinist) linguistic code they both refuse to speak and seek to crack.[13] In one way or another, too, many adopt strategies comparable to the one invented by Louie Pollit, the heroine of Christina Stead's *Kunstlerroman*, *The Man Who Loved Children*, who creates a witchlike private language that sounds suspiciously like a parodic mixture of Latin and Greek. TRAGOS: HERPES ROM. JOST 1, which means TRAGEDY: THE SNAKEMAN, ACT 1, is the play she produces in it, and when her father reacts in annoyance at his dependence on her translations – 'Why couldn't it be in English?' – she enlightens him: 'Did Euripides write in English?' Even as she ambitiously models herself on a classical playwright, however, she also believes that a 'secret language' allows her 'to write what she [wishes], she [can] invent an extensive language to express every shade of her ideas.'[14] In other words, like Dickinson, she believes that she can find illegitimate words in which to inscribe the history of her own consciousness.

While women like Dickinson and Stead's Louie Pollit produce terms they associate with female sorcery, their female cohorts from Edith Wharton to Willa Cather develop the female dream of linguistic witchcraft into other visions of female verbal power. In a short story called 'Xingu', for instance, Wharton hints at the existence of a language with Amazonian connections and Eleusinian connotations.[15] Renée Vivien, writing in the same period, learns Greek to read Sappho in the original, translates Sappho's lyrics into French, and writes her own 'sapphistries', poems about her love of women, which she composed and published in a French as foreign to her native English as her homosexuality was to the hegemonic heterosexual idiom.[16] Distancing herself chronologically rather than geographically from the sentences of patriarchy, Djuna Barnes composes in an English that predates the emergence of women writers, as if to reclaim lost dictions for her sex in works like *Ryder*, *Nightwood*, and *The Antiphon*. In addition, as if teasing out the intertextual significance of *The Bostonians*, she symbolises her desire to speak in tongues through explorative fantasies of the eroticism of the tongue.[17]

But perhaps most famously, Gertrude Stein remakes English

itself into a foreign language when she seems to speak in tongues, testifying to the authority of her own experience. For as most of her bemused readers realise, many of Stein's books are fantastic experiments in alternative tongues: in her *Tender Buttons*, for instance, she provides a new lexicon of old words; in *Three Lives*, she experiments with the continuous present; in *The Making of Americans*, she exchanges the sentence for the paragraph as the unit of meaning. Throughout her canon, clearly, she is attempting to follow her own advice to 'only, only excreate, only excreate a no since' in order to excrete a 'nonsense' language which would attack the causality of 'since' at the same time that it would X out those male definitions of female 'excrescence' which led to Joyce's demand for a female expression of pure excrement.[18] Furthermore, writing in France, happily surrounded by 'people who know no english,'[19] she dramatises her own (sexual) difference in poems like 'Lifting Belly', 'As a Wife Has a Cow', and 'Pink Melon Joy', where she creates an elaborate private code to describe the delights of an erotic linguistics that translates sacred cows into sexual 'cows'. Not surprisingly, then, even William Carlos Williams, who met her in Paris with some suspicion, observed that she had disentangled words from the weight of history, from 'the burden science, philosophy, and every higgledy-piggledy figment of law and order have been laying upon them in the past.'[20] By undertaking such a task, moreover, she, like Emily Dickinson, recovered the numinous names of an alternative history, for in plays like *Four Saints in Three Acts* and *The Mother of Us All*, she endows the voices of such heroines as Saint Theresa and Susan B. Anthony with fantastic exuberance.

A few decades later, in a very different mode but with what seems to have been the same purpose, Zora Neale Hurston creates a female protagonist nicknamed 'Alphabet', who recovers the black magic of what she calls 'de maiden language' over and over again, while Elinor Wylie proclaims that she was nurtured 'in the immaculate bosom of the mother tongue'.[21] But perhaps most strikingly, H.D. develops Dickinson's idea of witchcraft into an 'echoing spell' of what Robert Duncan has called her 'mothering language'.[22] In particular, at the centre of her book-length meditative poem *Trilogy*, she reconstitutes a new language through a magical, alchemical process. By recovering the 'candle and script and bell' that 'the new church spat upon,' she translates a word like 'venereous' into 'venerate' to resanctify the lost goddess Venus. Seasoning holy words for a liturgy that has gone misnamed or unnamed (she translates the Hebrew word *marah*, bitter, into 'Mother', for example), she whips up a batch of medicinal herbs from the poison she has etymologically uprooted. For H.D., a word is a jewel in a jar, incense in a bowl, a pearl in a shell, a sort of mystic egg that can 'hatch' multiple meanings. Therefore, she is multiply, almost endlessly inspired in *Tribute to Freud* by pictographic writing on a wall, and therefore she punningly revises words to turn 'ruins', say, into 'runes'. Indeed, all words, as she meditates on them, become palimpsests: in their palpable ambiguity, her hermetic redefinitions convert 'translation' into 'transubstantiation', 'fever' into 'fervour,' 'savour' into 'saviour,' and 'haven' into a 'heaven' of her own devising.[23]

Similar echoes and ambiguities haunt Virginia Woolf, a novelist who, even while in *A Room of One's Own* she cried out for a new 'woman's sentence', continually interpolated female linguistic fantasies into her revisionary narratives of women's histories. From *The Voyage Out*, in which Rachel Vinrace hears her lover reading the words of *Comus* and thinks that 'they sounded strange; they meant different things from what they usually meant',[24] to *Mrs Dalloway*, in which a sky-writing aeroplane produces an ambiguous trail of smoke which might mean 'Glaxo', 'Kreemo', 'toffee' or 'K E Y,' to *Between the Acts*, in which the mysterious Miss La Trobe imagines 'words without meaning' rising from mud – 'wonderful words' – Woolf's heroines, and sometimes even her heroes, experience themselves as alienated from the 'ordinary' sense of language.[25] At the same time, however, Woolf offers her heroines, and a few heroes, the amazing grace of fantastic new languages. In *Night and Day*, for instance, Katharine Hilbery articulates her feelings through enigmatic visions of 'algebraic symbols'.[26] Similarly, in *Mrs Dalloway* the shell-shocked Septimus expresses *his* strong emotions in pictographic 'writings', while an ancient woman 'opposite Regents Park Tube Station' sings a famously enigmatic song that goes 'ee um fah um so / foo

swee too eem oo.'[27] Again, in *Orlando* Woolf's androgynous
hero/heroine wires her husband a comically encoded comment
on the meaning of literary achievement: ' "Rattigan Glumph-
oboo," which summed it up precisely,' while in *The Years* the
two 'children of the caretaker' – descendants of the Tube
Station crone – provide a fitting climax to the Pargiters' family
reunion with a shrill ditty that begins: 'Etho passo tanno
hai, / Fai donk to tu do, / Mai to, kai to, lai to see / Toh dom
to tuh do—.'[28]

Finally, throughout her *oeuvre* Woolf emphasises the fact
that both the alienation from language her books describe and
the revision of lexicography her books detail are functions of
the dispossession of women, as well as of women's natural
resources in the face of this dispossession, and she does this
by presenting a dramatic succession of female figures whose
ancient voices seem to endure from a time before the neat
categories of culture restrained female energy. The most
notable of these figures is, of course, the Tube Station crone
in *Mrs Dalloway*. But clearly the ancestor of this woman is the
'old blind woman' who, in *Jacob's Room*, sits long past sunset
'singing out loud . . . from the depths of her gay wild heart.'[29]
And her descendants appear in *To the Lighthouse* as the force
that lurches through Mrs McNab's groaning and Mrs Bast's
creaking as they stay the corruption at work on the Ramsays'
one-time summer house. Speaking of a primal regeneration,
these ancient voices also resemble the source of voice that
empowers female singers in some of Willa Cather's stories and
novels. Thea Kronborg in *The Song of the Lark*, for instance,
finds her true soprano technique by visiting a 'cleft in the
world' called Panther Canyon, where the relics of an archaic
civilisation still remain intact.[30]

But to the fatherly priests who journey through Cather's
late *Death Comes for the Archbishop*, the earthy orifice that
sanctifies Thea's art is frankly terrifying. The Bishop, for
instance, who finds himself taking refuge from a snowstorm
inside 'two rounded ledges . . . with a mouthlike opening
between,' is revolted not only by a 'fetid odour' but also by
'a hole' between two 'stone lips' inside the cave, through which
he hears 'an extraordinary vibration'.[31] To this European man
of God, the speech of what was once an Indian oracle conveys

no more than the horror of its own enigmatic existence. How, Cather seems to ask, can a 'civilised' adult male come to terms with the terms Wallace Stevens once called 'words of the fragrant portals . . . / And of ourselves and of our origins.'[32] Her implicit question reminds us once again of the male modernist anxiety about female Babel to which so many of the women of letters we've discussed here were responding through their construction of fantasy languages. Perhaps more importantly, however, her awareness of the Bishop's dilemma as he listens to the speech of (Mother) earth also reminds us that male artists have long contended with their own linguistic anxieties through the invention of fantasy languages not just for women but for themselves – languages, that is, which did not primarily diminish femaleness but principally aggrandised maleness.

Of course, the historical range of male linguistic fantasies suggests that not all such variations on the theme of language function to confirm (masculinist) sexual self-definitions. However, as Walter Ong's recent account of the relationship between the common *materna lingua* (or mother tongue) and the 'civilised' *patrius sermo* (or father speech) implies, European male writers have, since the High Middle Ages, been deeply involved in a struggle into the vernacular which has continually forced them to usurp and transform the daily speech of women and children so as to make it into a suitable instrument for (cultivated) male art. 'Our first tongue,' writes Ong, 'is called our "mother tongue" in English and in many other languages,' adding that the only 'father speech' is a language such as, for example, Latin or Greek, 'inherited as land is, an external possession [which] refers to a [legalistic] line of conveyance, not to personal origins.'[33] (By such a distinction, we should note, we take him to mean that the mother tongue, far from being a unique women's language, is what we would ordinarily mean by the phrase 'ordinary language.') Certainly when, meditating on reading and writing in *Walden*, Henry David Thoreau contrasted the 'brutish . . . mother tongue' with the 'reserved and select' expression of the 'father tongue,' he implied that the spoken vernacular is as far below the written classics as dialect is below dialectic or as the literate is below the literary.[34] If men were anxious about the vernacular that their mothers, wives, and daughters also fluently spoke, however, it becomes necessary to speculate that since the thirteenth and fourteenth centuries male writers may have thought linguistic culture to be holding linguistic anarchy at bay because they have had to translate the 'high themes' of the classics into what they fear is a low language whose very accessibility might seem to vulgarise their noble subjects.

Still, although male intellectuals, from Dante and Chaucer on, composed their verses in a vernacular they defined as 'maternal,' their possession of the 'classics' diminished anxiety. Virgil was Dante's guide. Chaucer (as Pound approvingly observes) 'was more compendious than Dante' because he 'wrote while England was still a part of Europe,' and thus his language was still, if only metaphorically, a branch of a larger 'father speech' which constituted the (father) state rather than the (mother) nation. In fact, Pound goes on to say, Chaucer is '*Le Grand Translateur*' – that is, he is the man who brings over the *patrius sermo* of the Latin Middle Ages into the *materna lingua* of the vernacular Renaissance: 'He had found a new language, *he had it largely to himself*, with the grand opportunity. Nothing spoiled, nothing worn out.'[35] Similarly, says Pound, Milton, 'chock a block with Latin,' brings over that *patrius sermo* into English. That one turns to Pound's commentaries on these major male *translateurs* of classical culture into the vulgar vernacular, however, suggests the historical intensity of the linguistic issue that has haunted male writers since the nineteenth century, eliciting linguistic fantasies at least as forceful as those that many French feminists attribute uniquely to women. For, as Walter Ong has also noted, the teaching of Latin and Greek as part of the standard curriculum that functioned as a male initiation ritual had begun to die out by the end of the nineteenth century because, he speculates, of the entrance of women into higher education.[36] In addition, as Harold Bloom has argued, nineteenth-century men of letters increasingly experienced themselves as belated in relation to their great male precursors – and, we would add, threatened by their great female precursors and contemporaries.[37]

It is with special passion, therefore, that male writers from Tennyson to Joyce to Derrida and Hartman speculate on the linguistic possibilities available to them. To a man, they seem to feel themselves to be in the unenviable position of Tennyson's Merlin, who explains to Vivien in Book VI of *The Idylls of the King* that his magical powers derive from an ancient volume whose 'every square of text [has] an awful charm,' but then goes on to confess the secondary, belated character of his relationship to this paradigmatic book of patriarchal authority. It is, he notes,

> Writ in a language that has long gone by. . . .
> And every margin scribbled, crost, and crammed
> With comment, densest condensation, hard. . . .
> And none can read the text, not even I,
> And none can read the comment but myself,
> And in the comment did I find the charm.[38]

Tennyson's message is clear: even if he no longer knows the 'language that has long gone by,' the (male) magician must at all costs retain the charm that resides in the comment on the sacred text of power. Thus the transformation of the *materna lingua* into a new *patrius sermo* – that is, the occulting of common language, the transformation of the comment into the charm – seems to offer a definitive cure of the male linguistic wound.

Such a transformation is most notably accomplished in a number of different ways by even avant-garde fantasists of language, men who repossess the ancient strength of the *patrius sermo* through the creation of a literature of 'comment, densest condensation, hard.' The signatories of Eugene Jolas's 'Manifesto: The Revolution of the Word,' for instance, rebel against 'the spectacle of [literature] still under the hegemony of the banal word' with the assertion that 'the literary creator has the right to disintegrate the primal matter of words imposed on him. . . . He has the right to use words of his own fashioning.'[39] In just about every case, therefore, these linguistic revolutionaries became latter-day Merlins seeking, through 'densest condensation,' to (re)gain the mastery lost when male artists were forced by history to operate within the degrading confines of the vernacular mother tongue. But of course, if we have space to consider only one example, the twentieth century's greatest master of linguistic transformation – the man who definitively converted the comment into the charm – was James Joyce, whose 'densest condensation, hard,' with its proliferation of puns and parodies, transforms what Hélène Cixous calls 'the old single-grooved mothertongue'[40] into what we are calling a *patrius sermo* only comprehensible by those who, like Merlin and like Joyce himself, can translate what has been 'scribbled, crost, and crammed' on the margins of literature into a spell of power. *Finnegans Wake*, after all, condensed numerous Indo-European tongues into a neologistic language whose Viconian loops form a perfect Möbius strip of what we might call patrilinguistic history, but even before Joyce imagined that extravagant feat, *Ulysses* performed a similar task, transforming a comment on Homer's epic into a charm that inaugurated a new patrilinguistic epoch.

It would be impossible here to review all the strategies by which Joyce performed this feat of legerdemain. Perhaps for our purposes the most striking examples of his linguistic prestidigitation are the dazzling parodies of English style, from Anglo-Saxon alliteration to American slang, that he incorporates into the scene at the Lying-In Hospital and the dizzying puns he increasingly invents throughout his *oeuvre*. The so-called 'Oxen of the Sun' chapter, after all, records the conception, incubation, and birth – 'Hoopsa Boyaboy Hoopsa' – of a magical-sounding boy through a series of stylistic metamorphoses which seem to prove that (male) linguistic ontogeny recapitulates (male) linguistic phylogeny. The borning 'Boyaboy' *is* his language, a patriarchal word made flesh in the extended *patrius sermo* of history, and though he is undoubtedly torn out of the prostrate *materna lingua* represented by silent Mrs Purefoy, he is triumphantly flung, in a Carlylean birth passage, into 'God's air, the Allfather's air.'[41]

If the 'Oxen of the Sun' presents us with a wresting of patriarchal power from the mother tongue, moreover, Joyce's constantly expanding puns offer more instances of the ways in which male writers can transform the *materna lingua* into a *patrius sermo*. For, containing the powerful charm of etymological commentary within themselves, such multiple usages suggest not just a linguistic pleasure disrupting the decorum of the text, but also a linguistic power fortifying the writer's sentences with 'densest condensation, hard.' Provisionally, tentatively, we would suggest that a similar manoeuvre may be at the heart of what Geoffrey Hartman calls Derridadaism. Certainly, even while Hartman speculates that, for instance, *Glas* may be 'a fashionable meditation in the graveyard of Western culture,' he admits that though 'it may seem ingenious to characterise Derrida as a conservative thinker,' it is nevertheless the case that in *Glas*'s radical weave of radically unravelled significations 'the "*Monuments of unageing intellect*" *are not pulled down. . . .* the deconstructive activity becomes part of their structure.'[42] Exactly so, and exactly as in *Ulysses* or in the *Wake*. Mourning and waking a lost *patrius sermo*, male modernists and postmodernists transform the maternal vernacular into a new morning of patriarchy in which they can wake the old powers of the 'Allfather's' Word. The motto 'Hoopsa Boyaboy Hoopsa' is thus the (necessary) charm they consistently find in the commentary they ceaselessly study.

It hardly seems necessary to ask, therefore, what distinguishes the male linguistic fantasies we have reviewed here from the female fantasies we discussed earlier. By now it should be clear that women's imaginary languages arise out of a desire for linguistic primacy and are often founded on a celebration of the primacy of the mother tongue. For men, however, the case is different. 'Sexism in language,' as Christiane Olivier has pointed out, '[may be] the result of man's fear of using the same words as women, his fear of finding himself in the same place as the mother.'[43] Thus most male writers are either reacting against or appropriating the verbal fertility of the mother, and they are doing so precisely because, as Ong observes, 'there are no father tongues – a truth that calls for deeper reflection than it commonly commands.'[44] Clearly, it is this 'deeper reflection' that is reflected in the incongruent linguistic fantasies of male and female writers. For whether they are misogynistic deridings of female babble or self-valorising demands for 'the Allfather's air,' male vindications of the Name of the Father seem ultimately to be vilifications of the gnosis of the Mother.

Perhaps, too, we see the culmination of this tradition of

male discrediting of female originating in the extraordinary swerve Jacques Lacan has to perform as part of his attempt to make the moment of the child's accession to language coincide with the moment of the Oedipus complex, so that women can be defined 'as excluded by the nature of things which is the nature of words.' For as both Anika Lemaire and C. Stein observe, 'At the time of [the Oedipus] complex . . . linguistic communication has already been established, and logically, therefore, the complex itself cannot bring about the primal repression which establishes language.'[45] It is possible, then, that the Oedipal moment functions as a repetitive revision of an earlier moment, and that the power of the father, while obviously representing the law of patriarchy, need not be inextricably bound to the power of language. Indeed, the fact that the father is a supreme fiction in this now widely disseminated French Freudian theory points, paradoxically enough, to the primordial supremacy of the mother, for if, as language acquisition researchers have demonstrated, and as most mothers know, it is in most cultures the mother who feeds the child words even as she furnishes her or him with food, then, as Freud himself observed, the birth into language delivers the child from helplessness at the goings and the comings, the 'oo' and the 'ah,' the 'Fort' and the 'Da,' of the mother.[46]

In that case, if the primary moment of symbolisation occurs when the child identifies difference with distance from the mother, it is not only the presence of the mother's words that teaches the child words, but also the absence of the mother's flesh that requires the child to acquire words. As for the supposedly mediating and essential term of the father – the '*nom du père*' – we are suggesting that what makes this name secondary is precisely the fact that it symbolises no more than the autonomy of the mother – the '*aplomb de la mère*.' Moreover, if, as Lévi-Strauss concedes, a woman is not 'just a sign' but 'a generator of signs,' then it is the example of her self-possessed linguistic generations that impresses the child with the possibility that, because mom is not mum, one might bridge the grievous gulf of absence by expressing desire in language and reconstituting a lost presence through symbolisation.

Is it possible, then, that the idea that language is in its essence or nature patriarchal is a reaction-formation against the linguistic (as well as the biological) primacy of the mother? As long ago as 1954, after all, Bruno Bettelheim observed in *Symbolic Wounds* that 'penis envy in girls and castration anxiety in boys have been overemphasized, and a possibly much deeper psychological layer in boys has been relatively neglected. . . . a complex of desires and emotions which . . . might be called "vagina envy" [but which includes] . . . in addition, envy of and fascination with female breasts and lactation, with pregnancy and childbearing.'[47] Ten years earlier, too, Gregory Zilboorg had begun to call for further studies of 'the fundamental envy with which man treats woman.'[48] Suppose we follow out such insights by speculating that the biblical story of creation, with its linguistically powerful Adam and its anxious, tongue-tied Eve, is just a male fantasy devised to soothe men's feelings of secondariness, sexual dread, womb and breast envy. Suppose that instead of postulating a necessary linguistic connection between a lass and a lack we follow out Susan Lurie's speculation that 'the sight of woman as castrated is [a] mature male wish-fulfillment fantasy, designed to counter the real terror the sight of woman inspires: *that she is not castrated* despite the fact that she has "no penis," and does inspire male fear for his castration.' In that case, as Lurie observes, 'Psychoanalytic discourse participates in a broad cultural project . . . of constructing woman as castrated precisely because the sight of her does *not* signify her castration.'[49]

In *The Great Mother*, a useful text that has lately been too often ignored in favour of more fatherly works by Freud and Lacan, Erich Neumann points out that 'the positive femininity of the womb appears as a mouth . . . and on the basis of this positive symbolic equation the mouth, as "upper womb", is the birthplace of the breath and the word, the Logos.'[50] But the very fact that one can metaphorise the mouth as a womb, the Word as the child of female power, implies that women need not experience any ontological alienation from the idea of language as we know it. If the female does have a crucial linguistic role, moreover, isn't it also possible that the primordial self/other couple from whom we learn the couplings, doublings, splittings of 'hierarchy' is the couple called 'mother/child' rather than the one called 'man/woman'? If this is so, isn't it also possible that verbal signification arises not from a confrontation with the Law of the Father but from a consciousness of the lure and the lore of the mother? In other words, since boy and girl babies have the same relationship to the mother (as opposed to their relationship to the father), it may not be necessary to postulate (as Julia Kristeva does) that sexual difference issues in different (male/female) relationships to the symbolic contract. Indeed, it may be important to see that, since the symbolic contract is 'signed' before the social contract which in patriarchal culture constructs gender difference, these two contracts are notably different treaties with the world. The very fact that throughout this paper we have had to manoeuvre between theory and history, to contemplate the timeless questions of psychoanalysis while also confronting the time-bound constructions of literary history, would seem to reinforce this point, namely, the discontinuity between what *has to be* (that is, what is psychically essential) and what *has been* (that is, what is culturally determined). For if any of our speculations have any validity, we must also ask whether the whole structure of 'hierarchised' oppositions that some of us have thought essentially patriarchal has been historically erected as a massive defence against the deep throat of the mother and the astonishing autonomy of that mother tongue which is common to both genders.

In 'Thoughts on Writing,' the American feminist poet Susan Griffin expresses the exhilaration that such an intimation of female linguistic power has already begun to foster in some women writers: 'And now the words "mother tongue," language, widen out to me as I see that our relationship to the one who has given us birth, and to that universe which engendered our being, might be the same as our relationship to language; we must trust words and the coming of words.'[51] A century ago, moreover, Dickinson affirmed the same intuition of the mother tongue's nurturing primacy, declaring that 'a word made Flesh' can be 'tasted' with 'ecstasies of stealth' when 'the very food debated' is matched 'to our specific strength—.' For women writers in general, then, it may be this '*consent* of language' (our italics) that constitutes a 'loved Philology' (no. 1651), a philology whose implications even some male thinkers already understand.

To carry such an empowering intuition one step further and match it with Griffin's insight: can it be that feminist theorists must look beyond the traditional alphabetisings of history, with its masculinist syntax of subordination, to discover and recover the ways in which, as we have seen here, women have sometimes stealthily and sometimes ecstatically claimed the alphabet to capitalise (on) their own initials and their own initiatives? Can it be that, like the contemporary Spanish writer Maria Teresa Léon, women need only gaze into the common sustenance of our communal lives – a bowl, say, of alphabet soup – to create defiant and self-defining linguistic fantasies? Léon exuberantly records such a dream: 'Letters that float pursued by the spoon where they were going to die. Did they ever compose my name in the bowl? "Femme de lettres." I have never felt more reverence for the state of my uneasiness, for this daily itch within my flesh which writing gives me.'[52] The male reaction to such a vision may, as we have seen, be one of intensified misogyny. Yet at the same time, the very possibility that women might achieve such a vision implies that the relationship between anatomy and linguistic destiny, between sexual difference and the symbolic contract, may promise not just female *jouissance* but feminist *puissance*. For at last, in spite of feminist doubt and masculinist dread, we can affirm that woman has not been sentenced to transcribe male penmanship; rather, she commands sentences which inscribe her own powerful character.

7 Sorties: Out and Out: Attacks/Ways Out/Forays

Hélène Cixous

Where is she?
Activity/Passivity
Sun/Moon
Culture/Nature
Day/Night

Father/Mother
Head/Heart
Intelligible/Palpable
Logos/Pathos.
Form, convex, step, advance, semen, progress.
Matter, concave, ground – where steps are taken, holding-
and dumping-ground.
<u>Man</u>
Woman
  Always the same metaphor: we follow it, it carries us,
beneath all its figures, wherever discourse is organised. If we
read or speak, the same thread or double braid is leading
us throughout literature, philosophy, criticism, centuries of
representation and reflection.
Thought has always worked through opposition.
Speaking/Writing
Parole/Écriture
High/Low
  Through dual, hierarchical oppositions. Superior/Inferior.
Myths, legends, books. Philosophical systems. Everywhere

(where) ordering intervenes, where a law organises what is thinkable by oppositions (dual, irreconcilable; or sublatable, dialectical). And all these pairs of oppositions are *couples*. Does that mean something? Is the fact that Logocentrism subjects thought – all concepts, codes and values – to a binary system, related to 'the' couple, man/woman?

Nature/History
Nature/Art
Nature/Mind
Passion/Action

Theory of culture, theory of society, symbolic systems in general – art, religion, family, language – it is all developed while bringing the same schemes to light. And the movement whereby each opposition is set up to make sense is the movement through which the couple is destroyed. A universal battlefield. Each time, a war is let loose. Death is always at work.

Father/son   Relations of authority, privilege, force.
The Word/Writing   Relations: opposition, conflict, sublation, return.
Master/slave   Violence. Repression.

We see that 'victory' always comes down to the same thing: things get hierarchical. Organisation by hierarchy makes all conceptual organisation subject to man. Male privilege, shown in the opposition between *activity* and *passivity*, which he uses to sustain himself. Traditionally, the question of sexual difference is treated by coupling it with the opposition: activity/passivity.

The Masculine Future

There are some exceptions. There have always been those uncertain, poetic persons who have not let themselves be reduced to dummies programmed by pitiless repression of the homosexual element. Men or women: beings who are complex, mobile, open. Accepting the other sex as a component makes them much richer, more various, stronger, and – to the extent that they are mobile – very fragile. It is only in this condition that we invent. Thinkers, artists, those who create new values, 'philosophers' in the mad Nietzschean manner, inventors and wreckers of concepts and forms, those who change life cannot help but be stirred by anomalies – complementary or contradictory. That doesn't mean that you have to be homosexual to create. But it does mean that there is no *invention* possible, whether it be philosophical or poetic, without there being in the inventing subject an abundance of the other, of variety: separate-people, thought-/people, whole populations issuing from the unconscious, and in each suddenly animated desert, the springing up of selves one didn't know – our women, our monsters, our jackals, our Arabs, our aliases, our frights. That there is no invention of any other I, no poetry, no fiction without a certain homosexuality (the I/play of bisexuality) acting as a crystallisation of my ultrasubjectivities.[1] I is this exuberant, gay, personal matter, masculine, feminine or other where I enchants, I agonises me. And in the concert of personalisations called I, at the same time that a certain homosexuality is repressed, symbolically, substitutively, it comes through by various signs, conduct-character, behaviour-acts. And it is even more clearly seen in writing.

Thus, what is inscribed under Jean Genêt's name, in the movement of a text that divides itself, pulls itself to pieces, dismembers itself, regroups, remembers itself, is a proliferating, maternal femininity. A phantasmic meld of men, males, gentlemen, monarchs, princes, orphans, flowers, mothers, breasts gravitates about a wonderful 'sun of energy' – love, – that bombards and disintegrates these ephemeral amorous anomalies so that they can be recomposed in other bodies for new passions.

She is bisexual:

What I propose here leads directly to a reconsideration of *bisexuality*. To reassert the value of bisexuality;[2] hence to snatch it from the fate classically reserved for it in which it is conceptualised as 'neuter' because, as such, it would aim at warding off castration. Therefore, I shall distinguish between two bisexualities, two opposite ways of imagining the possibility and practice of bisexuality.

(1) Bisexuality as a fantasy of a complete being, which

replaces the fear of castration and veils sexual difference insofar as this is perceived as the mark of a mythical separation – the trace, therefore, of a dangerous and painful ability to be cut. Ovid's Hermaphrodite, less bisexual than asexual, not made up of two genders but of two halves. Hence, a fantasy of unity. Two within one, and not even two wholes.

(2) To this bisexuality that melts together and effaces, wishing to avert castration, I oppose the *other bisexuality*, the one with which every subject, who is not shut up inside the spurious Phallocentric Performing Theatre, sets up his or her erotic universe. Bisexuality – that is to say the location within oneself of the presence of both sexes, evident and insistent in different ways according to the individual, the nonexclusion of difference or of a sex, and starting with this 'permission' one gives oneself, the multiplication of the effects of desire's inscription on every part of the body and the other body.

For historical reasons, at the present time it is woman who benefits from and opens up within this bisexuality beside itself, which does not annihilate differences but cheers them on, pursues them, adds more: in a certain way *woman is bisexual* – man having been trained to aim for glorious phallic monosexuality. By insisting on the primacy of the phallus and implementing it, phallocratic ideology has produced more than one victim. As a woman, I could be obsessed by the sceptre's great shadow, and they told me: adore it, that thing you don't wield.

But at the same time, man has been given the grotesque and unenviable fate of being reduced to a single idol with clay balls. And terrified of homosexuality, as Freud and his followers remark. Why does man fear *being* a woman? Why this refusal (*Ablehnung*) of femininity? The question that stumps Freud. The 'bare rock' of castration. For Freud, the repressed is not the other sex defeated by the dominant sex, as his friend Fliess (to whom Freud owes the theory of bisexuality) believed; what is repressed is leaning toward one's own sex.

Psychoanalysis is formed on the basis of woman and has repressed (not all that successfully) the femininity of masculine sexuality, and now the account it gives is hard to disprove.

We women, the derangers, know it only too well. But nothing compels us to deposit our lives in these lack-banks;

to think that the subject is constituted as the last stage in a
drama of bruising rehearsals; to endlessly bail out the father's
religion. Because we don't desire it. We don't go round and
round the supreme hole. We have no *woman's* reason to pay
allegiance to the negative. What is feminine (the poets
suspected it) affirms: ... and yes I said yes I will Yes, says
Molly (in her rapture), carrying *Ulysses* with her in the
direction of a new writing; I said yes, I will Yes.

To say that woman is somehow bisexual is an apparently
paradoxical way of displacing and reviving the question of
difference. And therefore of writing as 'feminine' or 'masculine.'

I will say: today, writing is woman's. That is not a
provocation, it means that woman admits there is an other.
In her becoming-woman, she has not erased the bisexuality
latent in the girl as in the boy. Femininity and bisexuality
go together in a combination that varies according to the
individual, spreading the intensity of its force differently and
(depending on the moments of their history) privileging one
component or another. It is much harder for man to let the
other come through him. Writing is the passageway, the
entrance, the exit, the dwelling place of the other in me – the
other that I am and am not, that I don't know how to be, but
that I feel passing, that makes me live – that tears me apart,
disturbs me, changes me, who? – a feminine one, a masculine
one, some? – several, some unknown, which is indeed what
gives me the desire to know and from which all life soars. This
peopling gives neither rest nor security, always disturbs the
relationship to 'reality,' produces an uncertainty that gets in
the way of the subject's socialisation. It is distressing, it wears
you out; and for men this permeability, this nonexclusion is a
threat, something intolerable.

In the past, when carried to a rather spectacular degree, it
was called 'possession.' Being possessed is not desirable for a
masculine imaginary, which would interpret it as passivity –
a dangerous feminine position. It is true that a certain
receptivity is 'feminine.' One can, of course, as History has
always done, exploit feminine reception through alienation. A
woman, by her opening up, is open to being 'possessed,' which
is to say, dispossessed of herself.

But I am speaking here of femininity as keeping alive the other that is confided to her, that visits her, that she can love as other. The loving to be other, another, without its necessarily going the rout of abasing what is same, herself.

As for passivity, in excess, it is partly bound up with death. But there is a nonclosure that is not submission but confidence and comprehension; that is not an opportunity for destruction but for wonderful expansion.

Through the same opening that is her danger, she comes out of herself to go to the other, a traveller in unexplored places; she does not refuse, she approaches, not to do away with the space between, but to see it, to experience what she is not, what she is, what she can be.

Writing is working; being worked; questioning (in) the between (letting oneself be questioned) of same *and of* other without which nothing lives; undoing death's work by willing the togetherness of one-another, infinitely charged with a ceaseless exchange of one with another – not knowing one another and beginning again only from what is more distant, from self, from other, from the other within. A course that multiplies transformations by the thousands.

And that is not done without danger, without pain, without loss – of moments of self, of consciousness, of persons one has been, goes beyond, leaves. It doesn't happen without expense – of sense, time, direction.

But is that specifically feminine? It is men who have inscribed, described, theorised the paradoxical logic of an economy without reserve. This is not contradictory; it brings us back to asking about their femininity. Rare are the men able to venture onto the brink where writing, freed from law, unencumbered by moderation, exceeds phallic authority, and where the subjectivity inscribing its effects becomes feminine.

Where does difference come through in writing? If there is difference it is in the manner of spending, of valorising the appropriated, of thinking what is not-the-same. In general, it is in the manner of thinking any 'return,' the relationship of capitalisation, if this word 'return' (*rapport*) is understood in its sense of 'revenue.'

Today, still, the masculine return to the selfsame is narrower and more restricted than femininity's. It all happens as if man were more directly threatened in his being by the nonselfsame than woman. Ordinarily, this is exactly the cultural product described by psychoanalysis: someone who still has something to lose. And in the development of desire, of exchange, he is the en-grossing party: loss and expense are stuck in the commercial deal that always turns the gift into a gift-that-takes. The gift brings in a return. Loss, at the end of a curved line, is turned into its opposite and comes back to him as profit.

But does woman escape this law of return? Can one speak of another spending? Really, there is no 'free' gift. You never give something for nothing. But all the difference lies in the why and how of the gift, in the values that the gesture of giving affirms, causes to circulate; in the type of profit the giver draws from the gift and the use to which he or she puts it. Why, how, is there this difference?

When one gives, what does one give oneself?

What does he want in return – the traditional man? And she? At first what *he* wants, whether on the level of cultural or of personal exchanges, whether it is a question of capital or of affectivity (or of love, of *jouissance*) – is that he gain more masculinity: plus-value of virility, authority, power, money, or pleasure, all of which reinforce his phallocentric narcissism at the same time. Moreover, that is what society is made for – how it is made; and men can hardly get out of it. An unenviable fate they've made for themselves. A man is always proving something; he has to 'show off,' show up the others. Masculine profit is almost always mixed up with a success that is socially defined.

How does she give? What are her dealings with saving or squandering, reserve, life, death? She too gives *for*. She too, with open hands, gives herself – pleasure, happiness, increased value, enhanced self-image. But she doesn't try to 'recover her expenses.' She is able not to return to herself, never settling down, pouring out, going everywhere to the other. She does not flee extremes; she is not the being-of-the-end (the goal), but she is how-far-being-reaches.

If there is a self proper to woman, paradoxically it is her capacity to depropriate herself without self-interest: endless body, without 'end,' without principal 'parts'; if she is a whole, it is a whole made up of parts that are wholes, not simple, partial objects but varied entirety, moving and boundless change, a cosmos where eros never stops travelling, vast astral space. She doesn't revolve around a sun that is more star than the stars.

That doesn't mean that she is undifferentiated magma; it means that she doesn't create a monarchy of her body or her desire. Let masculine sexuality gravitate around the penis, engendering this centralised body (political anatomy) under the party dictatorship. Woman does not perform on herself this regionalisation that profits the couple head-sex, that only inscribes itself within frontiers. Her libido is cosmic, just as her unconscious is worldwide: her writing also can only go on and on, without ever inscribing or distinguishing contours, daring these dizzying passages in other, fleeting and passionate dwellings within him, within the hims and hers whom she inhabits just long enough to watch them, as close as possible to the unconscious from the moment they arise; to love them, as close as possible to instinctual drives, and then, further, all filled with these brief identifying hugs and kisses, she goes and goes on infinitely. She alone dares and wants to know from within where she, the one excluded, has never ceased to hear what-comes-before-language reverberating. She lets the other tongue of a thousand tongues speak – the tongue, sound without barrier or death. She refuses life nothing. Her tongue doesn't hold back but holds forth, doesn't keep in but keeps on enabling. Where the wonder of being several and turmoil is expressed, she does not protect herself against these unknown feminines; she surprises herself at seeing, being, pleasuring in her gift of changeability. I am spacious singing Flesh: onto which is grafted no one knows which I – which masculine or feminine, more or less human but above all living, because changing I.

I see her 'begin.' That can be written – these beginnings that never stop getting her up – can and must be written. Neither black on white nor white on black, not in this clash between paper and sign that en-graves itself there, not in this opposition of colours that stand out against each other. This is how it is:

There is a ground, it is her ground – childhood flesh,

shining blood – or background, depth. A white depth, a core, unforgettable, forgotten, and this ground, covered by an infinite number of strata, layers, sheets of paper – is her sun (*sol . . . soleil*). And nothing can put it out. Feminine light doesn't come from above, doesn't fall, doesn't strike, doesn't go through. It radiates, it is a slow, sweet, difficult, absolutely unstoppable, painful rising that reaches and impregnates lands, that filters, that wells up, that finally tears open, wets and spreads apart what is dull and thick, the stolid, the volumes. Fighting off opacity from deep within. This light doesn't plant, it spawns. And I see that she looks very closely with this light and she sees the veins and nerves of matter. Which he has no need of.

Her rising: is not erection. But diffusion. Not the shaft. The vessel. Let her write! And her text knows in seeking itself that it is more than flesh and blood, dough kneading itself, rising, uprising openly with resounding, perfumed ingredients, a turbulent compound of flying colours, leafy spaces, and rivers flowing to the sea we feed.

Writing femininity transformation:

And there is a link between the economy of femininity – the open, extravagant subjectivity, that relationship to the other in which the gift doesn't calculate its influence – and the possibility of love; and a link today between this 'libido of the other' and writing.

At the present time, defining a feminine practice of writing is impossible with an impossibility that will continue; for this practice will never be able to be *theorised*, enclosed, coded, which does not mean it does not exist. But it will always exceed the discourse governing the phallocentric system; it takes place and will take place somewhere other than in the territories subordinated to philosophical–theoretical domination. It will not let itself think except through subjects that break automatic functions, border runners never subjugated by any authority. But one can begin to speak. Begin to point out some effects, some elements of unconscious drives, some relations of the feminine imaginary to the real, to writing.

What I have to say about it is also only a beginning, because right from the start these features affect me powerfully.

First I sense femininity in writing by: a privilege of *voice*:

writing and voice are entwined and interwoven and writing's continuity/voice's rhythm take each other's breath away through interchanging, make the text gasp or form it out of suspenses and silences, make it lose its voice or rend it with cries.

In a way, feminine writing never stops reverberating from the wrench that the acquisition of speech, speaking out loud, is for her – 'acquisition' that is experienced more as tearing away, dizzying flight and flinging oneself, diving. Listen to woman speak in a gathering (if she is not painfully out of breath): she doesn't 'speak,' she throws her trembling body into the air, she lets herself go, she flies, she goes completely into her voice, she vitally defends the 'logic' of her discourse with her body; her flesh speaks true. She exposes herself. Really she makes what she thinks materialise carnally, she conveys meaning with her body. She *inscribes* what she is saying because she does not deny unconscious drives the unmanageable part they play in speech.

Her discourse, even when 'theoretical' or political, is never simple or linear or 'objectivised,' universalised; she involves her story in history.

Every woman has known the torture of beginning to speak aloud, heart beating as if to break, occasionally falling into loss of language, ground and language slipping out from under her, because for woman speaking – even just opening her mouth – in public is something rash, a transgression.

A double anguish, for even if she transgresses, her word almost always falls on the deaf, masculine ear, which can only hear language that speaks in the masculine.

We are not culturally accustomed to speaking, throwing signs out toward a scene, employing the suitable rhetoric. Also, it is not where we find our pleasure: indeed, one pays a certain price for the use of a discourse. The logic of communication requires an economy both of signs – of signifiers – and of subjectivity. The orator is asked to unwind a thin thread, dry and taut. We like uneasiness, questioning. There is waste in what we say. We need that waste. To write is always to make allowances for superabundance and uselessness while slashing the exchange value that keeps the spoken word on its track. That is why writing is good, letting the tongue try itself out – as one attempts a caress, taking the time a phrase or a thought needs to make oneself loved, to make oneself reverberate.

It is in writing, from woman and toward woman, and in accepting the challenge of the discourse controlled by the phallus, that woman will affirm woman somewhere other than in silence, the place reserved for her in and through the symbolic. May she get out of booby-trapped silence! And not have the margin or the harem foisted on her as her domain!

In feminine speech, as in writing, there never stops reverberating something that, having once passed through us, having imperceptibly and deeply touched us, still has the power to affect us – song, the first music of the voice of love, which every woman keeps alive.

The Voice sings from a time before law, before the symbolic took one's breath away and reappropriated it into language under its authority of separation. The deepest, the oldest, the loveliest Visitation. Within each woman the first, nameless love is singing.

In woman there is always, more or less, something of 'the mother' repairing and feeding, resisting separation, a force that does not let itself be cut off but that runs codes ragged. The relationship to childhood (the child she was, she is, she acts and makes and starts anew, and unties at the place where, as a same she even others herself), is no more cut off than is the relationship to the 'mother,' *as it consists of* delights and violences. Text, my body: traversed by lilting flows; listen to me, it is not a captivating, clinging 'mother'; it is the equivoice that, touching you, affects you, pushes you away from your breast to come to language, that summons *your* strength; it is the rhyth-me that laughs you; the one intimately addressed who makes all metaphors, all body(?) – bodies(?) – possible and desirable, who is no more describable than god, soul, or the other; the part of you that puts space between yourself and pushes you to inscribe your woman's style in language. Voice: milk that could go on forever. Found again. The lost mother/bitter-lost. Eternity: is voice mixed with milk.

Not the origin: she doesn't go back there. A boy's journey is the return to the native land, the *Heimweh* Freud speaks of, the nostalgia that makes man a being who tends to come back to the point of departure to appropriate it for himself and to die there. A girl's journey is farther – to the unknown, to invent.

How come this privileged relationship with voice? Because no woman piles up as many defences against instinctual drives as a man does. You don't prop things up, you don't brick things up the way he does, you don't withdraw from pleasure so 'prudently.' Even if phallic mystification has contaminated good relations in general, woman is never far from the 'mother' (I do not mean the role but the 'mother' as no-name and as source of goods). There is always at least a little good mother milk left in her. She writes with white ink.

Voice! That, too, is launching forth and effusion without return. Exclamation, cry, breathlessness, yell, cough, vomit, music. Voice leaves. Voice loses. She leaves. She loses. And that is how she writes, as one throws a voice – forward, into the void. She goes away, she goes forward, doesn't turn back to look at her tracks. Pays no attention to herself. Running breakneck. Contrary to the self-absorbed, masculine narcissism, making sure of its image, of being seen, of seeing itself, of assembling its glories, of pocketing itself again. The reductive look, the always divided look returning, the mirror economy; he needs to love himself. But she launches forth; she seeks to love. Moreover, this is what Valéry sensed, marking his Young Fate in search of herself with ambiguity, masculine in her jealousy of herself: 'seeing herself see herself,' the motto of all phallocentric speculation/specularisation, the motto of every Teste; and feminine in the frantic descent deeper deeper to where a voice that doesn't know itself is lost in the sea's churning.

Voice-cry. Agony – the spoken 'word' exploded, blown to bits by suffering and anger, demolishing discourse: this is how she has always been heard before, ever since the time when masculine society began to push her offstage, expulsing her, plundering her. Ever since Medea, ever since Electra.

Voice: unfastening, fracas. Fire! She shoots, she shoots away. Break. From their bodies where they have been buried, shut up and at the same time forbidden to take pleasure. Women have almost everything to write about femininity: about their sexuality, that is to say, about the infinite and mobile complexity of their becoming erotic, about the lightning ignitions of such a minuscule-vast region of their body, not about destiny but about the adventure of such an urge, the voyages, crossing, advances, sudden and slow awakenings, discoveries of a formerly timid region that is just now springing up. Woman's body with a thousand and one fiery hearths, when – shattering censorship and yokes – she lets it articulate the proliferation of meanings that runs through it in every direction. It is going to take much more than language for him to make the ancient maternal tongue sound in only one groove.

We have turned away from our bodies. Shamefully we have been taught to be unaware of them, to lash them with stupid modesty; we've been tricked into a fool's bargain: each one is to love the other sex. I'll give you your body and you will give me mine. But which men give women the body that they blindly hand over to him? Why so few texts? Because there are still so few women winning back their bodies. Woman must write her body, must make up the unimpeded tongue that bursts partitions, classes, and rhetorics, orders and codes, must inundate, run through, go beyond the discourse with its last reserves, including the one of laughing off the word 'silence' that has to be said, the one that, aiming for the impossible, stops dead before the word 'impossible' and writes it as 'end.'

In body/Still more: woman is body more than man is. Because he is invited to social success, to sublimation. More body hence more writing. For a long time, still bodily, within her body she has answered the harassment, the familial conjugal venture of domestication, the repeated attempts to castrate her. Woman, who has run her tongue ten thousand times seven times around her mouth before not speaking, either dies of it or knows her tongue and her mouth better than anyone. Now, I-woman am going to blow up the Law: a possible and inescapable explosion from now on; let it happen, right now, in language.

When '*The* Repressed' of their culture and their society come back, it is an explosive return, which is *absolutely* shattering, staggering, overturning, with a force never let loose before, on the scale of the most tremendous repressions: for at the end of the Age of the Phallus, women will have been either wiped out or heated to the highest, most violent, white-hot fire. Throughout their deafening dumb history, they have lived in dreams, embodied but still deadly silent, in silences, in voiceless rebellions.

And with what force in their fragility: 'fragility,' a vulner-abilty to match their matchless intensity. Women have not sublimated. Fortunately. They have saved their skins and their energy. They haven't worked at planning the impass of futureless lives. They have furiously inhabited these sumptuous bodies. Those wonderful hysterics, who subjected Freud to so many voluptuous moments too shameful to mention, bombarding his mosaic statue/law of Moses with their carnal, passionate body-words, haunting him with their inaudible thundering denunciations, were more than just naked beneath their seven veils of modesty – they were dazzling. In a single word of the body they inscribed the endless vertigo of a history loosed like an arrow from all men's history, from biblicocapitalist society. Following these yesterday's victims of torture, who anticipate the new women, no intersubjective relationship will ever be the same. It is you, Dora, you, who cannot be tamed, the poetic body, the true 'mistress' of the Signifier. Before tomorrow your effectiveness will be seen to work – when your words will no longer be retracted, pointed against your own breast, but will write themselves against the other and against men's grammar. Men must not have that place for their own any more than they have us for their own.

If woman has always functioned 'within' man's discourse, a signifier referring always to the opposing signifier that annihilates its particular energy, puts down or stifles its very different sounds, now it is time for her to displace this 'within,' explode it, overturn it, grab it, make it hers, take it in, take it into her woman's mouth, bite its tongue with her woman's teeth, make up her own tongue to get inside of it. And you will see how easily she will well up, from this 'within' where she was hidden and dormant, to the lips where her foams will overflow.

It is not a question of appropriating their instruments, their concepts, their places for oneself or of wishing oneself in their position of mastery. Our knowing that there is a danger of identification does not mean we should give in. Leave that to the worriers, to masculine anxiety and its obsessional relationship to workings they must control – knowing 'how it runs' in order to 'make it run'. Not taking possession to internalise or manipulate but to shoot through and smash the walls.

Feminine strength is such that while running away with syntax, breaking the famous line (just a tiny little thread, so they say) that serves men as a substitute cord, without which they can't have any fun (*jouir*), to make sure the old mother really is always behind them watching them play phallus, she goes to the impossible where she plays the other, for love, without dying of it.

De-propriation, depersonalisation, because she, exasperating, immoderate, and contradictory, destroys laws, the 'natural' order. She lifts the bar separating the present from the future, breaking the rigid law of individuation. Nietzsche, in *The Birth of Tragedy*, said that this is the privilege of divinatory, magical forces. What happens to the subject, to the personal pronoun, to its possessives when, suddenly, gaily daring her metamorphoses (because from her within – for a long time her world, she is in a pervasive relationship of desire with every being) she makes another way of knowing circulate? Another way of producing, of communicating, where each one is always far more than one, where her power of identification puts the same to rout. – And with the same traversing, dispersing gesture with which she becomes a feminine other, a masculine other, she breaks with explanation, interpretation, and all the authorities pinpointing localisation. She forgets. She proceeds by leaps and bounds. She flies/steals.

To fly/steal is woman's gesture, to steal into language to make it fly. We have all learned flight/theft, the art with many techniques, for all the centuries we have only had access to having by stealing/flying; we have lived in a flight/theft, stealing/flying, finding the close, concealed ways-through of desire. It's not just luck if the word 'voler' volleys between the 'vol' of theft and the 'vol' of flight, pleasuring in each and routing the sense police. It is not just luck: woman partakes of bird and burglar, just as the burglar partakes of woman and bird: hesheits pass, hesheits fly by, hesheits pleasure in scrambling spatial order, disorienting it, moving furniture, things, and values around, breaking in, emptying structures, turning the selfsame, the proper upside down.

What woman has not stolen? Who has not dreamed, savoured, or done the thing that jams sociality? Who has not dropped a few red herrings, mocked her way around the separating bar, inscribed what makes a difference with her body, punched holes in the system of couples and positions, and with a transgression screwed up whatever is successive, chain-linked, the fence of circumfusion?

A feminine text cannot not be more than subversive: if it writes itself it is in volcanic heaving of the old 'real' property crust. In ceaseless displacement. She must write herself because, when the time comes for her liberation, it is the invention of a *new, insurgent* writing that will allow her to put the breaks and indispensable changes into effect in her history. At first, individually, on two inseparable levels: – woman, writing herself, will go back to this body that has been worse than confiscated, a body replaced with a disturbing stranger, sick or dead, who so often is a bad influence, the cause and place of inhibitions. By censuring the body, breath and speech are censored at the same time.

To write – the act that will 'realise' the un-censored relationship of woman to her sexuality, to her woman-being giving her back access to her own forces; that will return her goods, her pleasures, her organs, her vast bodily territories kept under seal; that will tear her out of the superegoed, over-Mosesed structure where the same position of guilt is always reserved for her (guilty of everything, every time: of having desires, of not having any; of being frigid, of being 'too' hot; of not being both at once; of being too much of a mother and not enough; of nurturing and of not nurturing . . .). Write yourself: your body must make itself heard. Then the huge resources of the unconscious will burst out. Finally the inexhaustible feminine imaginary is going to be deployed. Without gold or black dollars, our naphtha will spread values over the world, un-quoted values that will change the rules of the old game.

8 Feminist, Female, Feminine
Toril Moi

What is the meaning of the word 'feminist' in 'feminist literary criticism'? Over the past decade, feminists have used the terms 'feminist', 'female' and 'feminine' in a multitude of different ways. One of the main points of this essay, however, is to urge that only a clear understanding of the differences between them can show what the crucial political and theoretical issues of contemporary feminist criticism really are. Initially, I will suggest that we distinguish between 'feminism' as a political position, 'femaleness' as a matter of biology and 'femininity' as a set of culturally defined characteristics.

Feminist

The words 'feminist' or 'feminism' are political labels indicating support for the aims of the new women's movement which emerged in the late 1960s. 'Feminist criticism', then, is a specific kind of political discourse: a critical and theoretical practice committed to the struggle against patriarchy and sexism, not simply a concern for gender in literature, at least not if the latter is presented as no more than another interesting critical approach on a par with a concern for sea-imagery or metaphors of war in medieval poetry. It is my view that, provided they are compatible with her politics, a feminist critic can use whichever methods or theories she likes. There are, of course, different political views within the feminist camp. My point here is not to try to unify or totalise these differences, but simply to insist that recognisable feminist criticism and theory must in some way be relevant to the study of the social, institutional and personal power relations between the sexes: what Kate Millett in her epochal study called *sexual politics*. For Millett, the 'essence of politics is power', and the task of feminist critics and theorists is to expose the way in which male dominance over females (which constitutes her simple and versatile definition of 'patriarchy') constitutes 'perhaps the most pervasive ideology of our culture and provides its most fundamental concept of power'.[1]

In keeping with Millett's approach, feminists have politicised existing critical methods (in much the same sort of way that Marxists have), and it is on this basis that feminist criticism has grown to become a new branch of literary studies. Feminists therefore find themselves in a position roughly similar to that of other radical critics: speaking from their marginalised positions on the outskirts of the academic establishment, they strive to make explicit the politics of the so-called 'neutral' or 'objective' works of their colleagues, as well as to act as cultural *critics* in the widest sense of the word. Like socialists, feminists can in a sense afford to be tolerantly pluralistic in their choice of literary methods and theories, precisely because any approach that can be successfully appropriated to their political ends must be welcome.

A key word here is *appropriation* in the sense of creative *transformation*. Given the feminist insistence on the dominant and all-pervasive nature of patriarchal power so far in history, feminists have to be pluralists: there is no pure feminist or female space from which we can speak. All ideas, including feminist ones, are in this sense 'contaminated' by patriarchal ideology. There is thus no reason to hide the fact that Mary Wollstonecraft was inspired by the male-dominated ideas of the French Revolution, or that Simone de Beauvoir was deeply influenced by Sartre's phallocentric categories when she wrote *The Second Sex*. Nor is it necessary to refuse to recognise John Stuart Mill's efforts to analyse the oppression of women simply because he was a male liberal. The point is not the origins of an idea (no provenance is pure), but the use to which it is put and the effects it can produce. What matters is therefore not so much whether a particular theory was formulated by a man or a woman, but whether its effects can be characterised as sexist or feminist in a given situation.

In this specific context, then, the fact that there are no purely female intellectual traditions available to us is not as depressing as it might have been. What is important is whether we can produce a recognisable feminist impact through our specific use (appropriation) of available material. This emphasis on the productive transformation of other thinkers' material in a way simply restates what creative thinkers and writers have always done: nobody thinks well in a vacuum, nor does anybody ever live in one. Feminists nevertheless often accuse male intellectuals of 'stealing' women's ideas, as for instance the title of one of Dale Spender's many books, *Women of Ideas and What Men Have Done to Them*, makes clear.[2] But can we accuse men of 'stealing' women's ideas if we at the same time argue vociferously for the feminist appropriation of *everybody*'s ideas? Spender's book examines cases of clear intellectual dishonesty: men presenting women's ideas as their own without any kind of acknowledgement of their borrowing, which must be said to constitute an obvious example of the widespread patriarchal effort to silence women. Feminists appropriating traditional thought explicitly discuss the assumptions and strategies of the material they want to use or transform: there can be no question of recommending *silent* appropriation of other theories. (Many feminists object to the idea that thoughts should be considered anybody's personal property. Although I agree with this view, it remains important to criticise the presentation of impulses received from others *as one's own*: this practice can only reinforce the ideology of intellectual property.) As politically motivated critics, feminists will try to make the political context and implications of their work explicit, precisely in order to counter the tacit acceptance of patriarchal power politics which is so often presented as intellectual 'neutrality' or 'objectivity'.

[margin note: explicit. oppress. aims]

The problem with Spender's approach is that it casts women as eternal victims of male ploys. While it is true that many women have been victimised intellectually, emotionally and physically by men, it is also true that some have managed efficiently to counter male power. Stressing our right, aggressively if necessary, to appropriate other people's ideas for our own political purposes, we may avoid a defeatist analysis of the situation of intellectually and culturally active women. As examples of this task of cultural transformation, we can point to the many women who have started the massive task of turning Freudian psychoanalysis into a source of truly feminist analyses of sexual difference and the construction of gender in patriarchal society, Hélène Cixous and Luce Irigaray who have put the philosophy of Jacques Derrida to illuminating feminist use, and Sandra Gilbert and Susan Gubar who have thoroughly rewritten the literary theory of Harold Bloom.[3]

Female

If feminist criticism is characterised by its *political* commitment to the struggle against all forms of patriarchy and sexism, it follows that the very fact of being *female* does not necessarily guarantee a feminist approach. As a political discourse feminist criticism takes its *raison d'être* from outside criticism itself. It is a truism, but it still needs to be said that not all books written by women on women writers exemplify anti-patri-archal commitment. This is particularly true for many early (pre-1960s) works on women writers, which often indulge in precisely the kind of patriarchal stereotyping feminists want to combat. A female tradition in literature or criticism is not necessarily a feminist one.

In her incisive essay 'Are Women's Novels Feminist Novels?' Rosalind Coward discusses the general confusion of *feminist* with *female* writing, both within the women's movement and in publishing and the other media. 'It is just not possible to say that woman-centred writings have any necessary relationship to feminism', Coward argues. 'The Mills and Boon romantic novels are written by, read by, marketed for, and are all about women. Yet nothing could be further from the aims of feminism than these fantasies based on sexual, racial, and class submission which so frequently characterize these novels'.[4] Behind the frequent confusion of feminist with female texts is a complex web of assumptions. It is, for example, often assumed that the very fact of describing experience typical of women is a feminist act. On the one hand this is obviously true: since patriarchy has always tried to silence and repress women and women's experience, rendering them visible is clearly an important anti-patriarchal strategy. On the other hand, however, women's experience can be made visible in alienating, deluded or degrading ways: the Mills and Boon accounts of female love or Anita Bryant's praise of heterosexual love and motherhood are not *per se* emancipatory reading for women. The mistaken belief in *experience* as the essence of feminist politics, stems from the early emphasis on consciousness-raising (c-r) as the main political base of the new women's movement. The point is that consciousness-raising, founded as it is on the notion of 'representative experience' cannot in itself ground a politics, since any experience is open to conflicting political interpretations.[5] It would seem that many feminists today have realised this. Rosalind Coward even argues that c-r groups are no longer central to the women's movement: 'For the most part, consciousness-raising no longer forms the heart of feminism; small groups which do still have a central place in feminist politics are now often either campaigning groups or study groups'.[6]

To believe that common female experience in itself gives rise to a feminist analysis of women's situation, is to be at once politically naive and theoretically unaware. The fact of having the same experience as somebody else in no way guarantees a common political front: the millions of soldiers who suffered in the trenches during the First World War did not all turn pacifist – or socialist or militarist – afterwards. Unfortunately, the experience of childbirth or period pains is neither common to all women nor particularly apt to inspire a deep desire for political liberation: if it did, women would long since have changed the face of the earth. Although crucially shaped by its anti-patriarchal emphasis on female experience, feminism as a political theory cannot be reduced to a reflection or a product of that experience. The Marxist view of the necessary dialectical relationship between theory and practice also applies to the relationship between female experience and feminist politics.

The fact that so many feminist critics have chosen to write about female authors, then, is a crucial political choice, but not a definition of feminist criticism. It is not its object, but its political perspective which gives feminist criticism its (relative) unity. Feminist critics, then, may well deal with books written by men, as they have done from the late 60s to the present day. Kate Millett, in her pioneering *Sexual Politics*, reveals the fundamental sexism of male writers such as Norman Mailer, Henry Miller and D. H. Lawrence; Mary Ellmann, in *Thinking About Women* wittily discusses the sexist habits of male literary critics, and Penny Boumelha analyses the sexual ideology of Thomas Hardy in her *Thomas Hardy and Women*, just to mention a few.[7]

A final problem raised by the distinction between feminist and female is the question of whether men can be feminists or feminist critics. If feminists do not have to work exclusively on female authors, perhaps they do not need to *be* females, either? In principle, the answer to this question is surely yes: men can be feminists – but they can't be women, just as whites can be anti-racist, but not black. Under patriarchy men will always speak from a different *position* than women, and their political strategies must take this into account. In practice, therefore, the would-be male feminist critic ought to ask himself whether he as a male is really doing feminism a service in our present situation by muscling in on the one cultural and intellectual space women have created for themselves within 'his' male-dominated discipline.

Feminine

If the confusion of *female* with *feminist* is fraught with political pitfalls, this is no less true of the consequences of the collapse of *feminine* into *female*. Among many feminists it has long been established usage to make 'feminine' (and 'masculine') represent *social constructs* (patterns of sexuality and behaviour imposed by cultural and social norms), and to reserve 'female' and 'male' for the purely biological aspects of sexual difference. Thus 'feminine' represents nurture, and 'female' nature in this usage. 'Femininity' is a cultural construct: one isn't born a woman, one becomes one, as Simone de Beauvoir puts it. Seen in this perspective, patriarchal oppression consists of imposing certain social standards of femininity on all biological women, in order precisely to make us believe that the chosen standards for 'femininity' are *natural*. Thus a woman who refuses to conform can be labelled both *unfeminine* and *unnatural*. It is in the patriarchal interest that these two terms (femininity and femaleness) stay thoroughly confused. Patriarchy, in other words, wants us to believe that there is such a thing as an essence of femaleness, called femininity. Feminists, on the contrary, have to disentangle this confusion, and must therefore always insist that though women undoubtedly are *female*, this in no way guarantees that they will be *feminine*. This is equally true whether one defines femininity in the old patriarchal ways or in a new feminist way. Essentialism (the belief in a given female nature) in the end always plays into the hands of those who want women to conform to predefined patterns of femininity. In this context *biologism* is the belief that such an essence is biologically given. It is not less *essentialist*, however, to hold that there is a historically or socially given female essence.

But if, as suggested, we define *feminism* as a political position and *femaleness* as a matter of biology, we are still confronted with the problem of how to define *femininity*. 'A set of culturally defined characteristics' or a 'cultural construct' may sound irritatingly vague to many. It would seem that any content could be poured into this container; it does not read like a 'proper' definition. The question is, however, whether it is desirable for feminists to try to fix the meaning of femininity at all. Patriarchy has developed a whole series of 'feminine' characteristics (sweetness, modesty, subservience, humility, etc.). Should feminists then really try to develop another set of 'feminine' virtues, however desirable? And even if we did want to define femininity normatively, would it then not just become a part of the metaphysical binary oppositions Hélène Cixous rightly criticises? There is also a danger of turning a positive, feminist definition of femininity into a definition of femaleness, and thereby falling back into another patriarchal trap. Gratifying though it is to be told that women really are strong, integrated, peace-loving, nurturing and creative beings, this plethora of new virtues is no less essentialist than the old ones, and no less oppressive to all those women who do not want to play the role of Earth Mother. It is after all patriarchy, not feminism, which has always believed in a true female/feminine nature: the biologism and essentialism which lurk behind the desire to bestow feminine virtues on all female bodies necessarily plays into the hands of the patriarchs.

The Deconstruction of Binary Oppositions

So far, we have looked at the terms female – feminine – feminist in relation only to each other. It is, however, equally important to be aware of the political and theoretical implications of assuming that they enter into automatic and static binary oppositions, such as female/male or feminine/masculine.

The case of *feminist* or *feminism*, however, would seem to be somewhat different. The relationship between words like feminism, sexism and patriarchy would seem to be more complex than in the case of female/male or feminine/masculine, possibly because of the political nature of these terms. I am therefore not assuming that the following discussion of the ideology of binary oppositions necessarily goes for sexist/feminist or patriarchal/feminist as well, since there seems to be no automatic homology with 'pairs' such as male/female or masculine/feminine.

Hélène Cixous has contributed a valuable discussion of the consequences of what she calls 'death-dealing binary thought'. Under the heading 'Where is she?', Cixous lines up a list of binary oppositions (see pp. 101–2 above). Corresponding as they do to the underlying opposition Man/Woman, these binary oppositions are heavily imbricated in the patriarchal value system: each opposition can be analysed as a hierarchy where the 'feminine' side is always seen as the negative, powerless instance. The biological opposition male/female, in other words, is used to construct a series of negative 'feminine' values which then are imposed on and confused with the 'female'. For Cixous, who at this point is heavily indebted to Jacques Derrida's work, Western philosophy and literary thought is and has always been caught up in this endless series of hierarchical binary oppositions, which always in the end come back to the fundamental 'couple' of male/female. Her examples show that it does not much matter which 'couple' one chooses to highlight: the hidden male/female opposition with its inevitable positive/negative evaluation can always be traced as the underlying paradigm.

In a typical move, Cixous then goes on to locate *death* at work in this kind of thought. For one of the terms to acquire meaning, she claims, it must destroy the other. The 'couple' cannot be left intact: it becomes a general battlefield where the struggle for signifying supremacy is forever re-enacted. In the end, victory is equated with activity and defeat with passivity; under patriarchy, the male is always the victor. Cixous passionately denounces such an equation of femininity with passivity and death as leaving no positive space for woman: 'Either woman is passive or she does not exist'.[8] Broadly inspired by the thinking and intellectual strategies of Jacques Derrida, her whole theoretical project can in one sense be summed up as the effort to undo this logocentric ideology: to proclaim woman as the source of life, power and energy and to hail the advent of a new, feminine language which ceaselessly subverts these patriarchal binary schemes where logocentrism colludes with phallocentrism in an effort to oppress and silence women. (*Phallocentrism* denotes a system that privileges the phallus as the symbol or source of power. The conjuncture of logocentrism and phallocentrism is often called, after Derrida, *phallogocentrism*.) This project is itself fraught with dangers: although more aware of the problems involved, Cixous often finds herself in great trouble when she tries to distinguish her concept of a *feminine* writing from the idea of a *female* writing. After an heroic struggle against the dangers of biologism, it is probably fair to say that Cixous's theories of an *écriture féminine* in the end fall back into a form of biological essentialism.[9]

But Cixous's 'deconstruction' of the feminine/masculine opposition remains valuable for feminists. If her analysis is correct, for a feminist to continue advocating binary thought, implicitly or explicitly, would seem to be tantamount to remaining inside patriarchal metaphysics. The idea of a unified *female* opposition pitting itself against a *male* front would thus not be a possible feminist strategy for the defeat of patriarchy: on the contrary, it would shore up the very system it seeks to undo. Against any binary scheme of thought, Cixous sets multiple, heterogeneous *difference*. In so doing, she is deeply influenced by the French philosopher Jacques Derrida's concept of difference, or, more correctly, *différance*. For Derrida, meaning (signification) is not produced in the static closure of the binary opposition. Rather it is achieved through the 'free play of the signifier'.[10] To enclose maleness and femaleness in an exclusive opposition to each other, Cixous argues, is thus precisely to force them to enter into the death-dealing power struggle she locates within the binary opposition. Following this logic, the feminist task *par excellence* becomes the deconstruction of patriarchal metaphysics (the belief in an inherent, present meaning in the sign). If, as Derrida has argued, we are still living under the reign of metaphysics, it is impossible to produce new concepts untainted by the metaphysics of presence. To propose a new definition of femininity is therefore necessarily to fall back into the metaphysical trap.

Femininity as Marginality

But doesn't all this theory leave feminists in a kind of double impasse? Is it really possible to remain in the realm of deconstruction when Derrida himself acknowledges that we still live in a 'metaphysical' intellectual space? And how can we continue our political struggle if we first have to deconstruct our own basic assumption of an opposition between male power and female submission? One way of answering these questions is to look at the French-Bulgarian linguist and psychoanalyst Julia Kristeva's considerations on the question of femininity. Flatly refusing to define 'femininity', she prefers to see it as a *position*. If femininity then can be said to have a definition at all in Kristevan terms, it is simply as 'that which is marginalised by the patriarchal symbolic order'. This relational 'definition' is as shifting as the various forms of patriarchy itself, and allows her to argue that men can also be constructed as marginal to the symbolic order, as her analyses of male avant-garde artists (Joyce, Céline, Artaud, Mallarmé, Lautréamont) have shown.[11]

Kristeva's emphasis on femininity as a patriarchal construct enables feminists to counter all forms of biologistic attacks from the defenders of phallocentrism. To posit all women as necessarily feminine and all men as necessarily masculine, is precisely the move which enables the patriarchal powers to define, not femininity, but all *women* as marginal to the symbolic order and to society. If, as Cixous has shown, femininity is defined as lack, negativity, absence of meaning, irrationality, chaos, darkness – in short, as non-Being – Kristeva's emphasis on marginality allows us to view this repression of the feminine in terms of *positionality* rather than of essences. What is perceived as marginal at any given time depends on the position one occupies. A brief example will illustrate this shift from essence to position: if patriarchy sees women as occupying a marginal position within the symbolic order, then it can construe them as the *limit* or border-line of that order. From a phallocentric point of view, women will then come to represent the necessary frontier between man and chaos, but because of their very marginality they will also always seem to recede into and merge with the chaos of the outside. Women seen as the limit of the symbolic order will in other words share in the disconcerting properties of *all* frontiers: they will be neither inside nor outside, neither known nor unknown. It is this position which has enabled male culture sometimes to vilify women as representing darkness and chaos, to view them as Lilith or the Whore of Babylon, and sometimes to elevate them as the representatives of a higher and purer nature, to venerate them as Virgins and Mothers of God. In the first instance the borderline is seen as part of the chaotic wilderness outside, and in the second it is seen as an inherent part of the inside: the part which protects and shields the symbolic order from the imaginary chaos. Needless to say, neither position corresponds to any essential truth of woman, much as the patriarchal powers would like us to believe that they did.[12]

Such a positional perspective on the meaning of femininity would seem to be the only way of escaping the dangers of biologism (conflation with femaleness). But it does not answer our basic political questions. For if we now have deconstructed the *female* out of existence, it would seem that the very foundations of the feminist struggle have disappeared. In her article 'Women's Time', Kristeva advocates a deconstructive approach to sexual difference. The feminist struggle, she argues, must be seen historically and politically as a three-tiered one, which can be schematically summarised as follows:

(1) Women demand equal access to the symbolic order. Liberal feminism. Equality.
(2) Women reject the male symbolic order in the name difference. Radical feminism. Femininity extolled.
(3) Women reject the dichotomy between masculine and feminine as metaphysical. (This is Kristeva's own position.)

The third position is one that has deconstructed the opposition between masculinity and femininity, and therefore necessarily challenges the very notion of identity. Kristeva writes:

> In this third attitude, which I strongly advocate – which I imagine? – the very dichotomy man/woman as an opposition between two rival entities may be understood as belonging to *metaphysics*. What can 'identity', even 'sexual identity', mean in a new theoretical and scientific space where the very notion of identity is challenged? (see below, pp. 214–15)

The relationship between these three positions requires some comments. Elsewhere in her article Kristeva clearly states that she sees them as simultaneous and non-exclusive positions in contemporary feminism, rather than as a feminist version of Hegel's philosophy of history. To advocate position 3 as exclusive of the first two is to lose touch with the political reality of feminism. We still need to claim our place in human society as equals, not as subordinate members, and we still need to emphasise that difference between male and female experience of the world. But that difference is shaped by the patriarchal structures feminists are opposing; and to remain faithful to it, is to play the patriarchal game. Nevertheless, as long as patriarchy is dominant, it still remains *politically* essential for feminists to defend women *as* women in order to counteract the patriarchal oppression that precisely despises women *as* women. But an 'undeconstructed' form of 'stage 2' feminism, unaware of the metaphysical nature of gender identities, runs the risk of becoming an inverted form of sexism. It does so by uncritically taking over the very metaphysical categories set up by patriarchy in order to keep women in their places, despite attempts to attach new feminist values to these old categories. An adoption of Kristeva's 'deconstructed' form of feminism therefore in one sense leaves everything as it was – our positions in the political struggle have not changed; but in another sense, it radically transforms our awareness of the nature of that struggle. A feminist appropriation of deconstruction is therefore both possible and politically productive as long as it does not lead us to repress the necessity of incorporating Kristeva's two first stages into our perspective.

Female Criticism and Feminine Theory

Against this background, the field of feminist criticism and theory today could helpfully be divided into two main categories: 'female' criticism and 'feminine' theory. 'Female' criticism, which *per se* only means criticism which in some way focuses on women, may then be analysed according to whether it is feminist or not, whether it takes female to mean feminist, or whether it conflates female with feminine. The apolitical study of female authors is obviously not in itself feminist: it could very well just be an approach which reduces women to the status of interesting scientific objects on a par with insects or nuclear particles. It is nevertheless important to stress that in a male-dominated context an interest in women writers must objectively be considered a support for the feminist project of making women visible. This would of course not be true for obviously sexist research on women. It is in other words possible to be a 'female' critic without necessarily being a feminist one.

The great majority of American feminist critics nevertheless write from an explicitly feminist position. The emphasis in the United States has been on 'gynocritics', or the study of women writers. Elaine Showalter's *A Literature of Their Own* and Sandra Gilbert and Susan Gubar's *The Madwoman in the Attic* are the most accomplished examples of this genre within feminist criticism.[13] In the context of this essay, Gilbert and Gubar's monumental study furnishes an instructive example of the consequences of the confusion not only of femaleness with femininity, but also of this amalgamated femaleness/femininity with feminism. In their investigation of typical motifs and patterns among nineteenth-century women writers, they persistently use the adjective *female*, discussing for instance the 'female tradition in literature', 'female writing', 'female creativity' or 'female anger', just to mention a few. One of their central arguments is that nineteenth-century women writers chose to express their own female anger in a series of duplicitous textual strategies whereby both the angel and the monster, the sweet heroine and the raging madwoman, are aspects of the author's self-image, as well as elements of her treacherous anti-patriarchal strategies. This is an extremely seductive theory, and strikingly productive, for instance when applied to the works of Charlotte Brontë, who of course created the eponymous madwoman in the first place. But if we unravel the probable meanings of the word *female* in Gilbert and Gubar's text, we find that this theory of 'female creativity' rests on the assumption that *female* authors always experience anti-patriarchal rage in their hearts and that this *feminist* anger will create a typically *feminine* pattern of writing, where a shrewd strategy of disguise is used to make the message from the marginalised group acceptable to the patriarchal powers. This *feminine* pattern, however, is not available to male authors, but common to all *female* writers. The patriarchal strategy of collapsing the feminine into the female can here be seen at work: the *écriture féminine* emerging from this kind of argument is more than tinged with biologism. Gilbert and Gubar's account homogenises all female creative utterances into *feminist* self-expression: a strategy which singularly fails to account for the ways in which women can come to take up a masculine subject position – that is to say, become solid defenders of the patriarchal status quo.

'Feminine' theory in its simplest definition would mean theories concerned with the construction of femininity. From a feminist perspective the problem with this kind of thought is that it is particularly prone to attacks of biologism and often unwittingly turns into theories about female essences instead. At the same time, even the most determinedly 'constructionist' of theories may very well not be feminist ones. The works of Sigmund Freud for example offer a splendid illustration of a theory formation which, while in no way feminist, provides a crucial foundation for a non-essentialist analysis of sexual difference. The alternative, a theory of essential female qualities, would, as we have seen, simply play the patriarchal game. Although psychoanalysis still needs to be creatively transformed for feminist purposes, the fact remains that feminism needs a non-essentialist theory of human sexuality and desire in order to understand the power relations between the sexes.

Much French feminist theory, as well as various feminist rereadings of psychoanalysis may be considered 'feminine theories' in this sense. But there is a paradox involved in my arguments here. Many French feminists, for example, would strongly take issue with my attempt to define 'femininity' at all. If they reject labels and names and 'isms' in particular – even 'feminism' and 'sexism' – it is because they see such labelling activity as betraying a phallogocentric drive to stabilise, organise and rationalise our conceptual universe. They argue that it is masculine rationality that has always privileged reason, order, unity and lucidity, and that it has done so by silencing and excluding the irrationality, chaos and fragmentation that has come to represent femininity. My own view is that such conceptual terms are at once politically crucial and ultimately metaphysical; it is necessary at once to deconstruct the opposition between traditionally 'masculine' and traditionally 'feminine' values *and* to confront the full political force and reality of such categories. We must aim for a society in which we have ceased to categorise logic, conceptualisation and rationality as 'masculine', not for one from which these virtues have been expelled altogether as 'unfeminine'.

To sum up this presentation of feminist literary theory

today, we can now define as *female*, writing by women, bearing in mind that this label does not say anything at all about the nature of that writing; as *feminist*, writing which takes a discernible anti-patriarchal and anti-sexist position; and as *feminine*, writing which seems to be marginalised (repressed, silenced) by the ruling social/linguistic order. The latter does not (*pace* Kristeva) entail any specific *political* position (no clear-cut feminism), although it does not exclude it either. Thus some feminists, such as Hélène Cixous, have tried to produce 'feminine' writing, and others (Simone de Beauvoir) have not. The problem with the 'feminine' label so far has been its tendency to privilege and/or overlap with existing forms of literary modernism and avant-gardism. This, I think, is only one possible way of being marginal in relation to the dominant order (in this case in relation to the traditional representational or realist forms of writing). 'Marginality' cannot or should not *only* be a matter of form.

Perhaps the most important point in all this is to realise that these three 'labels' are not essences. They are categories we as readers or critics operate. *We* produce texts as marginal by situating them in relation to other, dominant structures; we choose to read early texts by women as pre-feminist work; we decide to work on 'female' texts. The definitions proposed here are intended to be open for debate, not to put an end to it, although they are also supposed to say something about the terrain on which the debate might fruitfully be staged: politics, biology and marginality would seem to be key issues here. There is not, unfortunately, such a thing as an intrinsically feminist text: given the right historical and social context, all texts can be recuperated by the ruling powers – or appropriated by the feminist opposition. As Julia Kristeva might have argued, all forms of language are sites of struggle. As feminist critics our task is to prevent the patriarchs from getting away with their habitual trick of silencing the opposition. It is up to us to make the struggle over the meaning of the sign – the meaning of the text – an explicit and inevitable item on the cultural agenda.

9 Women and Madness: the Critical Phallacy
Shoshana Felman

> Silence gives the proper grace to women.
> Sophocles, Ajax

> *Dalila*: In argument with men a woman ever
> Goes by the worse, whatever be her
> cause.
> *Samson*: For want of words, no doubt, or
> lack of breath!
> Milton, Samson Agonistes

1 Woman as Madness

Is it by chance that hysteria (significantly derived, as is well known, from the Greek word for 'uterus') was originally conceived as an exclusively *female* complaint, as the lot and *prerogative* of women? And is it by chance that even today, between women and madness, sociological statistics establish a privileged relation and a definite correlation? 'Women,' writes Phyllis Chesler, in her book *Women and Madness*, 'Women more than men, and in greater numbers than their existence in the general population would predict, are involved in "careers" as psychiatric patients.'[1] How is this sociological fact to be analysed and interpreted? What is the nature of the relationship it implies between women and madness? Supported by extensive documentation, Phyllis Chesler proposes a confrontation between objective data and the subjective testimony of women: laced with the voices of women speaking in the first person – literary excerpts from the novels and autobiographies of women writers, and word-for-word interviews with female psychiatric patients – the book derives and disputes a 'female psychology' conditioned by an oppressive and patriarchal male culture. 'It is clear that for a woman to be healthy she must "adjust" to and accept the behavioural norms for her sex even though these kinds of behaviour are generally regarded as less socially desirable [. . .] The ethic of mental health is masculine in our culture.'[2] 'The *sine qua non* of "feminine" identity in patriarchal society is the violation of the incest taboo, i.e. the initial and continued "preference" for Daddy, followed by the approved falling in love and/or marrying of powerful father figures.'[3] From her initial family upbringing throughout her subsequent development, the social role assigned to the woman is that of *serving* an image, authoritative and central, of man: a woman is first and foremost a daughter/a mother/a wife. 'What we consider "madness", whether it appears in women or in men, is either the acting out of the devalued female role or the total or partial rejection of one's sex-role stereotype.'[4]

In contrast to the critical tendency currently in fashion in Europe, through which a certain French circle has allied itself philosophically with the controversial indictments of the English 'anti-psychiatry' movement, Phyllis Chesler, although protesting in turn against psychiatry as such, in no way seeks to bestow upon madness the romanticised glamour of political protest and of social and cultural contestation: 'It has never been my intention to romanticise madness, or to confuse it with political or cultural revolution.'[5] Depressed and terrified women are not about to seize the means of production and reproduction: quite the opposite of rebellion, madness is the impasse confronting those whom cultural conditioning has deprived of the very means of protest or self-affirmation. Far from being a form of contestation, 'mental illness' is a *request for help*, a manifestation both of cultural impotence and of political castration. This socially defined help-needing and help-seeking behaviour is itself part of female conditioning, ideologically inherent in the behavioural pattern and in the dependent and helpless role assigned to the woman as such.

It is not the material, social, and psychological female condition, but rather the very *status of womanhood* in Western *theoretical* discourse which concerns Luce Irigaray in her book, *Speculum de l'autre femme*.[6] In contrast to Phyllis Chesler, Luce Irigaray interrogates not the empirical voice of women and their subjective testimony, but the key theoretical writings of men – fundamental texts in philosophy and in psychoanalysis – which, in one way or another, involve the concept of femininity. Her study focuses on the text of Freud's (fictive) lecture entitled 'On Femininity' and on the feminine metaphors in Plato's myth of the Cave. A psychoanalyst herself, Luce Irigaray adopts the traditional feminist critique of the male-centred orientation and of the anti-feminine bias in psychoanalytical theory; but her elaboration and consolidation of these classical feminist arguments is derived from the current philosophical methods of thinking developed in France by Jacques Derrida and others in their attempt to work out a general critical 'deconstruction' of Western metaphysics. According to Derrida's radicalisation of the Nietzschean and Heideggerian critiques of traditional philosophy, Western metaphysics is based on the totalitarian principle of so-called 'logocentrism', that is, on the repressive predominance of 'logos' over 'writing', on the privileged status of the present and the consequent valorisation of presence. This *presence-to-itself* of a *centre* (given the name of Origin, God, Truth, Being, or Reason) centralises the world through the authority of its self-presence and subordinates to itself, in an agonistic, hierarchical manner, all the other cognisable elements of the same epistemological (or ontological) system. Thus, the metaphysical logic of dichotomous oppositions which dominates philosophical thought (Presence/Absence, Being/Nothingness, Truth/Error, Same/Other, Identity/Difference, etc.) is, in fact, a subtle mechanism of hierarchisation which assures the unique valorisation of the 'positive' pole (that is, of a *single* term) and, consequently, the repressive subordination of all 'negativity', the mastery of difference as such. It is by thus examining the mere illusion of duality and the repressive way in which the polarity Masculine/Feminine functions in Western thought so as to privilege a unique term, that Luce Irigaray proceeds to develop her critical argument. Theoretically subordinated to the concept of masculinity, the woman is viewed by the man as *his* opposite, that is to say, as *his* other, the negative of the positive, and not, in her own right, different, other, otherness itself. Throughout the Platonic metaphors which will come to dominate Western discourse and to act as a vehicle for meaning, Luce Irigaray points out a latent design to exclude the woman from the production of speech, since the woman, and the other as such, are philosophically subjugated to the logical principle of Identity – Identity being conceived as a solely *masculine* sameness, apprehended as *male* self-presence and consciousness-to-itself. The possibility of a thought which would neither spring from nor return to this masculine Sameness is simply unthinkable. Plato's text thus establishes the repressive systematisation of the logic of identity: the privilege of 'oneness', of the reproduction of likeness, of the repetition of sameness, of literal meaning, analogy, symmetry, dichotomous oppositions, teleological projects.

Freud, who for the first time freed thought from a certain conception of the present and of presence-to-oneself, whose notions of deferred action, of the unconscious, of the death instinct and of the repetition compulsion radically undermine the classical logic of identity, remains, nevertheless, himself a prisoner of philosophy when he determines the nature of sexual difference in function of the a priori of sameness, that is, of the male phallus. Female sexuality is thus described as an absence (of the masculine presence), as lack, incompleteness, deficiency, envy with respect to the only sexuality in which value resides. This symmetrical conception of otherness is a theoretical blindness to the woman's actual Difference, which is currently asserting itself, and asserting precisely its claim to a new kind of logic and a new type of theoretical reasoning.

A question could be raised: if 'the woman' is precisely the other of any conceivable Western theoretical locus of speech, how can the woman as such be speaking in this book? Who is speaking here, and who is asserting the otherness of the woman? If, as Luce Irigaray suggests, the woman's silence, or the repression of her capacity to speak, are constitutive of philosophy and of theoretical discourse as such, from what theoretical locus is Luce Irigaray herself speaking in order to develop her own theoretical discourse about the woman's exclusion? Is she speaking the language of men, or the silence of women? Is she speaking as a woman, or *in place of* the (silent) woman, *for* the woman, *in the name of* the woman? Is it enough to *be* a woman in order to *speak* as a woman? Is 'speaking as a woman' a fact determined by some biological *condition* or by a strategic, theoretical *position*, by anatomy[7] or by culture? What if 'speaking as a woman' were not a simple 'natural' fact, could not be taken for granted? With the increasing number of women and men alike who are currently choosing to share in the rising fortune of female misfortune, it has become all too easy to be a speaker '*for* women'. But what does 'speaking *for* women' imply? What is 'to speak *in the name of* the woman'? What, in a general manner, does 'speech in the name of' mean? Is it not a precise repetition of the oppressive gesture of *representation*, by means of which, throughout the history of logos, man has reduced the woman to the status of a silent and subordinate object, to something inherently *spoken for*? To 'speak in the name of,' to 'speak *for*', could thus mean, once again, to appropriate and to silence. This important theoretical question about the status of its own discourse and its own 'representation' of women, with which any feminist thought has to cope, is not thought out by Luce Irigaray, and thus remains the blind spot of her critical undertaking.

In a sense, the difficulty involved in any feminist enterprise is illustrated by the complementarity, but also by the incompatibility, of the two feminist studies which we have just examined: the works of Phyllis Chesler and Luce Irigaray. The interest of Chesler's book, its overwhelming persuasive power as an outstanding clinical document, lies in the fact that it *does not* speak *for* women: it lets women speak for themselves. Phyllis Chesler accomplishes thus the first symbolical step of the feminist revolution: she *gives voice* to the woman. But she can only do so in a pragmatic, empirical way. As a result, the book's theoretical contribution, although substantial, does not go beyond the classical feminist thought concerning the socio-sexual victimisation of women. On the other side of the coin, Irigaray's book has the merit of perceiving the problem on a theoretical level, of trying to think the feminist question through to its logical ends, reminding us that women's oppression exists not only in the material, practical organisation of economic, social, medical, and political structures, but also in the very foundations of logos, reasoning, and articulation – in the subtle linguistic procedures and in the logical processes through which meaning itself is produced. It is not clear, however, that statement and utterance here coincide so as to establish actual feminine difference, not only on the thematic, but also on the rhetorical level: although the otherness of the woman is here fully assumed as the subject of the statement, it is not certain whether that otherness can be taken for granted as positively occupying the unthought-out, problematical locus *from which* the statement is being *uttered*.

In the current attempt at a radical questioning and a general 'deconstruction' of the whole range of cultural codes, feminism encounters the major theoretical challenge of all contemporary thought. The problem, in fact, is common to the revaluation of madness as well as to the contention of women: how can one speak from the place of the other? How can the woman be thought about outside of the Masculine/Feminine framework, *other* than as opposed to man, without being subordinated to a primordial masculine model? How can madness, in a similar way, be conceived outside of its dichotomous opposition to sanity, without being subjugated to reason? How can difference as such be thought out as *non-subordinate* to identity? In other words, how can thought break away from the logic of polar oppositions?

In the light of these theoretical challenges, and in keeping with the feminist questioning of psychoanalytical and philosophical discourse, it could be instructive to examine the ideological effects of the very production of meaning in the language of literature and in its critical exegesis. We therefore propose here to undertake a reading of a text by Balzac which deals with the woman as well as with madness and to examine the way in which this text, and its portrayal of feminine madness, has been traditionally perceived and commented upon. The text – entitled *Adieu* – is a short story first published in 1830, and later included by Balzac in the volume of *Philosophical Studies* of the *Comédie humaine*.[8]

II   The Realistic Invisible

The story is divided into three parts. The first describes a mysterious domain into which have inadvertently wandered two lost hunters: Philippe de Sucy, a former colonel, and his friend d'Albon, a magistrate. Anxious to find out where they are, they turn to two women, the only human beings in the vicinity, but their questions meet only silence: one of the women, Geneviève, turns out to be a deaf-mute, and the other, an aphasic madwoman whose entire vocabulary consists of the word 'adieu'. On hearing this word, Philippe faints, recognising in the madwoman his former mistress, Countess Stéphanie de Vandières, who had accompanied him to Russia during the Napoleonic Wars but whom he has not seen again since their separation on the banks of the Berezina River and whose trace he has ever since been unable to recover.

The second part is a flashback to the war episode. Among the collapsing masses of the retreating French army, Stéphanie and Philippe are fighting against unbearable cold, inhuman exhaustion and debilitating hunger, in the midst of the snowy plains. Philippe heroically shields Stéphanie in the hope of crossing the Berezina and of thus reaching and having her reach the safety of the other side, free from the Russian threat. But when it turns out that only two places are left on the life raft, Philippe leaves them to Stéphanie and her husband, the Count of Vandières, sacrificing himself for the latter. The Count, however, never reaches the other side: in a violent jolt during the crossing, he is swept overboard and killed. Stéphanie cries out to Philippe, 'Adieu!': it is to be her last lucid word before she loses her reason. For two years thereafter, she continues to be dragged along by the army, the plaything of wretched riff-raff. Mad and cast off like an animal, she is discovered one day after the end of the war by her uncle, an elderly doctor, who takes her in and sees to her needs.

The third part describes the combined efforts of the two men – the doctor having been joined by Philippe – to save and to cure Stéphanie. Stéphanie, on seeing Philippe, fails to recognise him: her continuous repetition of the word 'adieu' implies no understanding and bears no relation to conscious memory. At the sight of the 'stranger' (Philippe), she runs

away like a frightened animal. Following the advice of the
doctor, Philippe learns how to 'tame' Stéphanie by giving her
sugar cubes, thus accustoming her to his presence. Philippe
still hopes that Stéphanie will some day recognise him. Driven
to despair, however, by the long wait, Philippe decides to
hasten Stéphanie's recognition of him by subjecting her to a
psycho-drama designed to restore her memory: he artificially
creates a replica of the Russian plains and of the Berezina
River; using peasants disguised as soldiers, he theoretically
reconstructs and replays before the madwoman's eyes the
exact scene of their wartime separation. Stéphanie is thus
indeed cured: overwhelmed, she recognises Philippe, smiles
to him, repeats once again 'adieu'; but at that very instant
she dies.

A current pocket edition of this amazing story (published
by Gallimard in the 'Folio' collection) ensures, in two different
ways, its critical presentation: the text is preceded and followed
by pedagogical commentary – a Preface by Pierre Gascan and
a 'Notice' by Philippe Berthier – which are supposed to
'explain' it and 'situate' its importance. It is striking that, of
the three chapters which constitute this short story – the
discovery of the madwoman in the mysterious domain, the
war scene, and the scene of the cure – *both* commentators
discuss only one: the chapter depicting the war. The main
plot, which consists of the story of a woman's madness
(episodes I and III), is somehow completely neglected in
favour of the subplot (episode II), a historical narrative
whose function is to describe the events which preceded and
occasioned the madness. The 'explication' thus excludes two
things: the madness and the woman. Viewed through the eyes
of the two academic critics, *Adieu* becomes a story about the
suffering of men in which the real protagonists are none but
'the soldiers of the Grand Army'. The Preface indeed makes
a great point of praising Balzac for 'the realism, unprecedented
in the history of literature, with which the war is here
depicted':[9] 'by showing us, in *Adieu*, the soldiers of the Grand
Army haggard, half dead with hunger and cold, draped in
rags, surging toward the pontoon bridge thrown across the
Berezina, he [Balzac] deals with the myth of military grandeur
[. . .] a blow whose repercussions extend well beyond the

post-Napoleonic era.'[10] This supposedly 'objective' reading of what is called Balzac's 'realism' in fact screens out and disguises an ideological pattern of textual amputations and cuts, in which only a *third* of the text is brought to the reader's attention. 'Indeed,' concedes the Preface's author, 'these scenes do not take up much room in [. . .] *Adieu*, where most of the action occurs subsequent to the historic events which they symbolise. *But they suffice* to give the war its true countenance.'[11] As for the author of the 'Notice', he does not even seek to justify the arbitrary, disproportionate cuts underlying his 'explication' – by putting forward a *truth* 'which suffices': 'the *true* countenance of the war.' In line with the academic tradition of 'selected passages', he proposes, simply and 'innocently', literally to *cut up* the text, to *extract* the second chapter, and truly materialise the operation of ideological extirpation with a serene pedagogical confidence: 'the second chapter, *which can be isolated from the work* as was the story of Goguelat from the *Country Doctor* (cf. our edition of this novel in Folio) marks the appearance in Balzac's work of the theme of the wartime disappearance of an officer who comes back many years later.'[12] The story is here explicitly summed up as being exclusively that of a man: that of 'the wartime disappearance of *an officer* who comes back many years later.' It is, therefore, by no means surprising to see the author of the 'Notice' taken aback by the fact – to him incomprehensible – that in its second version this text could have been, as he puts it, 'oddly entitled' *A Woman's Duty*.[13] Evident in an abandoned title, but in the text neither seen nor heard, the woman does not belong to the realm of the 'explicable'; her claim to commentary is solely an inexplicable piece of knowledge, an unusable article of erudition.

It is just in this manner that the institution of literary criticism pronounces its expert, professional discourse, without even noticing the conspicuousness of its flagrant misogyny. To the *sociological* sexism of the educational system corresponds, in this case, the naive, though by no means innocent, sexism of the exegetical system of *literary analysis*, of the academic and pedagogical fabrication of 'literary' and critical discourse. By guiding the reader, through the extirpation of 'explicable' facts, to the 'correct' perception, to the literal 'proper', so-called 'objective' level of textual interpretation, academic criticism conditions the very norms of 'legibility'. Madness and women, however, turn out to be the two outcasts of the establishment of readability. An ideological conditioning of literary and critical discourse, a political orientation of reading thus affirms itself, not so much through the negative treatment of women as through their total neglect, their pure and simple *omission*. This critical oversight, which appears as a *systematic* blindness to significant facts, functions as a censorship mechanism, as a symbolic eradication of women from the world of literature. It is therefore essential to examine the theoretical presuppositions which permit and sanction this kind of blindness.

We have seen that what is invoked so as to authorise the arbitrariness of the curtailment of the text is the critical concept of Balzac's 'realism': the realism of war, 'unprecedented' – as the Preface puts it – 'in the history of literature'. In the context of this manly realism, the woman is relegated to non-existence, since she is said to partake of the 'unreal': 'Beside the Berezina [. . .] Stéphanie's carriage, blocked among hordes of French soldiers savage with hunger and shock, becomes the *unwonted, almost unreal element* in which the whole absurdity of the situation bursts out.'[14] What, then, is this 'realism' the critic here ascribes to Balzac, if not the assumption, not shared by the text, that what happens to men is more important, and/or more 'real,' than what happens to women? A subtle boundary line, which gives itself as a 'natural frontier', is thus traced, in the critical vocabulary, between the realm of the 'real' and that of the 'unreal', between the category of 'realism' and that of the so-called 'supernatural':

While *Colonel Chabert* contains no *supernatural* elements [. . .] *Adieu* allots a great deal of space to psychic phenomena, with Stéphanie's madness, and even to parapsychic phenomena, with her death [. . .] It is noteworthy [. . .] that Balzac's short stories [. . .] devote infinitely more space to the *supernatural*, to the presence of the *invisible* [. . .] than do his novels. [. . .] In these four stories where it exists side by side with the most striking *realism, the marvellous* is in fact only represented by the *state of semi-unreality* which the main characters attain through the horror of their ordeal. We here come across [. . .] the romantic conception of the transfiguring power of suffering.[15]

The 'supernatural', as everyone knows, cannot be rationally explained and hence should not detain us and does not call for *thought*. Flattened out and banalised into the 'edifying conclusion'[16] of the beneficent power of suffering, Stéphanie's madness is *not problematic*, does not deserve to detain us, since it is but a 'state of semi-unreality'. Realism thus postulates a conception of 'nature' and of 'reality' which seeks to establish itself, tautologically, as 'natural' and as 'real'. Nothing, indeed, is less neutral than this apparent neutrality; nothing is less 'natural' than this frontier which is supposed to separate 'the real' from 'the unreal' and which in fact delimits only the inside and the outside of an ideological circle: an inside which is *inclusive* of 'reason' and men, i.e., 'reality' and 'nature'; and an outside which is *exclusive* of madness and women, i.e., the 'supernatural' and the 'unreal'. And since the supernatural is linked, as the critic would have it, to 'the presence of the invisible',[17] it comes as no surprise to find the woman predestined to be, precisely, *the realistic invisible*, that which realism as such is inherently unable to see.

It is the whole field of a problematic, which defines and structures the invisible as its definite outside – excluded from the domain of visibility and defined as excluded by the existence and the structure of the problematic field itself.[. . .] The invisible is defined by the visible as its invisible, its prohibited sight [. . .]. To see this invisible [. . .] requires something quite different from a sharp or attentive eye, it takes an *educated eye*, a revised, renewed way of looking, itself produced by the effect of a 'change of terrain' reflected back upon the act of seeing.[18]

With a 'revised' way of looking, 'educated' by the 'change of terrain' brought about by the feminist interrogation, let us now attempt to re-read Balzac's text and to reinterpret its relation to the woman as well as to madness.

III 'She? Who?'

From the very beginning the woman in this text stands out as a problem. The opening pages present the reader with a series of abstract questions concerning a female identity: the two lost hunters are trying to situate themselves, to ascertain the identity of the woman they have just glimpsed in the unknown place into which they have wandered: *'Where the devil are we? [. . .] / She, who? [. . .] / Where are we? What is that house? Whose is it? Who are you? Do you live here? [. . .] / But who is this lady? [. . .] / She? Who? [. . .]'*[19]

The reader, too, cannot get his/her bearings: deluged with questions, at the same time deprived systematically of information, not really knowing *who* is speaking, much less about whom, s/he is in turn as *lost* in the text as the two protagonists are in geographical space. The text thus originates in the *loss* of the very conditions of localisation and identification, in a general state of confusion from which, in an almost anonymous manner, a recurrent question emerges: 'She? Who?' The feminine pronoun preceding any proper denomination, the ambiguous question preceding any informative clarification, this preliminary inquiry takes on an abstractly emphatic and allegorical character, and seems to situate from the start the textual problematic within a systematic search for the nature of feminine identity. From the beginning, however, the question reaches a dead end: addressed to the women themselves, the query meets only silence, since both women here are deprived of the ability to speak. Addressed to others, the question obtains only distant and hypothetical answers: *'But who is this lady? [. . .] / It is presumed that she comes from Moulins [. . .]; she is said to be mad [. . .] I wouldn't guarantee you the truth of these rumours.'*[20]

The allegorical question, 'She? Who?' will thus remain unanswered. The text, nonetheless, will play out the question to its logical end, so as to show in what way it *precludes* any answer, in what way the question is set as a trap. The very *lack of the answer* will then write itself as a *different* question, through which the original question will find itself dislocated, radically shifted and transformed.

'She? Who?' The women cannot respond: mad, they do not

understand the men's questions. Nor do the rational men understand the senseless words of the women. But the women, though mad, understand each other. The doctor thus interprets the friendship that seems to unite Stéphanie and the peasant Geneviève: 'Here [. . .] she has found another creature she seems to get along with. It's an idiot peasant-woman [. . .] My niece and this poor girl are in a way united by the invisible chain of their common destiny, and by the feeling that causes their madness.'[21] Understanding occurs in this text only on one side or the other of the boundary line which, separating silence from speech, distinguishes madness from reason. It is nonetheless striking that the dichotomy Reason/Madness, as well as Speech/Silence, exactly coincides in this text with the dichotomy Men/Women. Women as such are associated both with madness and with silence, whereas men are identified with prerogatives of discourse and of reason. In fact, men appear not only as the possessors, but also as the dispensers, of reason, which they can at will mete out to – or take away from – others. While Philippe and the doctor undertake to 'restore Stéphanie's reason', the magistrate, on the other hand, brags: 'If you should ever bring a suit to court, *I would make you lose it, even if reason were a hundred per cent on your side.*'[22] The three men in the story in fact symbolically represent – by virtue of their professions: magistrate, doctor, soldier – the power to act *upon* others' reason, in the name of the law, of health or of force.

With respect to the woman's madness, man's reason reacts by trying to *appropriate* it: in the first place, by claiming to 'understand' it, but with an external understanding which reduces the madwoman to a spectacle, to an *object* which can be *known* and *possessed*. 'Go on, Sir, leave her alone,' the doctor recommends to Philippe, 'I know how to live with the dear little creature; I *understand* her madness, I *spy upon* her gestures, I am in on her secrets.'[23] To 'spy on' in order to 'know'; to 'tame' in order to 'cure': such are the methods used by masculine reason so as to *objectify* feminine madness, thereby mastering it. If the madwoman is throughout the story seen as and compared to an animal, this pervasive metaphor tells us less about Stéphanie's delirium than about the logic of her therapists. For the object is precisely to capture the animal and to tame it. Thus we see the symbolic import of the initial hunting scene. A metaphorical parody of the episode of war and of its martial logic (' "Come on, deputy, forward! Double time! Speed up [. . .] march over the ruts [. . .] Come on, march! [. . .] If you sit down, you're lost," '[24] the opening scene of the hunt already symbolically prefigures Philippe's attitude toward Stéphanie: 'Come on,' cries Philippe from the very first, not yet knowing whom he is talking about, but integrating as a matter of course the woman into his hunter's mentality, 'Come on, let's run after the white and black lady! Forward!'[25] But the hunter's chase will here be but the measure of the flight of his prey.

If masculine reason thus constitutes a scheme to capture and master, indeed, metaphorically *rape* the woman, by the same token, Stéphanie's madness is not contingent on but directly related to her femininity: consisting, precisely, in its loss. Several times Philippe, in fact, explicitly defines Stéphanie's madness as the loss of her womanhood. When the doctor advises him to tame her by feeding her pieces of sugar, Philippe sadly answers: '*When she was a woman*, she had no taste for sweets.'[26] And again, in a burst of sorrow, Philippe cries: 'I die a little more every day, every minute! My love is too great! I could bear everything if only, in her madness, she had kept some *semblance of femininity*.'[27] Madness, in other words, is precisely what makes a woman *not* a woman. But what is a 'woman'? Woman is a 'name', denied in fact to Geneviève in the same way as it is denied to Stéphanie: 'Then a *woman*, if such a *name* can be applied to the *undefinable being* who got up from under the bushes, pulled on the cow by its rope.'[28] 'Woman' is consequently a 'definable being' – chained to a 'definition' itself implying a model, a definition commanded by a *logic of resemblance*. Even in the war scene, Stéphanie had already lost her 'femininity'. '[When] all rolled around herself, *she really resembled nothing* [. . .] Was this that *charming woman, the glory of her lover, the queen of the Parisian ballrooms*? Alas! even the eyes of her most devoted friend could perceive *nothing feminine* left in that heap of linens and rags.'[29] If a 'woman' is strictly, exactly, 'what *resembles* a woman' ('she really resembled nothing [. . .] nothing feminine left'), it becomes apparent that 'femininity' is much less a 'natural' category than a rhetorical one, analogical and metaphorical: a metaphorical category which is explicitly bound, as perceived by Philippe, to a socio-sexual stereotype, to the 'definable' role of the mistress – 'the queen of the Parisian ballrooms'. Of course, the 'queen' here implies a king; the literal, *proper* meaning of metaphorical femininity, paradoxically enough, turns out to be a masculine property: the 'queen of the Parisian ballrooms', 'that charming woman', is above all '*The glory of her lover*'. 'Woman', in other words, is the exact metaphorical measure of the narcissism of man.

The Masculine thus turns out to be the universal equivalent of the opposition: Masculine/Feminine. It is insofar as Masculinity conditions Femininity as its universal equivalent, as what determines and measures its value, that the textual paradox can be created according to which the woman is 'madness', while at the same time 'madness' is the very 'absence of womanhood'. The woman is 'madness' to the extent that she is other, *different* from man. But 'madness' is the 'absence of womanhood' to the extent that 'womanhood' is what precisely resembles the Masculine universal equivalent, in the polar division of sexual roles. If so, the woman is 'madness' since the woman is *difference*; but 'madness' is 'non-woman' since madness is the *lack of resemblance*. What the narcissistic economy of the Masculine universal equivalent tries to eliminate, under the label 'madness', is nothing other than *feminine difference*.

IV   The Therapeutic Fallacy

Such is the male narcissistic principle on which the system of reason, with its therapeutic ambition, is based. For, to 'restore Stéphanie's reason' signifies, precisely, to reinstate her 'femininity': to make her *recognise* man, the 'lover' whose 'glory' she ought to be. 'I'm going to the Bons-Hommes,' says Philippe, 'to see her, speak to her, *cure* her [. . .] Do you think the poor woman would be able to *hear me* and *not recover her reason*?'[30] In Philippe's mind, 'to recover her reason' becomes synonymous with 'to hear *me*'. 'The cure of the madman,' writes Michel Foucault, 'is in the reason of the other – his

own reason being but the very truth of his madness.'[31]
Stéphanie's cure is in Philippe's reason. The 'recovery' of her
reason must thus necessarily entail an act of recognition:

> 'She doesn't recognise me,' cried the colonel in despair.
> Stéphanie! it's Philippe, your Philippe, Philippe!'[32]

> 'Her; not to recognise me, and to run away from me,'
> repeated the colonel.[33]

> 'My love,' he said, ardently kissing the countess's hands, 'I
> am Philippe.' 'Come,' he added, [. . .] 'Philippe is not dead,
> he is here, you are sitting on his lap. You are my Stéphanie,
> and I am your Philippe.' 'Adieu,' she said, 'adieu.'[34]

Stéphanie's recovery of her 'reason', the restoration of her
femininity as well as of her identity, depends then, in Philippe's
eyes, on her specular recognition of *him*, on her *reflection* of his
own name and of his own identity. If the question of female
identity remains in the text unanswered, it is simply because
it is *never* truly asked: in the guise of asking, 'She? Who?'
Philippe is in fact always asking 'I? Who?' – a false question,
the answer to which he believes he knows in advance: 'It's
Philippe.' The question concerning the woman is thereby
transformed into the question of a guarantee for men, a
question through which nothing is questioned, whose sole
function is to ensure the validity of its predefined answer:
'You are *my* Stéphanie.' The use of the possessive adjective
makes explicit the act of appropriation focused here on the
proper names. But it is from Stéphanie's own mouth that
Philippe must obtain his proper name, his guarantee of
the propriety of his own identity, and of hers:
Stéphanie = Philippe, 'You are my Stéphanie, and I am your
Philippe.' In Philippe's eyes, Stéphanie is viewed above all as
an object, whose role is to ensure, by an interplay of reflections,
his own self-sufficiency as a 'subject', to serve as a mediator
in his own specular relationship with himself. What Philippe
pursues in the woman is not a face, but a mirror, which,
reflecting his image, will thereby *acknowledge* his narcissistic
self-image. 'Women', writes Virginia Woolf, 'have served all

these centuries as looking-glasses possessing the magic and delicious power of reflecting the figure of man at twice its natural size.' Philippe, as it turns out, desires not *knowledge* of Stéphanie herself but her *acknowledgement* of him: his therapeutic design is to restore her not to *cognition*, but to *recognition*.

To this demand for recognition and for the restoration of identity through language, through the authority of proper names, Stéphanie opposes, in the figure of her madness, the dislocation of any transitive, communicative language, of 'propriety' as such, of any correspondence or transparency joining 'names' to 'things', the blind opacity of a lost signifier unmatched by any signified, the pure recurrent difference of a word detached from both its meaning and its context.

'Adieu,' she said in a soft harmonious voice, but whose melody, impatiently perceived by the expectant hunters, seemed to divulge not the slightest feeling or the least idea.[35]

'Adieu, adieu, adieu!' she said, without her soul's conferring any perceptible inflection upon the word.[36]

To this automatic repetition of senselessness and difference, Philippe in turn will oppose another type of repetition designed precisely to restore resemblance and identity: in order to cure Stéphanie, in order to restore to her demented, dislocated language its nominative and communicative function, he decides to *reproduce* the primal scene of the 'adieu' and thus to *re-present* theatrically the errant signifier's lost significance, its proper signified. Without her knowledge, Stéphanie will literally be forced to play herself, to return to her 'proper' role. Through the theatrical set-up, everything will end up making sense: and, with all difference thus erased, re-presentation necessarily will bring about the desired re-cognition.

The baron [de Sucy] had, inspired by a dream, conceived a plan to restore the countess's reason. [. . .] He devoted the rest of the autumn to the preparation of this immense enterprise. A small river flowed through his park where, in the winter, it flooded an extensive marsh which resembled [. . .] the one running along the right bank of the Berezina.

The village of Satou, set on a hill, added the final touch to put this scene of horror in its frame [. . .]. The colonel gathered a troop of workers to dig a canal which would represent the voracious river. [. . .] Thus aided by his memory, Philippe succeeded in copying in his park the riverbank where General Elbe had built his bridges. [. . .] The colonel assembled pieces of debris similar to what his fellow sufferers had used to construct their raft. He ravaged his park, in an effort to complete the illusion on which he pinned his last hopes. [. . .] In short, he had forgotten nothing that could reproduce the most horrible of all scenes, and he reached his goal. Toward the beginning of December, when the snow had blanketed the earth with a white coat, he recognised the Berezina. This false Russia was of such appalling truth that several of his comrades recognised the scene of their former sufferings. Monsieur de Sucy kept the secret of this tragic representation.[37]

The cure succeeds. However, so as to fulfil perfectly her 'Woman's Duty', to play her role correctly in this theatre of the identical, to recognise specularly and reflect perfectly Philippe's 'identity', Stéphanie herself must disappear: she has to *die* as *other*, as a 'subject' in her own right. The tragic outcome of the story is inevitable, inscribed as it is from the outset in the very logic of representation inherent in the therapeutic project. Stéphanie will die; Philippe will subsequently commit suicide. If, as ambiguous as it is, the cure turns out to be a murder, this murder, in its narcissistic dialectic, is necessarily suicidal,[38] since, killing Stéphanie in the very enterprise of 'saving' her,[39] it is also his own image that Philippe strikes in the mirror.

Through this paradoxical and disconcerting ending, the text subverts and dislocates the logic of representation which it has dramatised through Philippe's endeavour and his failure. Literature thus breaks away from pure representation: when transparency and meaning, 'reason' and 're-presentation' are regained, when madness ends, so does the text itself. Literature, in this way, seems to indicate its impuissance to dominate or to recuperate the madness of the signifier from which it speaks, its radical incapacity to master its own signifying repetition, to 'tame' its own linguistic difference, to 'represent' identity or truth. Like madness and unlike representation, literature can signify but not *make sense*.

Once again, it is amazing to what extent academic criticism, completely unaware of the text's irony, can remain blind to what the text says about itself. It is quite striking to observe to what extent the logic of the unsuspecting 'realistic' critic can reproduce, one after the other, all of Philippe's delusions, which the text deconstructs and puts in question. Like Philippe, the 'realistic' critic seeks representation, tries, by means of fiction, to reproduce 'the real thing', to reconstruct, minutely and exhaustively, the exact historical Berezina scene. Like Philippe, the 'realistic' critic is haunted by an obsession with proper names – identity and reference – sharing the same nostalgia for a transparent, transitive, communicative language, where everything possesses, unequivocally, a single meaning which can be consequently mastered and made clear, where each name 'represents' a thing, where each signifier, properly and adequately, corresponds both to a signified and to a referent. On the critical as well as on the literary stage, the same attempt is played out to appropriate the signifier and to reduce its differential repetition; we see the same endeavour to do away with difference, the same policing of identities, the same design of mastery, of *sense-control*. For the 'realistic' critic, as for Philippe, the readable is designed as a stimulus not for knowledge and cognition, but for acknowledge-ment and *re-cognition*, not for the *production* of a question, but for the *reproduction* of a foreknown answer – delimited within a pre-existing, pre-defined horizon, where the 'truth' to be discovered is reduced to the natural status of a simple *given*, immediately perceptible, directly 'representable' through the totally intelligible medium of transparent language. Exactly in the same way as Philippe, the commentators of *Adieu* are in turn taken in by the illusory security of a specularly structured act of recognition. Balzac's text, which applies as much to the 'realistic' critic as to Philippe, can itself be read as a kind of preface to its own Preface, as an ironic reading of its own academic reading.

For, what Philippe *misrecognises* in his 'realistic' recognition of the Berezina is, paradoxically enough, the *real*: the real not as a convergence of reflections, as an effect of mirroring focalisation, but as a radically de-centring resistance; the real as, precisely, other, the unrepresentable as such, the ex-centric residue which the specular relationship of vision cannot embrace.

Along with the illusions of Philippe, the 'realistic' critic thus repeats, in turn, his allegorical act of murder, his obliteration of the other: the critic also, in his own way, *kills the woman*, while killing, at the same time, the question of the text and the text as a question.

But, here again, as in Philippe's case, the murder is incorporated in an enterprise which can be seen as 'therapeutic'. For in obliterating difference, in erasing from the text the disconcerting and ex-centric features of a woman's madness, the critic seeks to 'normalise' the text, to banish and eradicate all trace of violence and anguish, of scandal or insanity, making the text a reassuring, closed retreat whose balance no upheaval can upset, where no convulsion is of any consequence. 'To drive these phantoms firmly back into their epoch, to close it upon them, by means of a historical narrative, this seems to have been the writer's intent.'[40] By reducing the story to a recognition scheme, familiar, snug and canny, the critic, like Philippe, 'cures' the text, precisely of that which in it is incurably and radically uncanny.

From this paradoxical encounter between literature's critical irony and the uncritical naivity of its critics, from this confrontation in which Balzac's text itself seems to be an ironic reading of its own future reading, the question arises: how *should* we read? How can a reading lead to something other than recognition, 'normalisation' and 'cure'? How can the critical project, in other words, be detached from the therapeutic projection?

This crucial theoretical question, which undermines the foundations of traditional thought and whose importance the feminist writings have helped to bring out, pinpoints at the same time the difficulty of the woman's position in today's critical discourse. If, in our culture, the woman is by definition associated with madness, her problem is how to break out of this (cultural) imposition of madness *without* taking up the critical and therapeutic positions of reason: how to avoid speaking both as *mad* and as *not mad*. The challenge facing the woman today is nothing less than to 're-invent' language, to *re-learn how to speak*: to speak not only against, but outside of the specular phallogocentric structure, to establish a discourse the status of which would no longer be defined by the phallacy of masculine meaning. An old saying would thereby be given new life: today more than ever, changing our minds – changing *the* mind – is a woman's prerogative.

10 Promises, Promises: the Fictional Philosophy in Mary Wollstonecraft's *Vindication of the Rights of Woman*

Jane Moore

i

This essay explores the possibility that deconstruction offers a useful mode of textual analysis both for feminist readings of past texts and relatedly, necessarily, for current feminist approaches to the politics of gender and literary criticism. I say necessarily related because how we read past representations of femininity and sexual difference has implications for understanding their present meanings. Also, I want to stress that although we always read past texts from the perspective of present-day concerns, knowledges and beliefs, there is, as Gillian Beer has noted, a significant difference between approaches which seek to convert the concerns of past texts into current categories, and those which attempt to read texts from the past in their historical difference from the present.[1]

At stake in these different approaches is the belief that meanings of femininity and sexual difference are multiple, contradictory and changing: the first way of reading fixes present meanings of sexual difference and current theoretical perspectives as the only source of authority from which to read the past, which often means judging the past; the second way of reading, which is the one I propose to adopt, foregrounds the specificity of historical meanings. This has the corresponding effect of unfixing the authority of current meanings, for to stress changes in past and present meanings is to locate the past and the present as moments in a continuous history of change. 'Now' may be the most familiar moment, but it is not any the more stable for that.

This is not meant to imply that we can somehow bypass the uncertain instabilities of the present in an effort to reach back through literary texts to an unadulterated 'true' version of the past which is untainted by the pre-conceptions of now. On the contrary, our interpretations of historical texts are always informed by present-day influences. But neither does it mean that as present-day readers we are inexorably compelled to abandon ourselves to the illusory authority of now, only that we should be alert to its imaginary effects, that is, to the way it masquerades as real. For, as Beer again notes, we will only read helplessly, 'merely hauling, without noticing, our own cultural baggage', if we 'read past texts solely for their grateful "relevance" to our expectations and to those of our circumstances that we happen to have noticed'.[2]

I have raised some of the problems and politics of reading history at the start of my paper for two reasons. The first and most obvious is that I have chosen to analyse a text from the 1790s. The second, perhaps less obvious, reason arises from the wish to use deconstructive theories in this task. By employing deconstructive textual strategies alongside a consideration of historical factors I hope to avoid the ahistoricism of certain, mainly American, deconstructors, whose inattention to the political implications of neglecting the historical limits of the texts they analyse has led Colin MacCabe to reaffirm Norman Mailer's remark that 'deconstruction–US style has been a "Reagan kind of radical theory"'; and Christopher Norris to speak of 'deconstruction on the wild side'.[3] Norris warns against a certain type of deconstructive free play which is concerned only with undoing the textual workings of the binary oppositions and metaphysical assumptions that underpin and distinguish one mode of writing, or genre, from the next. He does so on the grounds that this critical practice results in the collapse of all genre distinctions. Consequently, it becomes possible to claim, for example, that philosophy is 'simply another variety of literature, a text pervaded by the same ruses of figuration'.[4] And, by extension, it no longer makes any 'sense' for the critic to acknowledge a political preference for one discourse over another: all discourses are rendered the same, in that they are all 'pervaded by the same ruses of figuration' regardless of their different historical, cultural and sexual 'contexts'. Norris's warning against undoing all textual difference, all genre distinctions – a task which in the 1980s has perhaps become all too easy – is pertinent to an essay about feminist approaches to gender difference. For it is precisely on a recognition of genre difference that much late twentieth-century feminist theory, not to mention eighteenth-century explorations of gender difference, relies. Twentieth-century feminist criticism has identified an inextricable, though not inexorable, relationship between the taxonomy of genre and gender. This relationship occupies a privileged position in current feminist criticism's preoccupation with questioning the place from which women speak and the possibility of a specifically feminine language.

The French feminist Hélène Cixous thus begins her philosophical–poetical essay, 'Sorties', with the question 'Where is she?'; while the American theorists Sandra Gilbert and Susan Gubar start their paper in this volume by asking 'Is anatomy linguistic destiny?'[5] Cixous's essay suggests that woman's place in the history of Western thought has been at the negative pole of the series of binary oppositions which have structured that history. The examples given are 'Activity/Passivity, Sun/Moon, Culture/Nature, Day/Night, Father/Mother, Intelligible/Palpable, Logos/Pathos'.[6] All of these 'couples' come back to 'the' couple 'Man/Woman'. They also relate to another couple, which is 'Philosophy/Literature'.

'Literature', writes Cixous, 'is under the command of the philosophical and the phallocentric'.[7] Consequently, 'Sorties' concludes that women must reject a philosophical mode of writing if they are to 'write themselves', which is to write a specifically feminine discourse, and thereby resist identification with 'the [philosophical] discourse controlled by the phallus'.[8]

ii

In the eighteenth century the insistence on genre difference comes from the other side of the coin. The title of Mary Wollstonecraft's *Vindication of the Rights of Woman: with Strictures on Political and Moral Subjects*, published in 1792, immediately declares its philosophical status. The nascent feminist interests of this text result in a call to women to resist identification with dominant masculine assumptions on what it means to be a woman. This involves rejecting what the *Vindication* pinpoints as an artificial literary rhetoric of femininity and identifying instead with a philosophical rational discourse, which although controlled by the phallus is not inherently masculine.

The argument of the *Vindication* depends on maintaining a fundamental opposition between plain-speaking philosophy and fictional feminine figurality. It depends also, therefore, on the social and textual interrelation of genre and gender categories. From its beginning the *Vindication* stresses the determining influence of genre in shaping assumptions about gender; and, in line with the project to release women from false conceptions of their sex, the 'Author's Introduction' insists on discarding feminine ways of writing.

> Dismissing, then, those pretty feminine phrases, which the men condescendingly use to soften our slavish dependence, and despising that weak elegancy of mind, exquisite sensibility, and sweet docility of manners, supposed to be the sexual characteristics of the weaker vessel, I wish to show that elegance is inferior to virtue, that the first object of laudable ambition is to obtain a character as a human being, regardless of the distinction of sex, and that secondary views should be brought to this simple touchstone. (82)[9]

The *Vindication*'s call to women to reject a 'secondary', because culturally constituted, femininity and instead to 'obtain a character as a human being, regardless of the distinction of sex', appears to demand the complete effacement of sexual difference. But the 'human character' referred to here is not gender-neutral: it is male, in as much as it is the qualities *attributed* to masculinity which are lauded. In writing, these qualities are manifested in a straightforward rational prose, as opposed to the 'pretty feminine phrases' which Wollstonecraft associates only with women.

Wollstonecraft's plea to women to deny the specificity of their sex may seem misplaced, not to say anti-feminist, to twentieth-century readers. Mary Jacobus, for example, declares against what she sees as the text's cold logic. And she accuses Wollstonecraft of being a 'plain-speaking utilitarian', who 'speaks not so much *for* women, or *as* a woman, but *against* them – over their dead bodies'.[10] Certainly these charges are admissible, but, I suggest, they are the result of 'judging' the *Vindication* in isolation from the culture and history of which it forms a part. Moreover, their effect is to foreclose the possibility of reading the *Vindication* positively; that is, reading it for the challenge it poses to patriarchal assumptions, and not for the ways in which it complies with them.

In order to allow the radical edge of Wollstonecraft's project to come fully into view, which is the aim of my reading, it may be useful, necessary even, to consider the *Vindication*'s historical placement. Thus, before looking at the *Vindication* more closely, I want briefly to sketch some of the dominant (male) conceptions of gender and genre difference that were in circulation at the moment of the text's production. They are all assumptions which inform the *Vindication*'s discussion of the relationship between women and language.

In the late seventeenth and eighteenth centuries the categorisation of genre was instrumental in helping to formulate and coalesce received notions of sexual difference. The position of women in relation to men was roughly analogous to the position and function of figurative language in relation to a utilitarian one. Evidence of this relationship appears in chapter 10 of John Locke's *Essay Concerning Human Understanding* (1690), as well as in the mid-eighteenth century writings of Jean-Jacques Rousseau, and books by other later male educationists such as John Bennett.

Locke's *Essay* sets up a series of oppositions in order both to distinguish between and to privilege the capacity of language to instruct over its ability to entertain. Wit, fancy, pleasure, delight and eloquence are differentiated from truth, knowledge, improvement and lucidity. That these are oppositions not only of genre but also of gender is revealed by the following concluding sentences:

> Eloquence, like the fair sex, has too prevailing beauties in it to suffer itself ever to be spoken against. And it is in vain to find fault with those arts of deceiving wherein men find pleasure to be deceived.[11]

The implications for women of Locke's sentiments are fully spelt out in Rousseau's assertion:

> A man speaks of what he knows, a woman of what pleases her; the one requires knowledge, the other taste; the principal object of a man's discourse should be what is useful, that of a woman's what is agreeable.[12]

Even towards the end of the eighteenth century, by which time the need for reforms in female education was generally accepted, Rousseau's stress on women's ornamental role in society still influenced male educational reformers. John Bennett is a case in point.[13] In volume I of his two volumes of *Letters to a Young Lady*, first published in 1789 and reprinted in 1795, Bennett argues that women's education should be restricted to less arduous intellectual pursuits than men's. For, he claims,

> Whilst men, with solid judgement and a superior vigour are to combine ideas, to discriminate, and to examine a subject to the bottom, you are to give it all its brilliancy and all its charms. They provide the furniture; you dispose it with propriety. They build the house; you are to fancy, and to ornament the ceiling.[14]

It would be misleading, however, to suggest that these (male) views went uncontested. Certainly there were dissenting, mainly female, voices which countered the dominant, mainly male, ones. Along with Mary Wollstonecraft, Hannah More strongly advocated the need for a far broader system of female education. And although on other matters More spoke from the opposite end of the political spectrum to Wollstonecraft, Wollstonecraft probably would have approved of More's proposal that women's education should include reading such philosophical texts as Locke's *Essay*.[15] Also, some women's novels clearly supported a more extensive and more useful system of female education. Sarah Scott's *Millenium Hall* (1762), for example, describes a community of self-educated women living in the country, where they perform philanthropic work and read philosophical works.[16] And both Mary Hays's *Memoirs of Emma Courtney* (1796) and Mrs Opie's *Adeline Mowbray* (1804) have self-educated philosophical heroines.[17]

But in the moment of the *Vindication*'s production these voices were not dominant; indeed in some cases they hadn't even been articulated. Moreover, the 'fact' that the heroines of these women's novels are invariably self-educated suggests that, despite educational forms, women were obliged to look beyond male-controlled pedagogic practices for their education. It also suggests, of course, that women were capable of fulfilling greater tasks than the literal and metaphoric homemaking which John Bennett prescribes.

iii

To return, then, to the authorial preface of the *Vindication*, it now becomes clear why the text seeks to cement an opposition between 'pretty feminine phrases' designed to entertain, and unadorned utilitarian sentences designed to instruct, with the aim, of course, of rejecting the former.

Starting from this 'simple' conviction of difference, the text further distinguishes between primary and secondary discourses, which respectively relate to the binarism of natural/unnatural, true/false, good/bad. 'Pretty feminine phrases', a 'weak elegancy of mind', 'exquisite sensibility' and 'a sweet docility of manners', it is argued, are derivative from, or secondary to, a primordial self-evidently rational language which corresponds to a 'natural' state of being. The *Vindication* proposes that in order to return to the state where reason naturally reigns, women must throw off the artificial trappings – and tropings – of an unnatural culturally constituted femininity.

In making a distinction, however, between natural and unnatural uses of language, between a primary utilitarian language and a supplementary literarity, the *Vindication* immediately encounters the problem of its own textuality – its own wordiness: on the one hand it is argued that virtue is more natural than elegance, while on the other it is acknowledged that in order for the idea of virtue to be communicated it must be inscribed in language; and not only this, it is also hinted that meaning is itself an effect of language, including what it means to be a woman. The 'Author's Introduction' states that to be a human being one must first 'obtain a character as a human being'. In other words, one must take up a position in language. What is remarkable about the *Vindication*'s recognition of the way in which language shapes subjectivity is that it contradicts and effectively displaces the defining extra-textuality of the idea of reason, and of a 'natural' (pre-linguistic) state of being, on which the argument of that text depends. The opposition between natural and unnatural is undermined by their shared dependence for meaning on their (secondary) inscription in language, and the meaning of the word 'natural' consequently slides beyond the control of the primary/secondary opposition.

In an attempt, then, to bring the disruptive operations of language into line, the text vigorously reasserts a distinction between proper and improper uses of language. By arguing in a manner similar to William Godwin's *Enquiry Concerning Political Justice*, not that nature, virtue, truth, and reason are constitutive of an illusory referent, or a pre-linguistic essence, but rather that the language of reason *facilitates* direct access to an external order of those ideals, the *Vindication* defuses the threat which language poses to the belief that human beings have recourse to essential, primordial and natural ideals.[18] Thus, the emphasis of the 'Author's Introduction' increasingly falls on making a difference between the perceived transparency of a rational language and the deceptiveness and obscurity of a figural one. Hence, Wollstonecraft asserts:

I shall disdain to cull my phrases or polish my style. I aim at being useful, and sincerity will render me unaffected; for wishing rather to persuade by the force of my arguments than dazzle by the elegance of my language, I shall not waste my time in rounding periods, or in fabricating the turgid bombast of artificial feelings . . . (82)

As if this commitment to an 'unaffected' transparent mode of persuasion stands in need of further reassurance Wollstonecraft goes one step further: she announces her intention to abolish not only tropes but all words:

I shall be employed about things, not words! and, anxious to render my sex more respectable members of society, I shall try to avoid that flowery diction which has slided from essays into novels, and from novels into familiar letters and conversations. (82)

Seemingly untroubled, then, by its own insights about the discursive production of meaning and the mediating agency of language, the text confidently announces its project to instruct the reader by the persuasive force of rational argument, rather than dazzle and deceive her by the elegance of its language. Correspondingly, chapter 1 sets out 'to go back to first principles in search of the most simple truths' (91). It opens with a series of 'plain' questions – and answers – that enlist and instruct the reader in a peculiarly self-assured catechism, which reads as follows:

In what does man's pre-eminence over the brute creation consist? The answer is as clear as that a half is less than the whole, in Reason.

What acquirement exalts one being above another? Virtue, we spontaneously reply.

For what purpose were the passions implanted? That man by struggling with them might attain a degree of knowledge denied to the brutes, whispers Experience. (91)

The structure of these opening paragraphs at first sight appears to be a logical one. They offer the reader a rehearsal of the principles on which explanations and philosophical theories delivered later in the chapter will depend. It is paradoxical, then, that in order to communicate these principles, the text falls back on the tropic ruses it seeks to condemn. Transparency is re-placed by analogy and metaphor: reason is 'clear' only by analogy, while 'experience' 'whispers' to us as a personification.

Moreover, as the chapter continues, the already metaphoric language in which these 'plain' questions and answers are delivered very quickly runs out of control, thereby displacing the transparency earlier promised.

The 'first principles' outlined in the opening paragraphs become increasingly blurred at the edges by the 'dazzling' imagery of the rest of the chapter. Even by the second page it is evident that utilitarian prose has fallen victim to the wordiness of the language it is forced to communicate in: the obviousness, or transparency, of 'simple' truths is clouded by a continuous bodily metaphor of health and disease, beauty and deformity, which structures not only this chapter but all the succeeding ones. Thus, 'vice skulks with all its native deformity' and is 'rotten at the core'. (92) Aristocratic, monarchical and priestly powers constitute the 'pestilential vapour' (96) which hovers over society; while tyranny in all forms is a 'baneful lurking gangrene', a contagion spread by the unnatural state of the 'indolent puppet of court', who is the 'luxurious monster' and the 'fastidious sensualist'. (99) These metaphors culminate in the final potent image of the 'pestiferous purple' which sums up all that 'renders the progress of civilisation a curse, and warps the understanding.' (99)

Consequently, by the end of the chapter all that the reader can be certain of, all that she can glean from her instruction is that the transparent language and forceful reasoning promised earlier has become lost in a mist of words; and that, ironically, the text has reproduced the dazzling images and eloquent phrases it set out to avoid.

How, then, are we to interpret the apparent absence of clear rational argument in a chapter which aims to deliver precisely that? What is the epistemological status of a text that formally offers itself as a (philosophical) treatise 'on female rights and manners' (79), but which leaves the reader to wander unguided through the web of intertextual, often literary, allusions and sudden long digressions which comprise it? As one critic notes, another characteristic feature of this text is its hopelessly long sentences, imitative of the eighteenth-century rounded prose rejected by the 'Author's Introduction', where the reader comes panting to the end, a little unsure of what the subject was.[19] Moreover, what are we to make of the paradox that it is in the text's tropic supplementarity, and not in a forceful and rigorous 'philosophical' argument, that reason, or at least examples that help us to understand what the text means by reason, is found?[20] How, finally, should we approach the contradiction that the text reproduces what it most fears: metaphoricity, fictionality and, by extension, femininity, whereas reason – the effect of plain words – which is what the text most desires, constantly eludes it?

Not only is the light of reason eclipsed by metaphor, it is also displaced by the text's own rhetoric of temporality. This is indicated in the following assertion:

> Rousseau exerts himself to prove that all *was* right originally: a crowd of authors that all *is* now right: and I, that all will *be* right. (95)

Thus, there is produced the contradiction that the text wishes to rationally state the case for moving towards a society based on the principles of reason and sexual equality to the non-rational, because contemporary, female reader. This is an anachronism that haunts the *Vindication* throughout and returns with full force at its close, where it is stated:

> That women at present are by ignorance rendered foolish or vicious is, I think, not to be disputed; and that the most salutary effects tending to improve mankind might be expected from a REVOLUTION in female manners, appears, at least, with a face of probability, to rise out of the observation. (317)

Exactly like those 'silly' novels (308) which the *Vindication* reproves because they 'are only addressed to the imagination'

(307), and because they entice women with improbable fantasies worked up in 'stale tales' and 'meretricious scenes' (306), the *Vindication* itself can *only* address the imagination, since the possibility of women taking up a rational subject position in a language devoid of metaphor is deferred beyond the discursive limits of the present text.[21]

iv

Twentieth-century critics have shown a remarkable consistency in their approach to the contradictions I have outlined. They have unfailingly 'failed' the *Vindication* for its lack of a coherent argument, clear reasoning and a logical structure. Ralph Wardle's criticism of the text's 'lack of organisation', and of Wollstonecraft's inability to resist 'far-fetched metaphors which served only to cloud her meaning' is representative in this respect.[22] Miriam Brody is perhaps less so, for she remarks: 'It doesn't seem important any longer' to apologise for Wollstonecraft's style, 'since what she had to say was clear enough'.[23]

What is notable about the *Vindication*'s twentieth-century critics is their tendency not only to fail it, but also to fail its author. Even when critics are supportive, it is Wollstonecraft, not her text, who is implicitly critiqued. Invariably it is she, it is her temperament and her life, which critics turn to in order to account for what they perceive to be the *Vindication*'s chief 'flaw': namely, a lack of unity in content and structure. But if instead of seeking unity in Wollstonecraft's text, or more exactly her life, we focus our attention on how her text is produced from the range of meanings, beliefs and knowledges in circulation at the moment of its production, we are able to release the cultural relativity and historical instability, or disunity, of the system of differences which the text presents as self-evident and natural; for example, the difference of a philosophical from a literary rhetoric. Correspondingly, the project of interpretation shifts from a corrective position which bemoans a text's, or more often the author's failures, to one that, instead of employing the value-laden terms of success and failure, while claiming to undertake an 'objective', that is, value-free, assessment of 'good' writing, openly explores the political implications of the meanings of femininity and masculinity that are produced, and recognises that all critical practice is without objective criteria. One of the consequences of this way of reading is that culpability, especially authorial culpability, is no longer what is at issue, for the author is regarded not as the sovereign producer of meaning, but as the site where meanings converge and compete for a version of the 'truth'.

The *Vindication* may be read as a text that displays this conflict of meanings, thereby revealing their fundamental instability. Instead of attempting to unify the text's inconsistencies, or, alternatively, to mark it down because of them, I want to offer the thesis that the *Vindication* produces radical implications for an understanding of the historical construction of gendered meanings. Moreover, I propose that it does so precisely because of its inability to carry out the project of cementing an opposition between philosophical and literary uses of language, and its consequent incapacity to reason in the transparent 'unaffected' style promised by the 'Author's Introduction'. What is in question here is not whether the *Vindication* is a 'philosophical' failure, or even that it is, paradoxically, a 'literary' success; rather it is the possibility that the text radically subverts the extant binarism of genre and gender difference of the 1790s.

I have suggested that textual contradictions and uncertainties come into play in moments when the *Vindication*'s narrative oscillates between a rhetoric of 'philosophical rationalism' and a 'fictional feminine figurality'. At stake in this claim is the proposition that historical meanings are produced within a network of competing, unfixed and therefore changeable discourses. Also at stake is the historical specificity of those discourses and the meanings they produce. Eighteenth-century meanings of genre difference had precise implications for those of gender difference. For the twentieth-century critic to undo the genre differences in Wollstonecraft's text is simultaneously to collapse the gender difference inscribed in it. It is also, therefore, to side-step any consideration of the social power relations that inform those textual distinctions. This has not been my project. However, I would want to claim that we can reveal the instability of the opposition which the *Vindication* makes between fiction and philosophy. We can, for example, attend to the way in which a fictional or figural rhetoric displaces and subverts the seeming priority of philosophical argument, but in doing so we have always to be alert to the limits imposed on our interpretation of this past text by its own historical placement, and by the corresponding historical specificity of the meanings it constructs.

If this essay has privileged throughout the intertextual relationship between the *Vindication*'s literary and philosophical modes, it has done so not with the aim of collapsing these categories into one another, so that it becomes impossible to speak of literature and philosophy as such, but rather to emphasise the dialectical nature of their relationship. This relationship, then, is neither one of similitude nor one of mutual exclusivity. Each part of the opposition 'philosophy/literature' simultaneously defines and disrupts the other; the movement between them is never halted, the conflicts inscribed within it are never resolved; it is a movement which is precisely in process.

That the *Vindication* is ultimately unable to curtail and thereby contain its own textual operations of displacement and difference, with the result that it cannot produce a self-contained philosophical language, is evidenced by the constant invoking of a literary other within the text. It is also implied by the (literary) consequences of a 'Note' appended to the text. Here Wollstonecraft announces her intention to produce a second volume of the *Vindication*:

> When I began to write this work, I divided it into three parts, supposing that one volume would contain a full discussion of the arguments which seemed to me to rise naturally from a few simple principles; but fresh illustrations occurring as I advanced, I present only the first part to the public.
>
> Many subjects, however, which I have cursorily alluded to, call for further investigation, especially the laws relative to women, and the consideration of their peculiar duties. These will furnish ample matter for a second volume, which in due time will be published, to elucidate some of the

sentiments, and complete many of the sketches begun in
the first. (90)

The promised additional volume never appeared, at least not
as a philosophical treatise. What did appear – perhaps in its
place – was the fiction *The Wrongs of Woman: or, Maria* which,
unfinished at the time of Wollstonecraft's death, was edited
by William Godwin and published posthumously in 1789.[24]
As its title suggests and the authorial preface confirms, this
text can be read as a fictional reworking of its predecessor's
philosophical arguments. *The Wrongs of Woman* makes apparent
what the *Vindication* suppresses all along: this is the impossibility of treating literature and philosophy as self-enclosed
categories. *The Wrongs of Woman* is an eminently 'philosophical'
fiction: its project, like that of the *Vindication* is to '[exhibit]
the misery and oppression, peculiar to women, that arise out
of the partial laws and customs of society'.[25] And its arguments,
although inscribed in the language of fiction are no less
'philosophical' for that.

V

Why, though, should the 'flowery' prose of fiction seemingly
supplant the 'unaffected' prose of philosophy as the desired
and dominant language for the inscription of nascent feminist
beliefs in the short but climactic years from the publication
of *The Rights of Woman* in 1792 to *The Wrongs of Woman* in 1798?

Deconstructionist theory is useful in helping the critic
answer this question, but only up to a point, or rather a limit.
This limit is history; for, lacking a social theory, deconstruction
is correspondingly unable to offer historical explanations,
although it is not fundamentally incompatible with them. It
can, however, offer textual ones, the value of which to any
radical-minded critic I would not want to obscure.

Michael Ryan has suggested that the revolutionary potential
of deconstruction consists in its overturning of some of the
most treasured mainstays of bourgeois philosophy.[26] Used to
analyse a text like the *Vindication*, deconstructive strategies
enable the critic to question, for example, the primacy of

consciousness and the self-evidence of the text's binary oppositions, philosophy/literature, nature/culture, eloquent
language/elegant language and, implicitly, male/female. To
question the primacy of consciousness has the effect of displacing authorial intention as the source and guarantee of
meaning. This displacement produces a fundamentally
unstable text whose competing discursive modes struggle
for dominance. Consequently, it is the relation between
discourses, rather than the discourses themselves, which is
brought into the foreground, and it is the unknown, uncertain,
ceaselessly changing space between them which becomes the
new critical terrain. Meanings are unfixed and the status quo
is shown to be never quite that: the struggle between discourses
replaces the possibility of any balanced or harmonious existence, however temporary.

Similarly, recognition of the differential interconstitution of
a text's seemingly self-evident binary oppositions produces a
reading of the *Vindication* which focuses on the relations of
struggle that operate in the margins of the difference the text
has as its project to cement. For if the *Vindication*'s inability to
avoid what it condemns, namely 'pretty feminine phrases',
'flowery diction', rounded sentences and artificial, because
constructed, tropes indicates metaphoricity as norm rather
than anomaly, then the text produces not a theory of the
transparent capacity of language, nor evidence of the 'simple
truths' and 'first principles' assumed to pre-exist discursively
constituted meanings. Rather, it produces a theory of the
differential nature of textuality and offers a 'negative affirmation' of the infinite displacement and deferral of meaning.[27]
Starting with a conviction of difference, the text ends by
affirming differance (in the Derridean sense of to differ and to
defer).

A deconstructive analysis can, then, offer textual difference
as an explanation of why the *Vindication* is unable to reconcile
the conflict of its competing 'philosophical' and 'literary'
languages; and why, therefore, 'part two' was never produced
in the promised form of a (philosophical) treatise. But this
explanation points only to the impossibility of any self-enclosed
discourse or system of knowledge, which would equally
explain why fictions such as *The Wrongs of Woman* contain

'philosophical' passages and produce political insights.

Thus, in order to use deconstructive strategies for readings of past texts it may be useful, necessary even, to take account of history. Recourse to the historical specificity of meanings enables us to state the difference between eighteenth- and twentieth-century attitudes to genre and gender difference. It also has the corresponding effect of removing the temptation to endlessly deconstruct oppositions beyond the defining, albeit metaphysical, framework of meanings within which we make sense of the world – past and present. Could it be, then, that by temporarily limiting deconstruction's inherent lack of finality and fleetingly halting its capacity for limitless textual free play, so that, paradoxically, this limitlessness is curtailed and held to historical account, deconstruction is rendered more politically 'responsible' and more politically 'useful'?

This is a double-edged question. On the one hand it is this limitlessness, the indefinite sliding of signification that deconstruction identifies, which offers the most potentially revolutionary analysis of textual events; yet on the other, it also offers the most potentially reactionary ones. To acknowledge, for example, the open-ended possibility of metaphoric displacement in the *Vindication* usefully undoes the text's binary opposition of philosophy/literature, as well as challenging the surety of the gendered assumptions that inform it; but it also (potentially) collapses these terms and thereby effaces their historically specific meanings and political effects.

This is unsatisfactory, at least for me, because the distinction the *Vindication* makes between philosophical and literary genres is not only a textual but also a sexual one, which had precise political effects, delimiting what women were able to do, say and write. This is evidenced in part by the shift in popularity away from philosophical texts that occurred during the 1790s.

Marilyn Butler has observed that 'during the years 1797–8 the word "philosopher" becomes a term of abuse in popular fiction, drama and journalism, connoting atheist, seducer, plotter and revolutionary'.[28] In the context of Romanticism both philosophy and philosophers were denounced on the grounds that they were unnatural. The female philosopher was especially vulnerable to this charge. Lying behind the force of satiric attacks on female philosophers was the accusation that they unnaturally confused distinctions of sex. Mary Robinson's novel *The False Friend* offers one example of the combination of derision and fear which the idea of a female philosopher occasioned in men. In this novel a man accuses a woman of shortly becoming 'a he–she philosopher'.[29] Other examples include Mrs Opie's *Adeline Mowbray*, whose heroine of that ilk is, like Wollstonecraft, dubbed a hyena because of her refusal to adhere to the conventions of her sex.[30] Perhaps the best-known caricature of militant feminist philosophy in fiction is the figure cut by the significantly named Harriot Freake in Maria Edgeworth's popular novel *Belinda* (1801).[31]

The reaction against philosophy in general and philosophising women in particular did not take place in a vacuum. Rather, it emerged as one of the effects of the conservative backlash in British politics during the 1790s, which was in part a response to the increasing violence of the French Revolution. Wollstonecraft was not the only English radical to replace an attempt at the abstract reasoning of philosophy with the specific interrogations of a fictional mode increasingly concerned with subjectivity. The shift from the *Vindication*'s optimistic detailing of things as they might be to *The Wrongs of Woman*'s more pessimistic portrayal of 'things as they are' also characterises the difference of William Godwin's *Enquiry Concerning Political Justice* (1793) from his fiction *Things As They Are: or, The Adventures of Caleb Williams* (1794).[32]

On another level this shift can be described in terms of the transition from Radicalism to Romanticism. Both of Wollstonecraft's texts are products of this transitional period in British literature; *The Wrongs of Woman* in particular displays the conflict between this period's opposing discourses of collective radicalism and individual Romanticism.

To recognise the historical shifts of the 1780s–1790s and to account for the generic shaping of Wollstonecraft's texts in the light of them is not to re-fix historical meanings, thus lending to them the authority that deconstruction usefully denies, nor is it to offer totalising solutions from the hindsight made possible by reading from the perspective of 'now'; instead, it is to read past texts in their difference from the present. It is, perhaps, consciously to look in our readings of past texts for the textual operation of what is possibly deconstruction's most radical recognition: namely, differance. To attend to difference – both historical and sexual – is to release differance. It is also the first step towards denaturalising sexual difference, thereby exposing its historical relativity and cultural constitution, and so giving us a firmer grasp on understanding our own process of gender formation.

11 Three Women's Texts and a Critique of Imperialism

Gayatri Chakravorty Spivak

It should not be possible to read nineteenth-century British literature without remembering that imperialism, understood as England's social mission, was a crucial part of the cultural representation of England to the English. The role of literature in the production of cultural representation should not be ignored. These two obvious 'facts' continue to be disregarded in the reading of nineteenth-century British literature. This itself attests to the continuing success of the imperialist project, displaced and dispersed into more modern forms.

If these 'facts' were remembered, not only in the study of British literature but in the study of the literatures of the European colonising cultures of the great age of imperialism, we would produce a narrative, in literary history, of the 'worlding' of what is now called 'the Third World.' To consider the Third World as distant cultures, exploited but with rich intact literary heritages waiting to be recovered, interpreted, and curricularised in English translation fosters the emergence of 'the Third World' as a signifier that allows us to forget that 'worlding,' even as it expands the empire of the literary discipline.[1]

It seems particularly unfortunate when the emergent perspective of feminist criticism reproduces the axioms of imperialism. A basically isolationist admiration for the literature of the female subject in Europe and Anglo-America establishes the high feminist norm. It is supported and operated by an information-retrieval approach to 'Third

World' literature which often employs a deliberately 'non-theoretical' methodology with self-conscious rectitude.

In this essay, I will attempt to examine the operation of the 'worlding' of what is today 'the Third World' by what has become a cult text of feminism: *Jane Eyre*.[2] I plot the novel's reach and grasp, and locate its structural motors. I read *Wide Sargasso Sea* as *Jane Eyre*'s reinscription and *Frankenstein* as an analysis – even a deconstruction – of a 'worlding' such as *Jane Eyre*'s.[3]

I need hardly mention that the object of my investigation is the printed book, not its 'author.' To make such a distinction is, of course, to ignore the lessons of deconstruction. A deconstructive critical approach would loosen the binding of the book, undo the opposition between verbal text and the bio-graphy of the named subject 'Charlotte Brontë,' and see the two as each other's 'scene of writing.' In such a reading, the life that writes itself as 'my life' is as much a production in psychosocial space (other names can be found) as the book that is written by the holder of that named life – a book that is then consigned to what *is* most often recognised as genuinely 'social': the world of publication and distribution.[4] To touch Brontë's 'life' in such a way, however, would be too risky here. We must rather strategically take shelter in an essentialism which, not wishing to lose the important advantages won by US mainstream feminism, will continue to honour the suspect binary oppositions – book and author, individual and history – and start with an assurance of the following sort: my readings here do not seek to undermine the excellence of the individual artist. If even minimally successful, the readings will incite a degree of rage against the imperialist narrativisation of history, that it should produce so abject a script for her. I provide these assurances to allow myself some room to situate feminist individualism in its historical determination rather than simply to canonise it as feminism as such.

Sympathetic US feminists have remarked that I do not do justice to Jane Eyre's subjectivity. A word of explanation is perhaps in order. The broad strokes of my presuppositions are that what is at stake, for feminist individualism in the age of imperialism, is precisely the making of human beings, the constitution and 'interpellation' of the subject not only as individual but as 'individualist.'[5] This stake is represented on two registers: childbearing and soul making. The first is domestic-society-through-sexual-reproduction cathected as 'companionate love'; the second is the imperialist project cathected as civil-society-through-social-mission. As the female individualist, not-quite/not-male, articulates herself in shifting relationship to what is at stake, the 'native female' as such (*within* discourse, *as* a signifier) is excluded from any share in this emerging norm.[6] If we read this account from an isolationist perspective in a 'metropolitan' context, we see nothing here but the psychobiography of the militant female subject. In a reading such as mine, in contrast, the effort is to wrench oneself away from the mesmerising focus of the 'subject-constitution' of the female individualist.

To develop further the notion that my stance need not be an accusing one, I will refer to a passage from Roberto Fernández Retamar's 'Caliban.'[7] José Enrique Rodó had argued in 1900 that the model for the Latin American intellectual in relationship to Europe could be Shakespeare's Ariel.[8] In 1971 Retamar, denying the possibility of an identifiable 'Latin American Culture,' recast the model as Caliban. Not surprisingly, this powerful exchange still excludes any specific consideration of the civilisations of the Maya, the Aztecs, the Incas, or the smaller nations of what is now called Latin America. Let us note carefully that, at this stage of my argument, this 'conversation' between Europe and Latin America (without a specific consideration of the political economy of the 'worlding' of the 'native') provides a sufficient thematic description of our attempt to confront the ethno-centric and reverse-ethnocentric benevolent double bind (that is, considering the 'native' as object for enthusiastic information-retrieval and thus denying its own 'worlding') that I sketched in my opening paragraphs.

In a moving passage in 'Caliban,' Retamar locates both Caliban and Ariel in the postcolonial intellectual:

> There is no real Ariel–Caliban polarity: both are slaves in the hands of Prospero, the foreign magician. But Caliban is the rude and unconquerable master of the island, while

Ariel, a creature of the air, although also a child of the isle, is the intellectual.

The deformed Caliban – enslaved, robbed of his island, and taught the language by Prospero – rebukes him thus: 'You taught me language, and my profit on't / Is, I know how to curse.' ['C,' pp. 28, 11]

As we attempt to unlearn our so-called privilege as Ariel and 'seek from [a certain] Caliban the honour of a place in his rebellious and glorious ranks,' we do not ask that our students and colleagues should emulate us but that they should attend to us ('C,' p. 72). If, however, we are driven by a nostalgia for lost origins, we too run the risk of effacing the 'native' and stepping forth as 'the real Caliban,' of forgetting that he is a name in a play, an inaccessible blankness circumscribed by an interpretable text.[9] The stagings of Caliban work alongside the narrativisation of history: claiming to *be* Caliban legitimises the very individualism that we must persistently attempt to undermine from within.

Elizabeth Fox-Genovese, in an article on history and women's history, shows us how to define the historical moment of feminism in the West in terms of female access to individualism.[10] The battle for female individualism plays itself out within the larger theatre of the establishment of meritocratic individualism, indexed in the aesthetic field by the ideology of 'the creative imagination.' Fox-Genovese's presupposition will guide us into the beautifully orchestrated opening of *Jane Eyre*.

It is a scene of the marginalisation and privatisation of the protagonist: 'There was no possiblity of taking a walk that day. . . . Out-door exercise was now out of the question. I was glad of it,' Brontë writes (*JE*, p. 9). The movement continues as Jane breaks the rules of the appropriate top-ography of withdrawal. The family at the centre withdraws into the sanctioned architectural space of the withdrawing room or drawing room; Jane inserts herself – 'I slipped in' – into the margin – 'A small breakfast room *adjoined* the drawing room' (*JE*, p. 9; my emphasis).

The manipulation of the domestic inscription of space

within the upwardly mobilising currents of the eighteenth-
and nineteenth-century bourgeoisie in England and France is
well known. It seems fitting that the place to which Jane
withdraws is not only not the withdrawing room but also not
the dining room, the sanctioned place of family meals. Nor is
it the library, the appropriate place for reading. The breakfast
room 'contained a book-case' (*JE*, p. 9). As Rudolph Ackermann, wrote in his *Repository* (1823), one of the many manuals
of taste in circulation in nineteenth-century England, these
low bookcases and stands were designed to 'contain all the
books that may be desired for a sitting-room without reference
to the library.'[11] Even in this already triply off-centre place,
'having drawn the red moreen curtain nearly close, I [Jane]
was shrined in double retirement' (*JE*, pp. 9–10).

Here in Jane's self-marginalised uniqueness, the reader
becomes her accomplice: the reader and Jane are united –
both are reading. Yet Jane still preserves her odd privilege,
for she continues never quite doing the proper thing in its
proper place. She cares little for reading what is *meant* to be
read: the 'letter-press.' *She* reads the pictures. The power of
this singular hermeneutics is precisely that it can make the
outside inside. 'At intervals, while turning over the leaves of
my book, I studied the aspect of that winter afternoon.' Under
'the clear panes of glass,' the rain no longer penetrates, 'the
drear November day' is rather a one-dimensional 'aspect' to
be 'studied,' not decoded like the 'letter-press' but, like
pictures, deciphered by the unique creative imagination of the
marginal individualist (*JE*, p. 10).

Before following the track of this unique imagination, let us
consider the suggestion that the progress of *Jane Eyre* can be
charted through a sequential arrangement of the family/
counter-family dyad. In the novel, we encounter, first, the
Reeds as the legal family and Jane, the late Mr Reed's sister's
daughter, as the representative of a near incestuous counter-
family; second, the Brocklehursts, who run the school Jane is
sent to, as the legal family and Jane, Miss Temple, and Helen
Burns as a counter-family that falls short because it is only a
community of women; third, Rochester and the mad Mrs
Rochester as the legal family and Jane and Rochester as the
illicit counter-family. Other items may be added to the

thematic chain in this sequence: Rochester and Céline Varens as structurally functional counter-family; Rochester and Blanche Ingram as dissimulation of legality – and so on. It is during this sequence that Jane is moved from the counter-family to the family-in-law. In the next sequence, it is Jane who restores full family status to the as-yet-incomplete community of siblings, the Riverses. The final sequence of the book is a *community of families*, with Jane, Rochester, and their children at the centre.

In terms of the narrative energy of the novel, how is Jane moved from the place of the counter-family to the family-in-law? It is the active ideology of imperialism that provides the discursive field.

Let us consider the figure of Bertha Mason, a figure produced by the axiomatics of imperialism. Through Bertha Mason, the white Jamaican Creole, Brontë renders the human/animal frontier as acceptably indeterminate, so that a good greater than the letter of the Law can be broached. Here is the celebrated passage, given in the voice of Jane:

> In the deep shade, at the further end of the room, a figure ran backwards and forwards. What it was, whether beast or human being, one could not . . . tell: it grovelled, seemingly, on all fours; it snatched and growled like some strange wild animal: but it was covered with clothing, and a quantity of dark, grizzled hair, wild as a mane, hid its head and face. [*JE*, p. 295]

In a matching passage, given in the voice of Rochester speaking *to* Jane, Brontë presents the imperative for a shift beyond the Law as divine injunction rather than human motive. In the terms of my essay, we might say that this is the register not of mere marriage or sexual reproduction but of Europe and its not-yet-human other, of soul making. The field of imperial conquest is here inscribed as Hell:

> 'One night I had been awakened by her yells . . . it was a fiery West Indian night. . . .
> ' "This life," said I at last, "is hell! – this is the air – those are the sounds of the bottomless pit! *I have a right* to

deliver myself from it if I can. . . . Let me break away, and go home to God!" . . .

'A wind fresh from Europe blew over the ocean and rushed through the open casement: the storm broke, streamed, thundered, blazed, and the air grew pure. . . . It was true Wisdom that consoled me in that hour, and showed me the right path. . . .

'The sweet wind from Europe was still whispering in the refreshed leaves, and the Atlantic was thundering in glorious liberty. . . .

' "Go," said Hope, "and live again in Europe. . . . You have done all that God and Humanity require of you." '
[*JE*, pp. 310–11; my emphasis]

It is the unquestioned ideology of imperialist axiomatics, then, that conditions Jane's move from the counter-family set to the set of the family-in-law. Marxist critics such as Terry Eagleton have seen this only in terms of the ambiguous *class* position of the governess.[12] Sandra Gilbert and Susan Gubar, on the other hand, have seen Bertha Mason only in psychological terms, as Jane's dark double.[13]

I will not enter the critical debates that offer themselves here. Instead, I will develop the suggestion that nineteenth-century feminist individualism could conceive of a 'greater' project than access to the closed circle of the nuclear family. This is the project of soul making beyond 'mere' sexual reproduction. Here the native 'subject' is not almost an animal but rather the object of what might be termed the terrorism of the categorical imperative.

I am using 'Kant' in this essay as a metonym for the most flexible ethical moment in the European eighteenth century. Kant words the categorical imperative, conceived as the universal moral law given by pure reason, in this way: 'In all creation every thing one chooses and over which one has any power, may be used *merely as means*; man alone, and with him every rational creature, is an *end in himself.*' It is thus a moving displacement of Christian ethics from religion to philosophy. As Kant writes: 'With this agrees very well the possibility of such a command as: *Love God above everything, and thy neighbour as thyself.* For as a command it requires respect for a law which *commands love* and does not leave it to our own arbitrary choice to make this our principle.'[14]

The 'categorical' in Kant cannot be adequately represented in determinately grounded action. The dangerous transformative power of philosophy, however, is that its formal subtlety can be travestied in the service of the state. Such a travesty in the case of the categorical imperative can justify the imperialist project by producing the following formula: *make the heathen into a human so that he can be treated as an end in himself.*[15] This project is presented as a sort of tangent in *Jane Eyre*, a tangent that escapes the closed circle of the *narrative* conclusion. The tangent narrative is the story of St John Rivers, who is granted the important task of concluding the *text*.

At the novel's end, the *allegorical* language of Christian psychobiography – rather than the textually constituted and seemingly *private* grammar of the creative imagination which we noted in the novel's opening – marks the inaccessibility of the imperialist project as such to the nascent 'feminist' scenario. The concluding passage of *Jane Eyre* places St John Rivers within the fold of *Pilgrim's Progress*. Eagleton pays no attention to this but accepts the novel's ideological lexicon, which establishes St John Rivers' heroism by identifying a life in Calcutta with an unquestioning choice of death. Gilbert and Gubar, by calling *Jane Eyre* 'Plain Jane's progress,' see the novel as simply replacing the male protagonist with the female. They do not notice the distance between sexual reproduction and soul making, both actualised by the unquestioned idiom of imperialist presuppositions evident in the last part of *Jane Eyre*:

> Firm, faithful, and devoted, full of energy, and zeal, and truth, [St. John Rivers] labours for his race. . . . His is the sternness of the warrior Greatheart, who guards his pilgrim convoy from the onslaught of Apollyon. . . . His is the ambition of the high master-spirit[s] . . . who stand without fault before the throne of God; who share the last mighty victories of the Lamb; who are called, and chosen, and faithful. [*JE*, p. 455]

Earlier in the novel, St John Rivers himself justifies the project:

'My vocation? My great work? . . . My hopes of being numbered in the band who have merged all ambitions in the glorious one of bettering their race – of carrying knowledge into the realms of ignorance – of substituting peace for war – freedom for bondage – religion for superstition – the hope of heaven for the fear of hell?' (*JE*, p. 376). Imperialism and its territorial and subject-constituting project are a violent deconstruction of these oppositions.

When Jean Rhys, born on the Caribbean island of Dominica, read *Jane Eyre* as a child, she was moved by Bertha Mason: 'I thought I'd try to write her a life.'[16] *Wide Sargasso Sea*, the slim novel published in 1965, at the end of Rhys's long career, is that 'life.'

I have suggested that Bertha's function in *Jane Eyre* is to render indeterminate the boundary between human and animal and thereby to weaken her entitlement under the spirit if not the letter of the Law. When Rhys rewrites the scene in *Jane Eyre* where Jane hears 'a snarling, snatching sound, almost like a dog quarrelling' and then encounters a bleeding Richard Mason (*JE*, p. 210), she keeps Bertha's humanity, indeed her sanity as critic of imperialism, intact. Grace Poole, another character originally in *Jane Eyre*, describes the incident to Bertha in *Wide Sargasso Sea*: 'So you don't remember that you attacked this gentleman with a knife? . . . I didn't hear all he said except "I cannot interfere legally between yourself and your husband." It was when he said "legally" that you flew at him' (*WSS*, p. 150). In Rhys's retelling, it is the dissimulation that Bertha discerns in the word 'legally' – not an innate bestiality – that prompts her violent *re*action.

In the figure of Antoinette, whom in *Wide Sargasso Sea* Rochester violently renames Bertha, Rhys suggests that so intimate a thing as personal and human identity might be determined by the politics of imperialism. Antoinette, as a white Creole child growing up at the time of emancipation in Jamaica, is caught between the English imperialist and the black native. In recounting Antoinette's development, Rhys reinscribes some thematics of Narcissus.

There are, noticeably, many images of mirroring in the text. I will quote one from the first section. In this passage, Tia is the little black servant girl who is Antoinette's close companion: 'We had eaten the same food, slept side by side, bathed in the same river. As I ran, I thought, I will live with Tia and I will be like her. . . . When I was close I saw the jagged stone in her hand but I did not see her throw it. . . . We stared at each other, blood on my face, tears on hers. It was as if I saw myself. Like in a looking glass' (*WSS*, p. 38).

A progressive sequence of dreams reinforces this mirror imagery. In its second occurrence, the dream is partially set in a *hortus conclusus*, or 'enclosed garden' – Rhys uses the phrase (*WSS*, p. 50) – a Romance rewriting of the Narcissus topos as the place of encounter with Love.[17] In the enclosed garden, Antoinette encounters not Love but a strange threatening voice that says merely 'in here,' inviting her into a prison which masquerades as the legalisation of love (*WSS*, p. 50).

In Ovid's *Metamorphoses*, Narcissus' madness is disclosed when he recognises his other as his self: 'Iste ego sum.'[18] Rhys makes Antoinette see her *self* as her other, Brontë's Bertha. In the last section of *Wide Sargasso Sea*, Antoinette acts out *Jane Eyre*'s conclusion and recognises herself as the so-called ghost in Thornfield Hall: 'I went into the hall again with the tall candle in my hand. It was then that I saw her – the ghost. The woman with streaming hair. She was surrounded by a gilt frame but I knew her' (*WSS*, p. 154). The gilt frame encloses a mirror: as Narcissus' pool reflects the selfed other, so this 'pool' reflects the othered self. Here the dream sequence ends, with an invocation of none other than Tia, the other that could not be selfed, because the fracture of imperialism rather than the Ovidian pool intervened. (I will return to this difficult point.) 'That was the third time I had my dream, and it ended. . . . I called "Tia" and jumped and woke' (*WSS*, p. 155). It is now, at the very end of the book, that Antoinette/Bertha can say: 'Now at last I know why I was brought here and what I have to do' (*WSS*, pp. 155–6). We can read this as her having been brought into the England of Brontë's novel: 'This cardboard house' – a book between cardboard covers – 'where I walk at night is not England' (*WSS*, p. 148). In this fictive England, she must play out her role, act out the transformation of her 'self' into that fictive other, set fire to the house and kill herself, so that Jane Eyre can become the feminist individualist heroine of British fiction. I must read this as an allegory of the general epistemic violence of imperialism, the construction of a self-immolating colonial subject for the glorification of the social mission of the coloniser. At least Rhys sees to it that the woman from the colonies is not sacrificed as an insane animal for her sister's consolation.

Nevertheless, *Wide Sargasso Sea* marks with uncanny clarity the limits of its own discourse in Christophine, Antoinette's black nurse. We may perhaps surmise the distance between *Jane Eyre* and *Wide Sargasso Sea* by remarking that Christophine's unfinished story is the tangent to the latter narrative, as St John Rivers' story is to the former. Christophine is not a native of Jamaica; she is from Martinique. Taxonomically, she belongs to the category of the good servant rather than that of the pure native. But within these borders, Rhys creates a powerfully suggestive figure.

Christophine is the first interpreter and named speaking subject in the text. 'The Jamaican ladies had never approved of my mother, "because she pretty like pretty self" Christophine said,' we read in the book's opening paragraph (*WSS*, p. 15). I have taught this book five times, once in France, once to students who had worked on the book with the well-known Caribbean novelist Wilson Harris, and once at a prestigious institute where the majority of the students were faculty from other universities. It is part of the political argument I am making that all these students blithely stepped over this paragraph without asking or knowing what Christophine's patois, so-called incorrect English, might mean.

Christophine is, of course, a commodified person. ' "She was your father's wedding present to me" ' explains Antoinette's mother, ' "one of his presents" ' (*WSS*, p. 18). Yet Rhys assigns her some crucial functions in the text. It is Christophine who judges that black ritual practices are culture-specific and cannot be used by whites as cheap remedies for social evils, such as Rochester's lack of love for Antoinette. Most important, it is Christophine alone whom Rhys allows to offer a hard analysis of Rochester's actions, to challenge him in a face-to-face encounter. The entire extended passage is worthy of comment. I quote a brief extract:

'She is Creole girl, and she have the sun in her. Tell the truth now. She don't come to your house in this place England they tell me about, she don't come to your beautiful house to beg you to marry with her. No, it's you come all the long way to her house – it's you beg her to marry. And she love you and she give you all she have. Now you say you don't love her and you break her up. What you do with her money, eh?' [And then Rochester, the white man, comments silently to himself] Her voice was still quiet but with a hiss in it when she said 'money.' [*WSS*, p. 130]

Her analysis is powerful enough for the white man to be afraid: 'I no longer felt dazed, tired, half hypnotised, but alert and wary, ready to defend myself' (*WSS*, p. 130).

Rhys does not, however, romanticise individual heroics on the part of the oppressed. When the Man refers to the forces of Law and Order, Christophine recognises their power. This exposure of civil inequality is emphasised by the fact that, just before the Man's successful threat, Christophine had invoked the emancipation of slaves in Jamaica by proclaiming: 'No chain gang, no tread machine, no dark jail either. This is free country and I am free woman' (*WSS*, p. 131).

As I mentioned above, Christophine is tangential to this narrative. She cannot be contained by a novel which rewrites a canonical English text within the European novelistic tradition in the interest of the white Creole rather than the native. No perspective *critical* of imperialism can turn the other into a self, because the project of imperialism has always already historically refracted what might have been the absolutely other into a domesticated other that consolidates the imperialist self.[19] The Caliban of Retamar, caught between Europe and Latin America, reflects this predicament. We can read Rhys's reinscription of Narcissus as a thematisation of the same problematic.

Of course, we cannot know Jean Rhys's feelings in the matter. We can, however, look at the scene of Christophine's inscription in the text. Immediately after the exchange between her and the Man, well before the conclusion, she is simply driven out of the story, with neither narrative nor characterological explanation or justice. ' "Read and write I don't know.

Other things I know." She walked away without looking back'
(*WSS*, p. 133).

Indeed, if Rhys rewrites the madwoman's attack on the
Man by underlining of the use of 'legality,' she cannot deal
with the passage that corresponds to St John Rivers' own
justification of his martyrdom, for it has been displaced
into the current idiom of modernisation and development.
Attempts to construct the 'Third World Woman' as a signifier
remind us that the hegemonic definition of literature is itself
caught within the history of imperialism. A full literary
reinscription cannot easily flourish in the imperialist fracture
or discontinuity, covered over by an alien legal system
masquerading as Law as such, an alien ideology established
as only Truth, and a set of human sciences busy establishing
the 'native' as self-consolidating other.

In the Indian case at least, it would be difficult to find
an ideological clue to the planned epistemic violence of
imperialism merely by rearranging curricula or syllabi within
existing norms of literary pedagogy. For a later period of
imperialism – when the constituted colonial subject has firmly
taken hold – straightforward experiments of comparison can
be undertaken, say, between the functionally witless India of
Mrs Dalloway, on the one hand, and literary texts produced
in India in the 1920s, on the other. But the first half of the
nineteenth century resists questioning through literature or
literary criticism in the narrow sense, because both are
implicated in the project of producing Ariel. To reopen the
fracture without succumbing to a nostalgia for lost origins,
the literary critic must turn to the archives of imperial
governance.

In conclusion, I shall look briefly at Mary Shelley's *Frankenstein*, a text of nascent feminism that remains cryptic, I
think, simply because it does not speak the language of feminist
individualism which we have come to hail as the language of
high feminism within English literature. It is interesting that
Barbara Johnson's brief study tries to rescue this recalcitrant
text for the service of feminist autobiography.[20] Alternatively,
George Levine reads *Frankenstein* in the context of the creative
imagination and the nature of the hero. He sees the novel as
a book about its own writing and about writing itself, a

Romantic allegory of reading within which Jane Eyre as unself-conscious critic would fit quite nicely.[21]

I propose to take *Frankenstein* out of this arena and focus on it in terms of that sense of English cultural identity which I invoked at the opening of this essay. Within that focus we are obliged to admit that, although *Frankenstein* is ostensibly about the origin and evolution of man in society, it does not deploy the axiomatics of imperialism.

Let me say at once that there is plenty of incidental imperialist sentiment in *Frankenstein*. My point, within the argument of this essay, is that the discursive field of imperialism does not produce unquestioned ideological correlatives for the narrative structuring of the book. The discourse of imperialism surfaces in a curiously powerful way in Shelley's novel, and I will later discuss the moment at which it emerges.

Frankenstein is not a battleground of male and female individualism articulated in terms of sexual reproduction (family and female) and social subject-production (race and male). That binary opposition is undone in Victor Frankenstein's laboratory – an artificial womb where both projects are undertaken simultaneously, though the terms are never openly spelled out. Frankenstein's apparent antagonist is God himself as Maker of Man, but his real competitor is also woman as the maker of children. It is not just that his dream of the death of mother and bride and the actual death of his bride are associated with the visit of his monstrous homoerotic 'son' to his bed. On a much more overt level, the monster is a bodied 'corpse,' unnatural because bereft of a determinable childhood: 'No father had watched my infant days, no mother had blessed me with smiles and caresses; or if they had, all my past was now a blot, a blind vacancy in which I distinguished nothing' (*F*, pp. 57, 115). It is Frankenstein's own ambiguous and miscued understanding of the real motive for the monster's vengefulness that reveals his own competition with woman as maker:

I created a rational creature and was bound towards him to assure, as far as was in my power, his happiness and well-being. This was my duty, but there was another still paramount to that. My duties towards the beings of my own species had greater claims to my attention because they included a greater proportion of happiness or misery. Urged by this view, I refused, and I did right in refusing, to create a companion for the first creature. [*F*, p. 206)

It is impossible not to notice the accents of transgression inflecting Frankenstein's demolition of his experiment to create the future Eve. Even in the laboratory, the woman-in-the-making is not a bodied corpse but 'a human being.' The (il)logic of the metaphor bestows on her a prior existence which Frankenstein aborts, rather than an anterior death which he reembodies: 'The remains of the half-finished creature, whom I had destroyed, lay scattered on the floor, and I almost felt as if I had mangled the living flesh of a human being' (*F*, p. 163).

In Shelley's view, man's hubris as soul maker both usurps the place of God and attempts – vainly – to sublate woman's physiological prerogative.[22] Indeed, indulging a Freudian fantasy here, I could urge that, if to give and withhold to/from the mother a phallus is *the* male fetish, then to give and withhold to/from the man a womb might be the female fetish.[23] The icon of the sublimated womb in man is surely his productive brain, the box in the head.

In the judgment of classical psychoanalysis, the phallic mother exists only by virtue of the castration-anxious son; in *Frankenstein*'s judgment, the hysteric father (Victor Frankenstein gifted with his laboratory – the womb of theoretical reason) cannot produce a daughter. Here the language of racism – the dark side of imperialism understood as social mission – combines with the hysteria of masculism into the idiom of (the withdrawal of) sexual reproduction rather than subject-constitution. The roles of masculine and feminine individualists are hence reversed and displaced. Frankenstein cannot produce a 'daughter' because 'she might become ten thousand times more malignant than her mate ... [and because] one of the first results of those sympathies for which the demon thirsted would be children, and a race of devils would be propagated upon the earth who might make the very existence of the species of man a condition precarious and full of terror' (*F*, p. 158). This particular narrative strand also launches a thoroughgoing critique of the eighteenth-century European discourses on the origin of society through (Western Christian) man. Should I mention that, much like Jean-Jacques Rousseau's remark in his *Confessions*, Frankenstein declares himself to be 'by birth a Genevese' (*F*, p. 31)?

In this overtly didactic text, Shelley's point is that social engineering should not be based on pure, theoretical, or natural-scientific reason alone, which is her implicit critique of the utilitarian vision of an engineered society. To this end, she presents in the first part of her deliberately schematic story three characters, childhood friends, who seem to represent Kant's three-part conception of the human subject: Victor Frankenstein, the forces of theoretical reason or 'natural philosophy'; Henry Clerval, the forces of practical reason or 'the moral relations of things'; and Elizabeth Lavenza, that aesthetic judgment – 'the aerial creation of the poets' – which, according to Kant, is 'fit to be the mediating link between the realm of the natural and that of the concept of freedom . . . (which) promotes . . . *moral* feeling' [*F*, pp. 37, 36].[24]

This three-part subject does not operate harmoniously in *Frankenstein*. That Henry Clerval, associated as he is with practical reason, should have as his 'design . . . to visit India, in the belief that he had in his knowledge of its various languages, and in the views he had taken of its society, the means of materially assisting the progress of European colonisation and trade' is proof of this, as well as part of the incidental imperialist sentiment that I speak of above (*F*, pp. 151–2). I should perhaps point out that the language here is entrepreneurial rather than missionary:

> He came to the university with the design of making himself complete master of the Oriental languages, as thus he should open a field for the plan of life he had marked out for himself. Resolved to pursue no inglorious career, he turned his eyes towards the East as affording scope for his spirit of enterprise. The Persian, Arabic, and Sanskrit languages engaged his attention. [*F*, pp. 66–7]

But it is of course Victor Frankenstein, with his strange

itinerary of obsession with natural philosophy, who offers the strongest demonstration that the multiple perspectives of the three-part Kantian subject cannot co-operate harmoniously. Frankenstein creates a putative human subject out of natural philosophy alone. According to his own miscued summation: 'In a fit of enthusiastic madness I created a rational creature' (*F*, p. 206). It is not at all farfetched to say that Kant's categorical imperative can most easily be mistaken for the hypothetical imperative – a command to ground in cognitive comprehension what can be apprehended only by moral will – by putting natural philosophy in the place of practical reason.

I should hasten to add here that just as readings such as this one do not necessarily accuse Charlotte Brontë the named individual of harbouring imperialist sentiments, so also they do not necessarily commend Mary Shelley the named individual for writing a successful Kantian allegory. The most I can say is that it is possible to read these texts, within the frame of imperialism and the Kantian ethical moment, in a politically useful way. Such an approach presupposes that a 'disinterested' reading attempts to render transparent the interests of the hegemonic readership. (Other 'political' readings – for instance, that the monster is the nascent working class – can also be advanced.)

Frankenstein is built in the established epistolary tradition of multiple frames. At the heart of the multiple frames, the narrative of the monster (as reported by Frankenstein to Robert Walton, who then recounts it in a letter to his sister) is of his almost learning, clandestinely, to be human. It is invariably noticed that the monster reads *Paradise Lost* as true history. What is not so often noticed is that he also reads Plutarch's *Lives*, 'the histories of the first founders of the ancient republics,' which he compares to 'the patriarchal lives of my protectors' (*F*, pp. 123, 124). And his *education* comes through 'Volney's *Ruins of Empires*,' which purported to be a prefiguration of the French Revolution, published after the event and after the author had rounded off his theory with practice (*F*, p. 113). It is an attempt at an enlightened universal secular, rather than a Eurocentric Christian, history, written from the perspective of a narrator 'from below,' somewhat like the attempts of Eric Wolf or Peter Worsley in our own time.[25]

This Caliban's education in (universal secular) humanity takes place through the monster's eavesdropping on the instruction of an Ariel – Safie, the Christianised 'Arabian' to whom 'a residence in Turkey was abhorrent' (*F*, p. 121). In depicting Safie, Shelley uses some commonplaces of eighteenth-century liberalism that are shared by many today: Safie's Muslim father was a victim of (bad) Christian religious prejudice and yet was himself a wily and ungrateful man not as morally refined as her (good) Christian mother. Having tasted the emancipation of woman, Safie could not go home. The confusion between 'Turk' and 'Arab' has its counterpart in present-day confusion about Turkey and Iran as 'Middle Eastern' but not 'Arab.'

Although we are a far cry here from the unexamined and covert axiomatics of imperialism in *Jane Eyre*, we will gain nothing by celebrating the time-bound pieties that Shelley, as the daughter of two anti-evangelicals, produces. It is more interesting for us that Shelley differentiates the other, works at the Caliban/Ariel distinction, and *cannot* make the monster identical with the proper recipient of these lessons. Although he had 'heard of the discovery of the American hemisphere and *wept with Safie* over the helpless fate of its original inhabitants,' Safie cannot reciprocate his attachment. When she first catches sight of him, 'Safie, unable to attend to her friend [Agatha], rushed out of the cottage' (*F*, pp. 114 [my emphasis], 129).

In the taxonomy of characters, the Muslim-Christian Safie belongs with Rhys's Antoinette/Bertha. And indeed, like Christophine the good servant, the subject created by the fiat of natural philosophy is the tangential unresolved moment in *Frankenstein*. The simple suggestion that the monster is human inside but monstrous outside and only provoked into vengefulness is clearly not enough to bear the burden of so great a historical dilemma.

At one moment, in fact, Shelley's Frankenstein does try to tame the monster, to humanise him by bringing him within the circuit of the Law. He 'repair[s] to a criminal judge in the town and . . . relate[s his] history briefly but with firmness' – the first and disinterested version of the narrative of Frankenstein – 'marking the dates with accuracy and never deviating into invective or exclamation. . . . When I had concluded my narration I said, "This is the being whom I accuse and for whose seizure and punishment I call upon you to exert your whole power. It is your duty as a magistrate"' (*F*, pp. 189, 190). The sheer social reasonableness of the mundane voice of Shelley's 'Genevan magistrate' reminds us that the absolutely other cannot be selfed, that the monster has 'properties' which will not be contained by 'proper' measures:

> 'I will exert myself [he says], and if it is in my power to seize the monster, be assured that he shall suffer punishment proportionate to his crimes. But I fear, from what you have yourself described to be his properties, that this will prove impracticable; and thus, while every proper measure is pursued, you should make up your mind to disappointment.'
> [*F*, p. 190]

In the end, as is obvious to most readers, distinctions of human individuality themselves seem to fall away from the novel. Monster, Frankenstein, and Walton seem to become each others' relays. Frankenstein's story comes to an end in death; Walton concludes his own story within the frame of his function as letter writer. In the *narrative* conclusion, he is the natural philosopher who learns from Frankenstein's example. At the end of the *text*, the monster, having confessed his guilt toward his maker and ostensibly intending to immolate himself, is borne away on an ice raft. We do not see the conflagration of his funeral pile – the self-immolation is not consummated in the text: he too cannot be contained by the text. In terms of narrative logic, he is 'lost in darkness and distance' (*F*, p. 211) – these are the last words of the novel – into an existential temporality that is coherent with neither the territorialising individual imagination (as in the opening of *Jane Eyre*) nor the authoritative scenario of Christian psychobiography (as at the end of Brontë's work). The very relationship between sexual reproduction and social subject-production – the dynamic nineteenth-century topos of feminism-in-imperialism – remains problematic within the limits of Shelley's text and, paradoxically, constitutes its strength.

Earlier, I offered a reading of woman as womb holder in *Frankenstein*. I would now suggest that there is a framing woman in the book who is neither tangential, nor encircled, nor yet encircling. 'Mrs Saville,' 'excellent Margaret,' 'beloved Sister' are her address and kinship inscriptions (*F*, pp. 15, 17, 22). She is the occasion, though not the protagonist, of the novel. She is the feminine *subject* rather than the female individualist: she is the irreducible *recipient*-function of the letters that constitute *Frankenstein*. I have commented on the singular appropriative hermeneutics of the reader reading with Jane in the opening pages of *Jane Eyre*. Here the reader must read with Margaret Saville in the crucial sense that she must *intercept* the recipient-function, read the letters *as* recipient, in order for the novel to exist.[26] Margaret Saville does not respond to close the text as frame. The frame is thus simultaneously not a frame, and the monster can step 'beyond the text' and be 'lost in darkness.' Within the allegory of our reading, the place of both the English lady and the unnamable monster are left open by this great flawed text. It is satisfying for a postcolonial reader to consider this a noble resolution for a nineteenth-century English novel. This is all the more striking because, on the anecdotal level, Shelley herself abundantly 'identifies' with Victor Frankenstein.[27]

I must myself close with an idea that I cannot establish within the limits of this essay. Earlier I contended that *Wide Sargasso Sea* is necessarily bound by the reach of the European novel. I suggested that, in contradistinction, to reopen the epistemic fracture of imperialism without succumbing to nostalgia for lost origins, the critic must turn to the archives of imperialist governance. I have not turned to those archives in these pages. In my current work, by way of a modest and inexpert 'reading' of 'archives,' I try to extend, outside of the reach of the European novelistic tradition, the most powerful suggestion in *Wide Sargasso Sea*: that *Jane Eyre* can be read as the orchestration and staging of the self-immolation of Bertha Mason as 'good wife.' The power of that suggestion remains unclear if we remain insufficiently knowledgeable about the history of the legal manipulation of widow-sacrifice in the entitlement of the British government in India. I would hope that an informed critique of imperialism, granted some attention from readers in the First World, will at least expand the frontiers of the politics of reading.

12 Women's Time
Julia Kristeva

Two Generations

In its beginnings, the women's movement, as the struggle of suffragists and of existential feminists, aspired to gain a place in linear time as the time of project and history. In this sense, the movement, while immediately universalist, is also deeply rooted in the sociopolitical life of nations. The political demands of women; the struggles for equal pay for equal work, for taking power in social institutions on an equal footing with men; the rejection, when necessary, of the attributes traditionally considered feminine or maternal insofar as they are deemed incompatible with insertion in that history – all are part of the *logic of identification* with certain values: not with the ideological (these are combated, and rightly so, as reactionary) but, rather, with the logical and ontological values of a rationality dominant in the nation-state. Here it is unnecessary to enumerate the benefits which this logic of identification and the ensuing struggle have achieved and continue to achieve for women (abortion, contraception, equal pay, professional recognition, etc.): these have already had or will soon have effects even more important than those of the Industrial Revolution. Universalist in its approach, this current in feminism *globalises* the problems of women of different milieux, ages, civilisations, or simply of varying psychic structures, under the label 'Universal Woman.' A consideration of *generations* of women can only be conceived of in this global way as a succession, as a progression in the accomplishment of the initial programme mapped out by its founders.

In a second phase, linked, on the one hand, to the younger

women who came to feminism after May 1968 and, on the other, to women who had an aesthetic or psychoanalytic experience, linear temporality has been almost totally refused, and as a consequence there has arisen an exacerbated distrust of the entire political dimension. If it is true that this more recent current of feminism refers to its predecessors and that the struggle for sociocultural recognition of women is necessarily its main concern, this current seems to think of itself as belonging to another generation – qualitatively different from the first one – in its conception of its own identity and, consequently, of temporality as such. Essentially interested in the specificity of female psychology and its symbolic realisations, these women seek to give a language to the intra-subjective and corporeal experiences left mute by culture in the past. Either as artists or writers, they have undertaken a veritable exploration of the *dynamic of signs*, an exploration which relates this tendency, at least at the level of its aspirations, to all major projects of aesthetic and religious upheaval. Ascribing this experience to a new generation does not only mean that other, more subtle problems have been added to the demands for sociopolitical identification made in the beginning. It also means that, by demanding recognition of an irreducible identity, without equal in the opposite sex and, as such, exploded, plural, fluid, in a certain way nonidentical, this feminism situates itself outside the linear time of identities which communicate through projection and revindication. Such a feminism rejoins, on the one hand, the archaic (mythical) memory and, on the other, the cyclical or monumental temporality of marginal movements. It is certainly not by chance that the European and trans-European problematic has been posited as such at the same time as this new phase of feminism.

Finally, it is the mixture of the two attitudes – *insertion* into history and the radical *refusal* of the subjective limitations imposed by this history's time on an experiment carried out in the name of the irreducible difference – that seems to have broken loose over the past few years in European feminist movements, particularly in France and in Italy.

If we accept this meaning of the expression 'a new generation of women,' two kinds of questions might then be posed. What sociopolitical processes or events have provoked this mutation? What are its problems: its contributions as well as dangers?

Socialism and Freudianism

One could hypothesise that if this new generation of women shows itself to be more diffuse and perhaps less conscious in the United States and more massive in Western Europe, this is because of a veritable split in social relations and mentalities, a split produced by socialism and Freudianism. I mean by *socialism* that egalitarian doctrine which is increasingly broadly disseminated and accepted as based on common sense, as well as that social practice adopted by governments and political parties in democratic regimes which are forced to extend the zone of egalitarianism to include the distribution of goods as well as access to culture. By *Freudianism* I mean that lever, inside this egalitarian and socialising field, which once again poses the question of sexual difference and of the difference among subjects who themselves are not reducible one to the other.

Western socialism, shaken in its very beginnings by the egalitarian or differential demands of its women (e.g., Flora Tristan), quickly got rid of those women who aspired to recognition of a specificity of the female role in society and culture, only retaining from them, in the egalitarian and universalistic spirit of Enlightenment Humanism, the idea of a necessary identification between the two sexes as the only and unique means for liberating the 'second sex.' I shall not develop here the fact that this 'ideal' is far from being applied in practice by these socialist-inspired movements and parties and that it was in part from the revolt against this situation that the new generation of women in Western Europe was born after May 1968. Let us just say that in theory, and as put into practice in Eastern Europe, socialist ideology, based on a conception of the human being as determined by its place in *production* and the *relations of production*, did not take into consideration this same human being according to its place in *reproduction*, on the one hand, or in the *symbolic order*, on the other. Consequently, the specific character of women could

only appear as nonessential or even nonexistent to the totalising and even totalitarian spirit of this ideology.[1] We begin
to see that this same egalitarian and in fact censuring treatment
has been imposed, from Enlightenment Humanism through
socialism, on religious specificities and, in particular, on Jews.[2]

What has been achieved by this attitude remains nonetheless
of capital importance for women, and I shall take as an
example the change in the destiny of women in the socialist
countries of Eastern Europe. It could be said, with only
slight exaggeration, that the demands of the suffragists and
existential feminists have, to a great extent, been met in these
countries, since three of the main egalitarian demands of early
feminism have been or are now being implemented despite
vagaries and blunders: economic, political, and professional
equality. The fourth, sexual equality, which implies permiss-
iveness in sexual relations (including homosexual relations),
abortion, and contraception, remains stricken by taboo in
Marxian ethics as well as for reasons of state. It is, then, this
fourth equality which is the problem and which therefore
appears *essential* in the struggle of a new generation. But
simultaneously and as a consquence of these socialist
accomplishments – which are in fact a total deception – the
struggle is no longer concerned with the quest for equality
but, rather, with difference and specificity. It is precisely at
this point that the new generation encounters what might be
called the *symbolic* question. Sexual difference – which is at
once biological, physiological, and relative to reproduction –
is translated by and translates a difference in the relationship
of subjects to the symbolic contract which *is* the social contract:
a difference, then, in the relationship to power, language, and
meaning. The sharpest and most subtle point of feminist
subversion brought about by the new generation will henceforth be situated on the terrain of the inseparable conjunction
of the sexual and the symbolic, in order to try to discover,
first, the specificity of the female, and then, in the end, that
of each individual woman.

A certain saturation of socialist ideology, a certain exhaustion of its potential as a programme for a new social contract
(it is obvious that the effective realisation of this programme
is far from being accomplished, and I am here treating only

its system of thought) makes way for . . . Freudianism. I am, of course, aware that this term and this practice are somewhat shocking to the American intellectual consciousness (which rightly reacts to a muddled and normatising form of psychoanalysis) and, above all, to the feminist consciousness. To restrict my remarks to the latter: Is it not true that Freud has been seen only as a denigrator or even an exploiter of women? as an irritating phallocrat in a Vienna which was at once Puritan and decadent – a man who fantasised women as sub-men, castrated men?

Castrated and/or Subject to Language

Before going beyond Freud to propose a more just or more modern vision of women, let us try, first, to understand his notion of castration. It is, first of all, a question of an *anguish* or *fear* of castration, or of correlative penis *envy*; a question, therefore, of *imaginary* formations readily perceivable in the *discourse* of neurotics of both sexes, men and women. But, above all, a careful reading of Freud, going beyond his biologism and his mechanism, both characteristic of his time, brings out two things. First, as presupposition for the 'primal scene,' the castration fantasy and its correlative (penis envy) are hypotheses, a priori suppositions intrinsic to the theory itself, in the sense that these are not the ideological fantasies of their inventor but, rather, logical necessities to be placed at the 'origin' in order to explain what unceasingly functions in neurotic discourse. In other words, neurotic discourse, in man and woman, can only be understood in terms of its own logic when its fundamental causes are admitted as the fantasies of the primal scene and castration, even if (as may be the case) nothing renders them present in reality itself. Stated in still other terms, the reality of castration is no more real than the hypothesis of an explosion which, according to modern astrophysics, is at the origin of the universe: Nothing proves it, in a sense it is an article of faith, the only difference being that numerous phenomena of life in this 'big-bang' universe are explicable only through this initial hypothesis. But one is infinitely more jolted when this kind of intellectual method concerns inanimate matter than when it is applied to our own subjectivity and thus, perhaps, to the fundamental mechanism of our epistemophilic thought.

Moreover, certain texts written by Freud (*The Interpretation of Dreams*, but especially those of the second topic, in particular the *Metapsychology*) and their recent extensions (notably by Lacan), imply that castration is, in sum, the imaginary construction of a radical operation which constitutes the symbolic field and all beings inscribed therein. This operation constitutes signs and syntax: that is, language, as a *separation* from a presumed state of nature, of pleasure fused with nature so that the introduction of an articulated network of differences, which refers to objects henceforth and only in this way separated from a subject, may constitute *meaning*. This logical operation of separation (confirmed by all psycholinguistic and child psychology) which preconditions the binding of language which is already syntactical, is therefore the common destiny of the two sexes, men and women. That certain biofamilial conditions and relationships cause women (and notably hysterics) to deny this separation and the language which ensues from it, whereas men (notably obsessionals) magnify both and, terrified, attempt to master them – this is what Freud's discovery has to tell us on this issue.

The analytic situation indeed shows that it is the penis which, becoming the major referent in this operation of separation, gives full meaning to the *lack* or to the *desire* which constitutes the subject during his or her insertion into the order of language. I should only like to indicate here that, in order for this operation constitutive of the symbolic and the social to appear in its full truth and for it to be understood by both sexes, it would be just to emphasise its extension to all that is privation of fulfilment and of totality; exclusion of a pleasing, natural, and sound state: in short, the break indispensable to the advent of the symbolic.

It can now be seen how women, starting with this theoretical apparatus, might try to understand their sexual and symbolic difference in the framework of social, cultural, and professional realisation, in order to try, by seeing their position therein, either to fulfil their own experience to a maximum or – but always starting from this point – to go further and call into question the very apparatus itself.

Living the Sacrifice

In any case, and for women in Europe today, whether or not they are conscious of the various mutations (socialist and Freudian) which have produced or simply accompanied their coming into their own, the urgent question on our agenda might be formulated as follows: *What can be our place in the symbolic contract?* If the social contract, far from being that of equal men, is based on an essentially sacrificial relationship of separation and articulation of differences which in this way produces communicable meaning, what is our place in this order of sacrifice and/or of language? No longer wishing to be excluded or no longer content with the function which has always been demanded of us (to maintain, arrange, and perpetuate this sociosymbolic contract as mothers, wives, nurses, doctors, teachers . . .), how can we reveal our place, first as it is bequeathed to us by tradition, and then as we want to transform it?

It is difficult to evaluate what in the relationship of women to the symbolic as it reveals itself now arises from a sociohistorical conjuncture (patriarchal ideology, whether Christian, humanist, socialist or so forth), and what arises from a structure. We can speak only about a structure observed in a sociohistorical context, which is that of Christian, Western civilisation and its lay ramifications. In this sense of psychosymbolic structure, women, 'we' (is it necessary to recall the warnings we issued at the beginning of this article concerning the totalising use of this plural?)[3] seem to feel that they are the casualties, that they have been left out of the sociosymbolic contract, of language as the fundamental social bond. They find no affect there, no more than they find the fluid and infinitesimal significations of their relationships with the nature of their own bodies, that of the child, another woman, or a man. This frustration, which to a certain extent belongs to men also, is being voiced today principally by women, to the point of becoming the essence of the new feminist ideology.

A therefore difficult, if not impossible, identification with the sacrificial logic of separation and syntactical sequence at the foundation of language and the social code leads to the rejection of the symbolic – lived as the rejection of the paternal function and ultimately generating psychoses.

But this limit, rarely reached as such, produces two types of counterinvestment of what we have termed the sociosymbolic contract. On the one hand, there are attempts to take hold of this contract, to possess it in order to enjoy it as such or to subvert it. How? The answer remains difficult to formulate (since, precisely, any formulation is deemed frustrating, mutilating, sacrificial) or else is in fact formulated using stereotypes taken from extremist and often deadly ideologies. On the other hand, another attitude is more lucid from the beginning, more self-analytical which – without refusing or sidestepping this sociosymbolic order – consists in trying to explore the constitution and functioning of this contract, starting less from the knowledge accumulated about it (anthropology, psychoanalysis, linguistics) than from the very personal effect experienced when facing it as subject and as a woman. This leads to the active research,[4] still rare, undoubtedly hesitant but always dissident, being carried out by women in the human sciences; particularly those attempts, in the wake of contemporary art, to break the code, to shatter language, to find a specific discourse closer to the body and emotions, to the unnameable repressed by the social contract. I am not speaking here of a 'woman's language,' whose (at least syntactical) existence is highly problematical and whose apparent lexical specificity is perhaps more the product of a social marginality than of a sexual-symbolic difference.[5]

Nor am I speaking of the aesthetic quality of productions by women, most of which – with a few exceptions (but has this not always been the case with both sexes?) – are a reiteration of a more or less euphoric or depressed romanticism and always an explosion of an ego lacking narcissistic gratification.[6] What I should like to retain, nonetheless, as a mark of collective aspiration, as an undoubtedly vague and unimplemented intention, but one which is intense and which has been deeply revealing these past few years, is this: The new generation of women is showing that its major social concern has become the sociosymbolic contract as a sacrificial contract. If anthropologists and psychologists, for at least a century, have not stopped insisting on this in their attention to 'savage thought,' wars, the discourse of dreams, or writers, women are today affirming – and we consequently face a mass phenomenon – that they are forced to experience this sacrificial contract against their will.[7] Based on this, they are attempting a revolt which they see as a resurrection but which society as a whole understands as murder. This attempt can lead us to a not less and sometimes more deadly violence. Or to a cultural innovation. Probably to both at once. But that is precisely where the stakes are, and they are of epochal significance.

The Terror of Power or the Power of Terrorism

First in socialist countries (such as the USSR and China) and increasingly in Western democracies, under pressure from feminist movements, women are being promoted to leadership positions in government, industry, and culture. Inequalities, devalorisations, under-estimations, even persecution of women at this level continue to hold sway in vain. The struggle against them is a struggle against archaisms. The cause has nonetheless been understood, the principle has been accepted. What remains is to break down the resistance to change. In this sense, this struggle, while still one of the main concerns of the new generation, is not, strictly speaking, *its* problem. In relationship to *power*, its problem might rather be summarised as follows: What happens when women come into power and identify with it? What happens when, on the contrary, they refuse power and create a parallel society, a counterpower which then takes on aspects ranging from a club of ideas to a group of terrorist commandos.

The assumption by women of executive, industrial, and cultural power has not, up to the present time, radically changed the nature of this power. This can be clearly seen in the East, where women promoted to decision-making positions suddenly obtain the economic as well as the narcissistic advantages refused them for thousands of years and become the pillars of the existing governments, guardians of the status quo, the most zealous protectors of the established order.[8] This identification by women with the very power structures previously considered as frustrating, oppressive, or inaccessible has often been used in modern times by totalitarian regimes: the German National-Socialists and the Chilean junta are examples of this.[9] The fact that this is a paranoid type of counterinvestment in an initially denied symbolic order can perhaps explain this troubling phenomenon; but an explanation does not prevent its massive propagation around the globe, perhaps in less dramatic forms than the totalitarian ones mentioned above, but all moving toward levelling, stabilisation, conformism, at the cost of crushing exceptions, experiments, chance occurrences.

Some will regret that the rise of a libertarian movement such as feminism ends, in some of its aspects, in the consolidation of conformism; others will rejoice and profit from this fact. Electoral campaigns, the very life of political parties, continue to bet on this latter tendency. Experience proves that too quickly even the protest or innovative initiatives on the part of women inhaled by power systems (when they do not submit to them right off) are soon credited to the system's account; and that the long-awaited democratisation of institutions as a result of the entry of women most often comes down to fabricating a few 'chiefs' among them. The difficulty presented by this logic of integrating the second sex into a value system experienced as foreign and therefore counterinvested is how to avoid the centralisation of power, how to detach women from it, and how then to proceed, through their critical, differential, and autonomous interventions, to render decision-making institutions more flexible.

Then there are the more radical feminist currents which, refusing homologation to any role of identification with existing power no matter what the power may be, make of the second sex a *countersociety*. A 'female society' is then constituted as a sort of alter ego of the official society, in which all real or fantasised possibilities for *jouissance* take refuge. Against the sociosymbolic contract, both sacrificial and frustrating, this countersociety is imagined as harmonious, without prohibitions, free and fulfilling. In our modern societies which have no hereafter or, at least, which are caught up in a transcendency either reduced to this side of the world (Protestantism) or crumbling (Catholicism and its current challenges), the countersociety remains the only refuge for fulfilment since it is precisely an a-topia, a place outside the law, utopia's floodgate.

As with any society, the countersociety is based on the expulsion of an excluded element, a scapegoat charged with the evil of which the community duly constituted can then purge itself; a purge which will finally exonerate that community of any future criticism. Modern protest movements have often reiterated this logic, locating the guilty one – in order to fend off criticism – in the foreign, in capital alone, in the other religion, in the other sex. Does not feminism become a kind of inverted sexism when this logic is followed to its conclusion? The various forms of marginalism – according to sex, age, religion, or ideology – represent in the modern world this refuge for *jouissance*, a sort of laicised transcendence. But with women, and insofar as the number of those feeling concerned by this problem has increased, although in less spectacular forms than a few years ago, the problem of the countersociety is becoming massive: It occupies no more and no less than 'half of the sky'.

It has, therefore, become clear, because of the particular radicalisation of the second generation, that these protest movements, including feminism, are not 'initially libertarian' movements which only later, through internal deviations or external chance manipulations, fall back into the old ruts of the initially combated archetypes. Rather, the very logic of counterpower and of countersociety necessarily generates, by its very structure, its essence as a simulacrum of the combated society or of power. In this sense and from a viewpoint undoubtedly too Hegelian, modern feminism has only been but a moment in the interminable process of coming to consciousness about the implacable violence (separation, castration, etc.) which constitutes any symbolic contract.

Thus the identification with power in order to consolidate it or the constitution of a fetishist counterpower – restorer of the crises of the self and provider of a *jouissance* which is always already a transgression – seem to be the two social forms which the face-off between the new generation of women and the social contract can take. That one also finds the problem of terrorism there is structurally related.

The large number of women in terrorist groups (Palestinian commandos, the Baader-Meinhoff Gang, Red Brigades, etc.) has already been pointed out, either violently or prudently according to the source of information. The exploitation of women is still too great and the traditional prejudices against them too violent for one to be able to envisage this phenomenon with sufficient distance. It can, however, be said from now on that this is the inevitable product of what we have called a denial of the sociosymbolic contract and its counterinvestment as the only means of self-defence in the struggle to safeguard an identity. This paranoid-type mechanism is at the base of any political involvement. It may produce different civilising attitudes in the sense that these attitudes allow a more or less flexible reabsorption of violence and death. But when a subject is too brutally excluded from this sociosymbolic stratum; when, for example, a woman feels her effective life as a woman or her condition as a social being too brutally ignored by existing discourse or power (from her family to social institutions); she may, by counterinvesting the violence she has endured, make of herself a 'possessed' agent of this violence in order to combat what was experienced as frustration – with arms which may seem disproportional, but which are not so in comparison with the subjective or more precisely narcissistic suffering from which they originate. Necessarily opposed to the bourgeois democratic regimes in power, this terrorist violence offers as a programme of liberation an order which is even more oppressive, more sacrificial than those it combats. Strangely enough, it is not against totalitarian regimes that these terrorist groups with women participants unleash themselves but, rather, against liberal systems, whose essence is, of course, exploitative, but whose expanding democratic legality guarantees relative tolerance. Each time, the mobilisation takes place in the name of a nation, of an oppressed group, of a human essence imagined as good and sound; in the name, then, of a kind of fantasy of archaic fulfilment which an arbitrary, abstract, and thus even bad and ultimately discriminatory order has come to disrupt.

While that order is accused of being oppressive, is it not actually being reproached with being too weak, with not measuring up to this pure and good, but henceforth lost, substance? Anthropology has shown that the social order is sacrificial, but sacrifice orders violence, binds it, tames it. Refusal of the social order exposes one to the risk that the so-called good substance, once it is unchained, will explode, without curbs, without law or right, to become an absolute arbitrariness.

Following the crisis of monotheism, the revolutions of the past two centuries, and more recently fascism and Stalinism, have tragically set in action this logic of the oppressed goodwill which leads to massacres. Are women more apt than other social categories, notably the exploited classes, to invest in this implacable machine of terrorism? No categorical response, either positive or negative, can currently be given to this question. It must be pointed out, however, that since the dawn of feminism, and certainly before, the political activity of exceptional women, and thus in a certain sense of liberated women, has taken the form of murder, conspiracy, and crime. Finally, there is also the connivance of the young girl with her mother, her greater difficulty than the boy in detaching herself from the mother in order to accede to the order of signs as invested by the absence and separation constitutive of the paternal function. A girl will never be able to reestablish this contact with her mother – a contact which the boy may possibly rediscover through his relationship with the opposite sex – except by becoming a mother herself, through a child, or through a homosexuality which is in itself extremely difficult and judged as suspect by society; and, what is more, why and in the name of what dubious symbolic benefit would she want to make this detachment so as to conform to a symbolic system which remains foreign to her? In sum, all of these considerations – her eternal debt to the woman-mother – make a woman more vulnerable within the symbolic order, more fragile when she suffers within it, more virulent when she protects herself from it. If the archetype of the belief in a good and pure substance, that of utopias, is the belief in the omnipotence of an archaic, full, total, englobing mother with no frustration, no separation, with no break-producing symbolism (with no castration, in other words), then it becomes evident that we will never be able to defuse the violences mobilised through the counterinvestment necessary to carrying out this phantasm, unless one challenges precisely this myth of the archaic mother. It is in this way that we can understand the warnings against the recent invasion of the women's movements by paranoia, as in Lacan's scandalous sentence 'There is no such thing as Woman.'[10] Indeed, she does *not* exist with a capital 'W,' possessor of some mythical unity – a supreme power, on which is based the terror of power and terrorism as the desire for power. But what an unbelievable force for subversion in the modern world! And, at the same time, what playing with fire!

Creatures and Creatresses

The desire to be a mother, considered alienating and even reactionary by the preceding generation of feminists, has obviously not become a standard for the present generation. But we have seen in the past few years an increasing number of women who not only consider their maternity compatible with their professional life or their feminist involvement (certain improvements in the quality of life are also at the origin of this: an increase in the number of day-care centres and nursery schools, more active participation of men in child care and domestic life, etc.) but also find it indispensable to their discovery, not of the plenitude, but of the complexity of the female experience, with all that this complexity comprises in joy and pain. This tendency has its extreme: in the refusal of the paternal function by lesbian and single mothers can be seen one of the most violent forms taken by the rejection of the symbolic outlined above, as well as one of the most fervent divinisations of maternal power – all of which cannot help but trouble an entire legal and moral order without, however, proposing an alternative to it. Let us remember here that Hegel distinguished between female right (familial and religious) and male law (civil and political). If our societies know well the uses and abuses of male law, it must also be recognised that female right is designated, for the moment by a blank. And if these practices of maternity, among others, were to be generalised, women themselves would be responsible for elaborating the appropriate legislation to check the violence to which, otherwise, both their children and men would be subject. But are they capable of doing so? This is one of the important questions that the new generation of women encounters, especially when the members of this new generation refuse to ask those questions, seized by the same rage with which the dominant order originally victimised them.

Faced with this situation, it seems obvious – and feminist groups become more aware of this when they attempt to broaden their audience – that the refusal of maternity cannot be a mass policy and that the majority of women today see the possibility for fulfilment, if not entirely at least to a large degree, in bringing a child into the world. What does this desire for motherhood correspond to? This is one of the new questions for the new generation, a question the preceding generation had foreclosed. For want of an answer to this question, feminist ideology leaves the door open to the return of religion, whose discourse, tried and proved over thousands of years, provides the necessary ingredients for satisfying the anguish, the suffering, and the hopes of mothers. If Freud's affirmation – that the desire for a child is the desire for a penis and, in this sense, a substitute for phallic and symbolic dominion – can be only partially accepted, what modern women have to say about this experience should nonetheless be listened to attentively. Pregnancy seems to be experienced as the radical ordeal of the splitting of the subject: redoubling up of the body, separation and coexistence of the self and of an other, of nature and consciousness, of physiology and speech. This fundamental challenge to identity is then accompanied by a fantasy of totality – narcissistic completeness – a sort of instituted, socialised, natural psychosis. The arrival of the child, on the other hand, leads the mother into the labyrinths of an experience that, without the child, she would only rarely encounter: love for an other. Not for herself, nor for an identical being, and still less for another person with whom 'I' fuse (love or sexual passion). But the slow, difficult, and delightful apprenticeship in attentiveness, gentleness, forgetting oneself. The ability to succeed in this path without masochism and without annihilating one's affective, intellectual, and professional personality – such would seem to be the stakes to be won through guiltless maternity. It then becomes a creation in the strong sense of the term. For this moment, utopian?

On the other hand, it is in the aspiration toward artistic and, in particular, literary creation that woman's desire for affirmation now manifests itself. Why literature?

Is it because, faced with social norms, literature reveals a certain knowledge and sometimes the truth itself about an otherwise repressed, nocturnal, secret, and unconscious universe? Because it thus redoubles the social contract by exposing the unsaid, the uncanny? And because it makes a game, a space of fantasy and pleasure, out of the abstract and frustrating order of social signs, the words of everyday communication? Flaubert said, 'Madame Bovary, c'est moi.' Today many women imagine, 'Flaubert, c'est moi.' This identification with the potency of the imaginary is not only an identification, an imaginary potency (a fetish, a belief in the maternal penis maintained at all costs), as a far too normative view of the social and symbolic relationship would have it. This identification also bears witness to women's desire to lift the weight of what is sacrificial in the social contract from their shoulders, to nourish our societies with a more flexible and free discourse, one able to name what has thus far never been an object of circulation in the community: the enigmas of the body, the dreams, secret joys, shames, hatreds of the second sex.

It is understandable from this that women's writing has lately attracted the maximum attention of both 'specialists' and the media.[11] The pitfalls encountered along the way, however, are not to be minimised: For example, does one not read there a relentless belittling of male writers whose books, nevertheless, often serve as 'models' for countless productions by women? Thanks to the feminist label, does one not sell numerous works whose naive whining or market-place romanticism would otherwise have been rejected as anachronistic? And does one not find the pen of many a female writer being devoted to phantasmic attacks against Language and Sign as the ultimate supports of phallocratic power, in the name of a semi-aphonic corporality whose truth can only be found in that which is 'gestural' or 'tonal'?

And yet, no matter how dubious the results of these recent productions by women, the symptom is there – women are writing, and the air is heavy with expectation: What will they write that is new?

In the Name of the Father, the Son . . . and the Woman?

These few elements of the manifestations by the new generation of women in Europe seem to me to demonstrate that, beyond the sociopolitical level where it is generally inscribed (or inscribes itself), the women's movement – in its present stage, less aggressive but more artful – is situated within the very framework of the religious crisis of our civilisation.

I call 'religion' this phantasmic necessity on the part of speaking beings to provide themselves with a *representation* (animal, female, male, parental, etc.) in place of what constitutes them as such, in other words, symbolisation – the double articulation and syntactic sequence of language, as well as its preconditions or substitutes (thoughts, affects, etc.). The elements of the current practice of feminism that we have just brought to light seem precisely to constitute such a representation which makes up for the frustrations imposed on women by the anterior code (Christianity or its lay humanist variant). The fact that this new ideology has affinities, often revindicated by its creators, with so-called matriarchal beliefs (in other words, those beliefs characterising matrilinear societies) should not overshadow its radical novelty. This ideology seems to me to be part of the broader antisacrificial current which is animating our culture and which, in its protest against the constraints of the sociosymbolic contract, is no less exposed to the risks of violence and terrorism. At this level of radicalism, it is the very principle of sociality which is challenged.

Certain contemporary thinkers consider, as is well known, that modernity is characterised as the first epoch in human history in which human beings attempt to live without religion.

In its present form, is not feminism in the process of becoming one?

Or is it, on the contrary and as avant-garde feminists hope, that having started with the idea of difference, feminism will be able to break free of its belief in Woman. Her power. Her writing, so as to channel this demand for difference into each and every element of the female whole, and, finally, to bring out the singularity of each woman, and beyond this, her multiplicities, her plural languages, beyond the horizon, beyond sight, beyond faith itself?

A factor for ultimate mobilisation? Or a factor for analysis?

Imaginary support in a technocratic era where all narcissism is frustrated? Or instruments fitted to these times in which the cosmos, atoms, and cells – our true contemporaries – call for the constitution of a fluid and free subjectivity?

The question has been posed. Is to pose it already to answer it?

Another Generation Is Another Space

If the preceding can be *said* – the question whether all this is *true* belongs to a different register – it is undoubtedly because it is now possible to gain some distance on these two preceding generations of women. This implies, of course, that a *third* generation is now forming, at least in Europe. I am not speaking of a new group of young women (though its importance should not be underestimated) or of another 'mass feminist movement' taking the torch passed on from the second generation. My usage of the word 'generation' implies less a chronology than a *signifying space*, a both corporeal and desiring mental space. So it can be argued that as of now a third attitude is possible, thus a third generation, which does not exclude – quite to the contrary – the *parallel* existence of all three in the same historical time, or even that they be interwoven one with the other.

In this third attitude, which I strongly advocate – which I imagine? – the very dichotomy man/woman as an opposition between two rival entities may be understood as belonging to *metaphysics*. What can 'identity,' even 'sexual identity,' mean in a new theoretical and scientific space where the very notion of identity is challenged? I am not simply suggesting a very hypothetical bisexuality which, even if it existed, would only, in fact, be the aspiration toward the totality of one of the sexes and thus an effacing of difference. What I mean is, first of all, the demassification of the problematic of *difference*, which would imply, in a first phase, an apparent de-dramatisation of the 'fight to the death' between rival groups and thus between the sexes. And this not in the name of some reconciliation – feminism has at least had the merit of showing what is irreducible and even deadly in the social contract – but in order that the struggle, the implacable difference, the violence be conceived in the very place where it operates with the maximum intransigence, in other words, in personal and sexual identity itself, so as to make it disintegrate in its very nucleus.

It necessarily follows that this involves risks not only for what we understand today as 'personal equilibrium' but also for social equilibrium itself, made up as it now is of the counterbalancing of aggressive and murderous forces massed in social, national, religious, and political groups. But is it not the insupportable situation of tension and explosive risk that the existing 'equilibrium' presupposes which leads some of those who suffer from it to divest it of its economy, to detach themselves from it, and to seek another means of regulating difference?

To restrict myself here to a personal level, as related to the question of women, I see arising, under the cover of a relative indifference toward the militance of the first and second generations, an attitude of retreat from sexism (male as well as female) and, gradually, from any kind of anthropo-morphism. The fact that this might quickly become another form of spiritualism turning its back on social problems, or else a form of repression ready to support all status quos, should not hide the radicalness of the process. This process could be summarised as an *interiorisation of the founding separation of the sociosymbolic contract*, as an introduction of its cutting edge into the very interior of every identity whether subjective, sexual, ideological, or so forth. This in such a way that the habitual and increasingly explicit attempt to fabricate a scapegoat victim as foundress of a society or a countersociety may be replaced by the analysis of the potentialities of *victim/executioner* which characterise each identity, each subject, each sex.

What discourse, if not that of a religion, would be able to support this adventure which surfaces as a real possibility, after both the achievements and the impasses of the present ideological reworkings, in which feminism has participated? It seems to me that the role of what is usually called 'aesthetic practices' must increase not only to counterbalance the storage and uniformity of information by present-day mass media, data-bank systems, and, in particular, modern communications technology, but also to demystify the identity of the symbolic bond itself, to demystify, therefore, the *community* of language as a universal and unifying tool, one which totalises and equalises. In order to bring out – along with the *singularity* of each person and, even more, along with the multiplicity of every person's possible identifications (with atoms, e.g., stretching from the family to the stars) – the *relativity of his/her symbolic as well as biological existence*, according to the variation in his/her specific symbolic capacities. And in order to emphasise the *responsibility* which all will immediately face of putting this fluidity into play against the threats of death which are unavoidable whenever an inside and an outside, a self and an other, one group and another, are constituted. At this level of interiorisation with its social as well as individual stakes, what I have called 'aesthetic practices' are undoubtedly nothing other than the modern reply to the eternal question of morality. At least, this is how we might understand an ethics which, conscious of the fact that its order is sacrificial, reserves part of the burden for each of its adherents, therefore declaring them guilty while immediately affording them the possibility for *jouissance*, for various productions, for a life made up of both challenges and differences.

Spinoza's question can be taken up again here: Are women subject to ethics? If not to that ethics defined by classical philosophy – in relationship to which the ups and downs of feminist generations seem dangerously precarious – are women not already participating in the rapid dismantling that our age is experiencing at various levels (from wars to drugs to artificial insemination) and which poses the *demand* for a new ethics? The answer to Spinoza's question can be affirmative only at the cost of considering feminism as but a *moment* in the thought of that anthropomorphic identity which currently blocks the horizon of the discursive and scientific adventure of our species.

Summaries and Notes

1 Catherine Belsey and Jane Moore, Introduction: The Story So Far

1. She was long believed to have been the editor, but see Margaret Maison, 'Mary Wollstonecraft and Mr Cresswick', *Notes and Queries*, n.s. 34 (1987), pp. 467–8.

2. Kate Millett, *Sexual Politics* (London, 1971), p. xii.

3. Eva Figes, *Patriarchal Attitudes: Women in Society* (London, 1986), p. 15.

4. Dale Spender, *Man Made Language* (London, 1980), p. 101.

5. Jacqueline Rose, *Sexuality in the Field of Vision* (London, 1986), p. 91.

6. Elaine Showalter, 'Toward a Feminist Poetics', in *Women Writing and Writing About Women* (ed.) Mary Jacobus (London, 1979), pp. 22–41; reprinted in Elaine Showalter (ed.) *The New Feminist Criticism* (New York, 1985 and London, 1986), pp. 125–43.

7. Ellen Moers, *Literary Women* (London, 1977). See especially pp. 119, 170–2, 126.

8. Moers, *Literary Women*, p. 44.

9. Rosalind Coward, *Female Desire: Women's Sexuality Today* (London, 1984), p. 13.

10. Coward, *Female Desire*, p. 13.

11. Rachel Bowlby, *Just Looking: Consumer Culture in Dreiser, Gissing and Zola* (New York and London, 1985), p. 34.

12. Stephen Heath, *The Sexual Fix* (London, 1982), p. 3. See also Heath's essay, 'Difference', *Screen*, 19 (1978), 3, pp. 51–112. This essay gives an account of the difficult, mainly French, theories invoked in *The Sexual Fix*.

13. Heath, *The Sexual Fix*, p. 3.

14. Alice Jardine and Paul Smith (eds), *Men In Feminism* (New York and London, 1987).

15. Hélène Cixous, 'The Laugh of the Medusa', in Elaine Marks and Isabelle de Courtivron (eds), *New French Feminisms: An Anthology* (Brighton, 1981), p. 250.

16. Luce Irigaray, 'This Sex which is Not One', in Marks and de Courtivron (eds), *New French Feminisms*, p. 103.

17. Mary Jacobus, *Reading Woman: Essays in Feminist Criticism* (London, 1986), p. 5.

18. Jacobus, *Reading Woman*, p. 109.

19. Bonnie Zimmerman, 'What Has Never Been: An Overview of Lesbian Feminist Criticism', in Gayle Greene and Coppélia Kahn (eds), *Making a*

Difference: Feminist Literary Criticism (London, 1985), 177–210, p. 183; also in Showalter (ed.), *The New Feminist Criticism*, 200–24, p. 204.

20. Barbara Smith, 'Toward a Black Feminist Criticism', in Showalter (ed.), *The New Feminist Criticism*, 168–85, p. 175.

21. Deborah E. McDowell, 'New Directions for Black Feminist Criticism', in Showalter (ed.), *The New Feminist Criticism*, 186–99, p. 192.

22. Susan Willis, 'Black Women Writers: Taking a Critical Perspective', in Greene and Kahn (eds), *Making a Difference*, 211–37, p. 220.

23. See, for example, Spivak's translations of and commentaries on stories by Mahasweta Devi. Devi is a Bengali woman writer; examples of her work can be found in Gayatri Chakravorty Spivak, *In Other Worlds: Essays in Cultural Politics* (New York and London, 1987), pp. 179–96, 222–68.

24. Spivak, *In Other Worlds*, p. 150.

25. Alice Jardine, *Gynesis: Configurations of Woman and Modernity* (Ithaca, N.Y., 1985), p. 25.

26. Ibid., p. 36.

27. Ibid., p. 25.

28. Julia Kristeva, 'Women's Time', p. 215 above.

29. Jardine, *Gynesis*, p. 258.

2   Dale Spender, 'Women and Literary History' (From *Mothers of the Novel* (London, 1986), pp. 115–18 and 138–44.)

Summary

'Women and Literary History' raises questions concerning the disappearance of so much writing by women from the literary canon and literary history. How and why has woman's writing been excluded? Does it matter? The extract (from a book on eighteenth-century women writers) suggests that the suppression of women's writing entails the corresponding suppression not only of women's achievements but of women's meanings and values.

Notes

1. I have since checked the current course offerings of the English Department of Sydney University; in 1985, of twenty-five courses only *one* is devoted to a woman writer, and *only three include women writers*! What is more, the course entitled 'The Place of Women' gives pride of place to men, with three out of the four texts used being by male authors. I am indebted to Debra Adelaide for her assistance in gaining these figures and I deplore the fact that in twenty-five years and with the pressure of the contemporary women's movement, no progress has been made to give women recognition in this reputable university establishment.

2. Ian Watt, *The Rise of the Novel: Studies in Defoe, Richardson and Fielding* (London, 1957), p. 296.

3. Ibid., p. 290.

4. Ibid., p. 298.

5. Germaine Greer, 'Flying Pigs and Double Standards', *Times Literary Supplement*, 26 July 1974, p. 784.

6. Matilda Joslyn Gage, *Woman, Church and State: the Original Exposé of Male Collaboration Against the Female Sex* (Chicago, 1873; reprinted Watertown, Mass., 1980).

7. Hilary Simpson, 'A Literary Trespasser: D. H. Lawrence's Use of Women's Writing', *Women's Studies International Quarterly*, 2 (1979), pp. 155–79.

8. Nancy Milford, *Zelda Fitzgerald* (London, 1975).

9. Marion Glastonbury, 'Holding the Pens', in Sarah Elbert and Marion Glastonbury, *Inspiration and Drudgery: Notes on Literature and Domestic Labour in the Nineteenth Century* (London, 1978), pp. 27–47.

10. Dora Russell, *The Religion of the Machine Age* (London, 1984); Elizabeth Robins, *Ancilla's Share: an Indictment of Sex Antagonism* (London, 1924); Kate Millett, *Sexual Politics* (London, 1971); Adrienne Rich, *On Lies, Secrets and Silence* (London, 1980).

3   Rosalind Coward, 'The True Story of How I Became My Own Person' (From *Female Desire* (London: 1984), pp. 175–86.)

Summary

Focusing on women's novels, the essay traces a shift from the centrality of marriage in the narrative structure of nineteenth-century fiction, towards the prominence of sexual confession in novels of the late 1960s and early 1970s – a period marked by the increasing influence of feminism and the so-called sexual revolution. In this context questions are raised concerning the relation of women's novels about sexuality to feminism. Are they automatically feminist novels? Do they contribute to a more progressive understanding of female sexuality? The essay suggests that fictional inscriptions of female sexuality construct historically-specific subject positions for women which correspond to the structures of power in society at large.

Notes

1. Samuel Richardson, *Pamela*, 1740–1; *Clarissa Harlowe*, 1746–7.

2. See Ian Watt, *The Rise of the Novel: Studies in Defoe, Richardson and Fielding* (London, 1957).

3. Maxine Hong Kingston, *The Woman Warrior* (London, 1981).

4. See, for example, 'Walter', *My Secret Life*, in Phyllis and Eberhard Kronhausen (eds), *Walter the English Casanova* (London, 1967).

4   Mary Jacobus, 'The Difference of View' (From Mary Jacobus (ed.), *Women Writing and Writing About Women* (London: 1979), pp. 10–21.)

Summary

'The Difference of View' poses the question of women's writing. How can we write and retain our difference, without reproducing the patriarchal differentiation which has either confined women to incoherence or silenced them altogether? On the one hand, in an effort to resist patriarchal meanings, French feminist writing has proposed inscribing the feminine as non-sense, but with the effect of denying to women the coherence of accepted definitions. On the other hand there is the problem that the production of (patriarchal) sense necessarily reproduces patriarchy itself. As a way out of this impasse the essay proposes an alternative way of reading women's texts. This involves the identification of moments in writing when structures are shaken, and when literary boundaries are transgressed as a result of the marginal being brought into focus. The effect is the disruption of familiar stabilities: the insistence of what is normally excluded throws into relief both the otherness of the transgressive material and the precariousness of the structures which usually hold it at bay.

Notes

1. Virginia Woolf, *Collected Essays*, vol. 1 (London, 1966), p. 204; my italics.

2. Ibid., vol. 1, p. 204.

3. See Elaine Marks, 'Women and Literature in France', *Signs: Journal of Women in Culture and Society*, 3 (1978), pp. 833–42, for a discussion of the work of recent French feminist literary and psychoanalytic theorists, especially Hélène Cixous, *La Jeune née*, Paris, 1975 (*The Newly Born Woman*, trans. Betsy Wing, Minneapolis and Manchester, 1986), and 'Le Rire de la Méduse' ('The Laugh of the Medusa', trans. Keith and Paula Cohen, *Signs*, 1 (1976), pp. 875–93); Luce Irigaray, *Speculum de l'autre femme*, Paris, 1974 (*Speculum of the Other Woman*, trans. Gillian C. Gill (Ithaca, N.Y., 1985)?, and *Ce Sexe qui n'en est pas un*, Paris, 1977 (*This Sex Which is Not One*, trans. Catherine Porter with Carolyn Burke (Ithaca, N.Y., 1985)?; Julia Kristeva, *La Révolution du language poétique* (Paris, 1974), *Polylogue* (Paris, 1977) and, from *La Révolution du language poétique*, 'Phonétique, phonologie et bases pulsionelles', translated as 'Phonetics, Phonology and Impulsional Bases' by Caren Greenberg, *Diacritics*, 4 (Fall 1974), pp. 33–7. See also Michèle Montrelay, 'Inquiry into Femininity', trans. Parveen Adams, *m/f*, 1 (1978), pp. 83–101, from *L'Ombre et le nom: sur la féminité* (Paris, 1977). The work of Luce Irigaray and Julia Kristeva is reviewed and compared by Josette Ferral, 'Antigone or *The Irony of the Tribe*', *Diacritics*, 8 (Fall 1978), pp. 2–14. See also Stephen Heath, 'Difference', *Screen*, 19, 3 (1978), pp. 51–112, especially pp. 78–83 for a discussion of the theoretical implications raised by these writers.

4. See 'Study of Thomas Hardy', in E. D. Macdonald (ed.), *Phoenix: The Posthumous Papers of D. H. Lawrence* (London, 1967), p. 496.

5. Mary Wollstonecraft, *Mary, A Fiction and The Wrongs of Woman*, ed. Gary Kelly (London, 1976), pp. 83–4; my italics.

6. Virginia Woolf, *A Room of One's Own* (London, 1929), p. 104. (*Jane Eyre*, XII); my italics.

7. George Eliot, *Middlemarch* (4 vols., Edinburgh and London, 1871–2), vol. iv, pp. 369–70.

8. Woolf, *A Room of One's Own*, p. 7.

9. Ibid., p. 9.

10. Ibid., p. 146.

11. Ibid., p. 148.

5   Gillian Beer, 'Representing Women: Re-presenting the Past' (First given at the Oxford English Limited conference on 'Re-thinking Literary History', May 1987.)

Summary

The essay addresses the problem of how to read or, more precisely, reread the past from the unavoidable perspective of present cultural influences and knowledges, without denying the specificity and difference of the past on the one hand or, on the other, pretending to have escaped the preconceptions of the present, which shape our readings of the past. To adopt the first of these alternatives is to succumb to what the essay calls 'presentism'. This is the belief that 'now' offers the only authoritative source of meaning, and that history is to be read for its relevance to present-day concerns. The problem with this approach is that it naturalises and fixes culturally constituted contemporary meanings of femininity; it also militates against seeing the past or the present as sites where meaning can change. The second way of thinking goes to the other extreme by attempting to ignore the present altogether. Yet in each case the effect is the same: the collapse of historical difference.

In place of these strategies, the essay proposes an alternative way of interpreting or re-presenting the past. This involves recognising difference – historical and sexual. For to emphasise the difference of past writings and past concerns from present-day beliefs and meanings is better to understand the historical processes of gender formation and gender change. Correspondingly, it is also to expose the present as unstable, not fixed, not timeless, a site of shifts in the meanings of femininity and masculinity. In practice, this means analysing writing by men alongside women's writing, in order first to recognise sexual difference and then to denaturalise it – to expose masculinity and femininity as historically and culturally specific.

Notes

1. Hélène Cixous, 'The Laugh of the Medusa', in Elaine Marks and

Isabelle de Courtivron (eds), *New French Feminisms: An Anthology* (Brighton, 1981) pp. 245–64. Cixous retains the metaphoric contradiction: 'Even if phallic mystification has generally contaminated good relationships, a woman is never far from "mother" (I mean outside her role functions: the mother as non-name and as source of goods). There is always within her at least a little of that good mother's milk. She writes in white ink.' (cf. p. 112 above.) Note the combination of mothering and trading metaphors here, which I discuss in relation to *Moll Flanders*.

2. Nancy Chodorow, *The Reproduction of Mothering: Psychoanalysis and the Sociology of Gender* (Berkeley, 1978); Dorothy Dinnerstein, *The Rocking of the Cradle and the Ruling of the World* (London, 1978); Coppélia Kahn, 'The Hand that Rocks the Cradle: Recent Gender Theories and their Implications', in Shirley Nelson Garner et al. (eds), *The (M)other Tongue* (Ithaca and London, 1985), pp. 72–88.

3. The descriptions and prescriptions concerning hysteria and menopause are cases in point.

4. Robert Halsband, 'Women and Literature in Eighteenth-Century England', in Paul Fritz and Richard Morton (eds), *Woman in the Eighteenth Century and Other Essays* (Toronto, 1976), 55–71, p. 64.

5. Mary Hays, *Appeal to the Men of Great Britain in Behalf of Women* (London, 1798; reprinted New York and London, 1974), G. Luria (ed.), p. 50.

6. See Gillian Beer, *Darwin's Plots* (London, 1983); George Lakoff and Mark Johnson, *Metaphors We Live By* (Chicago, 1980).

7. Hélène Cixous, in Marks and de Courtivron (eds), *New French Feminisms*, p. 90. See also pp. 101–2 above.

8. The original sponsors of the paper were Lisa Jardine, Jill Mann, Gillian Beer, Stephen Heath, Tony Tanner.

9. Patrick Wright, *On Living in an Old Country: the National Past in Contemporary Britain* (London, 1985); Simon Barker, 'Images of the Sixteenth and Seventeenth Centuries as a History of the Present', in Francis Barker et al. (eds), *Literature, Politics and Theory: Papers from the Essex Conference 1976–84* (London and New York, 1986), pp. 173–89.

10. For discussion of this question see Gillian Beer, *George Eliot* (Key Women Writers) (Brighton, 1986), pp. 17–20, 42–3.

11. See Peter Stallybrass and Allon White, *The Politics and Poetics of Transgression* (London, 1986).

12. For further discussion see Carolyn Merchant, *The Death of Nature: Women, Ecology and the Scientific Revolution* (London, 1980); Ludmilla Jordanova (ed.), *Languages of Nature* (London, 1986); Evelyn Fox Keller, *Reflections on Gender and Science* (New Haven and London, 1985), especially 'Baconian Science: The Arts of Mastery and Obedience', pp. 33–42.

13. Virginia Woolf, *A Room of One's Own* (London, 1929), p. 125.

14. Virginia Woolf, *Three Guineas* (London, 1938), pp. 252, 253.

15. Catherine Macaulay, *Letters on Education* (Dublin, 1790), pp. 127, 130.

16. Katharine Rogers, 'The Feminism of Daniel Defoe', in Fritz and Morton (eds), *Woman in the Eighteenth Century and Other Essays*, pp. 3–24 passim.

17. Luce Irigaray, *Ce sexe qui n'en est pas un* (Paris, 1977). See 'Le Marché des femmes', pp. 167–85 and 'Des Marchandises entre elles', pp. 189–93.

18. Quoted by Luce Irigaray, 'Le Marché des femmes', pp. 170–1.

19. Spiro Peterson (ed.), *The Counterfeit Lady Unveiled and Other Criminal Fiction of Seventeenth-Century England* (Garden City, New York, 1961), pp. 15, 97.

20. Juliet Mitchell (ed.), Daniel Defoe, *The Fortunes and Misfortunes of the Famous Moll Flanders* (Harmondsworth, 1978), pp. 315, 317.

21. Defoe, *Moll Flanders*, p. 262.

22. Ibid., p. 28.

23. In French, mother-earth is *'la terre-mère'*. In 'Le Marché des femmes' Irigaray asserts that the mother cannot become part of a mercantile system of circulation without undermining the social order: *'Valeur naturelle et valeur d'usage, la mère ne peut circuler sous forme de marchandise sous peine d'abolir l'ordre social.'* p. 180.

24. G. M. Trevelyan, *The History of England* (London, 1926). Woolf discusses Trevelyan's representation of women in history in *A Room of One's Own*, London, 1929; see especially pp. 63–73. I am grateful to Hazel Mills and the members of our seminar on women's history for making me realise how closely Trevelyan is linked to *Orlando* as well as to *A Room of One's Own*.

25. Virginia Woolf, *Orlando* (London, 1928), pp. 123–6.

6   Sandra M. Gilbert and Susan Gubar, 'Sexual Linguistics: Gender, Language, Sexuality' (From *New Literary History*, 16 (1985), pp. 515–16, 523–4, 525–43.)

Summary

'Is anatomy linguistic destiny?' Is the language we speak man-made, and, if so, are women necessarily alienated from the words they write and speak? The essay begins by exploring the ways in which contemporary feminist theorists have treated these questions, and argues that their investigations so far have taken two forms: Anglo-American research, in an effort to make language work for, not against, women, seeks a place for women within the existing range of meanings. On the other hand, French feminists have speculated on the possibility of a feminine body-language, a writing of the body, which would break with the authority of patriarchal speech.

The extract reprinted here takes to task the notion, shared by both schools, that language is in essence patriarchal. Locating distinct male (misogynist) and female (feminist) literary traditions, the essay challenges the assumption that language is man-made, and proposes that male linguistic sexism arose out of a fear precisely of female linguistic primacy. Arguing that the mother occupies a primordial position in the symbolic contract, the essay suggests that women are not necessarily alienated from language, which, although corrupted by the father, originates from the voice of the mother. The very existence of a distinct female literary tradition, it is argued, suggests the possibility that women are able to command language, rather than be commanded by it.

Notes

1. See Julia Kristeva, 'Women's Time', p. 200 above.
2. William Faulkner, *Mosquitoes* (New York, 1927), p. 26. See also the crucially important chapter on the twentieth century in Katharine Rogers's *The Troublesome Helpmate: A History of Misogyny in Literature* (Seattle, 1966), pp. 226–64.
3. James Joyce, *Finnegans Wake* (New York, 1939), p. 628; see, for instance, James Joyce, *Selected Letters* (ed.) Richard Ellmann (New York, 1975), p. 186, in which the author-to-be of *Ulysses* admonishes his sweetheart to 'write the dirty words big and underline them and kiss them and hold them for a moment to your sweet hot cunt, darling, and also pull up your dress a moment and hold them in under your dear little farting bum.'
4. See James Joyce, *Ulysses* (New York, 1961), pp. 346–83. Hawthorne's comments on Fanny Fern are quoted in Caroline Ticknor, *Hawthorne and His Publishers* (Boston, 1913), p. 142. As Anthony Burgess observes, Gertie has read Marie Cummins's sentimental bestseller *The Lamplighter*, 1854, whose style is closely akin to that of her own stream of consciousness and whose heroine, significantly, is named *Gertie* (*Joyceprick: An Introduction to the Language of James Joyce* (New York, 1973), p. 103).
5. Henry James, *The Bostonians* (ed.) Alfred Habegger (Indianapolis, 1976), p. 318.
6. T. S. Eliot, 'Hysteria', in *The Collected Poems of T. S. Eliot, 1909–1961* (New York, 1970), p. 24; the original draft of 'The Love Song of J. Alfred Prufrock', entitled 'Prufrock Among the Women', is held in the Berg Collection of the New York City Public Library.
7. See Conrad Aiken, *Ushant* (New York and Boston, 1952), p. 233. See also Ezra Pound, 'Hugh Selwyn Mauberley' and 'Portrait d'une Femme', in *Selected Poems* (New York, 1957), pp. 64 and 16–17, in which civilisation is an 'old bitch gone in the teeth' and woman ('your mind and you are our Sargasso Sea') is herself botched.
8. See Richard Ellmann, *James Joyce* (New York, 1959), p. 510. For a more extended discussion of the sexual anxiety implicit in *The Waste Land*, see Sandra M. Gilbert, 'Costumes of the Mind: Transvestism as Metaphor in Modern Literature', *Critical Inquiry*, 7 (1980).
9. Ernest Hemingway, 'The Lady Poets With Foot Notes', in *88 Poems* (ed.) Nicholas Georgiannis (New York, 1979), p. 77. (To add real footnotes, we might note that behind the misogyny of this catalogue lurk Edna St Vincent Millay, Alice Kilmer, Sara Teasdale, Zoe Atkins, Lola Ridge, and Amy Lowell.) We are indebted to Cara Chell for bringing this poem to our attention.
10. Nathanael West, *Miss Lonelyhearts and The Day of the Locust* (New York, 1962), pp. 13–14.
11. Emily Dickinson, *The Complete Poems of Emily Dickinson* (ed.) Thomas

H. Johnson (Boston, 1960), no. 593. Subsequent Johnson numbers are cited in the text.

12. The phrase 'daughters of educated men' is continually used by Virginia Woolf in *Three Guineas* (New York, 1938). Walter Ong's *Fighting for Life* (Ithaca, N.Y., 1981), is crucial for an understanding of masculine competition and sexual anxiety in general and for a discussion of the mother tongue (as opposed to the *patrius sermo*) in particular (see esp. pp. 36–7). Also important for an analysis of the function of the classics in male education is Ong's *The Presence of the Word: Some Prolegomena for Cultural and Religious History* (New Haven, 1967), esp. pp. 249–50.

13. Virginia Woolf, 'On Not Knowing Greek', in *The Common Reader* (New York, 1925), p. 24. See also Sandra M. Gilbert and Susan Gubar, *The Madwoman in the Attic* (New Haven, 1979), pp. 133–4, 215, and Mary Jacobus, 'The Question of Language: Men of Maxims and *The Mill on the Floss*', *Critical Inquiry*, 7 (1981), pp. 207–22. Significantly, in *The Mill on the Floss* (1860; reprinted Boston, 1961), Eliot praises 'the mother tongue of our imagination, the language that is laden with all the subtle inextricable associations the fleeting hours of our childhood left behind them', p. 38.

14. Christina Stead, *The Man Who Loved Children* (1940; reprinted New York, 1966), p. 360.

15. Edith Wharton, 'Xingu', in *Xingu* (New York, 1916).

16. Renée Vivien's volumes include the novel *Une Femme m'apparut* (1904), and the verse collection *A l'heure des mains jointes* (1906), which have been reprinted recently by The Naiad Press as *A Woman Appeared to Me*, trans. Jeannette H. Foster (Reno, Nev., 1976), and *At the Sweet Hour of Hand in Hand*, trans. Sandia Belgrade (Reno, Nev., 1979). See also Susan Gubar, 'Sapphistries', *Signs*, 10 (1984), pp. 43–62.

17. See Susan Sniader Lanser, 'Speaking in Tongues: *Ladies Almanack* and the Language of Celebration', *Frontiers*, 4 (Autumn 1979), 3, pp. 39–46; also Carolyn Allen, ' "Dressing the Unknowable in the Garments of the Known": The Style of Djuna Barnes's *Nightwood*', in Douglas Buttiuff and Edmund L. Epstein (eds), *Women's Language and Style, Studies in Contemporary Language* (Akron, Ohio, 1976), no. 1, pp. 106–18.

18. Gertrude Stein, 'Tender Buttons', in Carl Van Vechten (ed.), *Selected Writings of Gertrude Stein* (1914; reprinted New York, 1962), p. 496.

19. Stein, 'The Autobiography of Alice B. Toklas', in *Selected Writings of Gertrude Stein*, p. 66. See Catharine Stimpson, 'The Mind, the Body and Gertrude Stein', *Critical Inquiry*, 3 (1977), pp. 491–6, and Elizabeth Fifer, 'Is Flesh Advisable? The Interior Theatre of Gertrude Stein', *Signs*, 4 (1979), pp. 472–83.

20. William Carlos Williams, 'The Work of Gertrude Stein', in *Selected Essays of William Carlos Williams* (New York, 1954), p. 116.

21. Zora Neale Hurston's Janie is nicknamed 'Alphabet' in *Their Eyes Were Watching God* (1937; reprinted Urbana, Ill., 1979), p. 21; Elinor Wylie, 'Dedication', in *Collected Poems* (New York, 1932), pp. 109–10.

22. Robert Duncan, 'The H. D. Book, Part Two: Nights and Days, Chapter 9', *Chicago Review*, 30 (Winter 1979), 3, p. 88.

23. H. D. describes her vision of 'the writing on the wall' in *Tribute to Freud* (1945–6; reprinted New York, 1974), pp. 44–56; her alchemical redefinition of words appears in *Tribute to the Angels*, the middle book of *Trilogy* (1944; reprinted New York, 1973), pp. 63, 71, 75; revisionary spellings also appear in H.D.'s *Hermetic Definition* (New York, 1972), pp. 12, 14, 36. See also Susan Gubar, 'The Echoing Spell of H. D.'s *Trilogy*, in Sandra M. Gilbert and Susan Gubar (eds), *Shakespeare's Sisters: Feminist Essays on Women Poets* (Bloomington, 1979), pp. 200–218.

24. Virginia Woolf, *The Voyage Out* (New York, 1920), p. 326.

25. Virginia Woolf, *Mrs Dalloway* (New York, 1925), pp. 29–32; *Between the Acts* (New York, 1941), p. 212.

26. Virginia Woolf, *Night and Day* (New York, 1919), p. 300.

27. Woolf, *Mrs Dalloway*, p. 122.

28. Virginia Woolf, *Orlando* (New York, 1928, p. 282); *The Years* (New York, 1937), p. 429.

29. Virginia Woolf, *Jacob's Room* (New York, 1978), p. 67.

30. Willa Cather, *The Song of the Lark* (1915; reprinted Lincoln, Neb., 1978), p. 301.

31. Willa Cather, *Death Comes for the Archbishop* (1927; reprinted New York, 1971), pp. 125–8.

32. Wallace Stevens, 'The Idea of Order at Key West', in *The Collected Poems of Wallace Stevens* (New York, 1955), p. 130.

33. Ong, *Fighting for Life*, p. 37.

34. Henry David Thoreau, 'Reading', in *Walden and Selected Essays* (1854; reprinted New York, 1973), p. 95.

35. Ezra Pound, *The ABC of Reading* (1934; reprinted New York, 1960), p. 101; our italics.

36. See Ong, *The Presence of the Word*, pp. 250–55.

37. Harold Bloom, *The Anxiety of Influence* (New York, 1973), passim.

38. Alfred, Lord Tennyson, 'Merlin and Vivien', in Jerome H. Buckley (ed.), *Poems of Tennyson* (Boston, 1958), p. 381. We are grateful to Elliot Gilbert for bringing this passage to our attention; for a different but related analysis of its implications see his 'The Female King: Tennyson's Arthurian Apocalypse', *PLMA*, 98 (1983), pp. 863–78.

39. 'Manifesto: The Revolution of the Word', in Eugene Jolas (ed.), *Transition Workshop* (New York, 1949), p. 174.

40. Hélène Cixous, 'The Laugh of the Medusa', in Elaine Marks and Isabelle de Courtivron (eds), *New French Feminisms* (Amherst, Mass., 1980), p. 256.

41. Joyce, *Ulysses*, p. 416.

42. Geoffrey Hartman, *Saving the Text: Literature, Derrida, Philosophy* (Baltimore, 1981), pp. 9, 24; our italics.

43. Christiane Olivier, *Les Enfants de Jocaste* (Paris, 1980), p. 143; translated by Elyse Bankley, to whom we are grateful for calling this passage to our attention.

44. Ong, *Fighting for Life*, p. 36.

45. Anika Lemaire, *Jacques Lacan*, trans. David Macey (London, 1977), pp. 88–9.

46. Sigmund Freud, *Beyond the Pleasure Principle* (1920; reprinted New York, 1963), especially pp. 32–36.

47. Bruno Bettleheim, *Symbolic Wounds* (Glencoe, Ill., 1954), p. 20.

48. Cited by Bettleheim, p. 22, but see also Gregory Zilboorg, 'Masculine and Feminine', *Psychiatry*, 7 (1944), pp. 257–96, and Ralph Greenson, 'The Mother Tongue and the Mother', *International Journal of Psychoanalysis*, 31 (1950), p. 22.

49. Susan Lurie, 'Pornography and the Dread of Women: The Male Dilemma', in Laura Lederer (ed.), *Take Back the Night* (New York, 1980), pp. 159–78, and Susan Lurie, 'The Construction of the "Castrated Woman" in Psychoanalysis and Cinema', *Discourse*, 4 (Winter 1981–2), p. 53.

50. Erich Neumann, *The Great Mother*, trans. Ralph Manheim (Princeton, 1963), p. 168.

51. Susan Griffin, 'Thoughts on Writing', in Janet Sternburg (ed.), *The Writer On Her Work* (New York, 1980), p. 110.

52. Maria Teresa León, *Memoria de la melancolia* (Barcelona, 1977), p. 308.

7 Hélène Cixous, 'Sorties: Out and Out: Attacks/Ways Out/Forays'

(From *The Newly Born Woman*, trans. Betsy Wing (Minneapolis and Manchester, 1986), pp. 63–4, 83–8, 91–7. *The Newly Born Woman* was first published as *La Jeune née*, Paris, 1975.)

Summary

'Where is she?' To what place has the feminine been allocated in the history of Western patriarchal thought? How has sexual difference – the relation of women to men and of femininity to masculinity – been conceived? What is the association between gendered or culturally constituted sexual identities and anatomical sexuality? Can we distinguish between femaleness and femininity, maleness and masculinity? If we can, what are the consequences for the relationship between sexuality and textuality?

All of these questions relate to a recurrent concern of Cixous's work in general: namely, the connections between the female body and feminine writing or *écriture féminine*. In the following extracts from her long philosophic-al-poetical-autobiographical essay 'Sorties', these issues are channelled through an exploration of the possible 'ways out', or *sorties*, for women from their culturally marginal position.

The essay begins by investigating the hierarchical oppositions which have structured the history of Western philosophy – a history in which women have traditionally been placed on the side of negativity, passivity, power-lessness. The alienation of women from their bisexually charged bodily selves is identified as the most damaging effect of the subjection of the feminine to a masculine order, for what is also repressed is women's capacity for endless and boundless sexual pleasure, or *jouissance*, which is seen to arise from their recognition of the (masculine) other within themselves. 'Sorties' suggests that the way for women not only to break from but to un-do their cultural repression is to begin writing their bodies, since it is in *écriture féminine* that women are at once able to reclaim the specificity of their sex, to affirm difference, and to challenge 'the discourse controlled by the phallus'.

Thus, feminine writing is identified as the liberatory act which resists patriarchal definitions of femininity as lack or negativity, and which will 'change the rules of the old game' by celebrating the affirmative power of a feminine sexual/textual aesthetic of difference. Although this aesthetic presently belongs to women writers, with the exception of some homosexual male writers such as Jean Genêt, or modernists like James Joyce, the essay envisages a utopian future in which the plurality and difference of each person's possible sexual/textual identities will be released.

Notes

1. Cixous, 'Les Comtes de Hoffmann' ('Tales of Hoffmann'), in *Prénoms de personne* (*Nobody's First Names*) (Paris, 1974), p. 112ff.
2. See 'Bisexualité et difference des sexes', *Nouvelle Revue de Psychanalyse*, 7 (Spring 1973).

8   Toril Moi, 'Feminist, Female, Feminine' (Edited extracts from 'Feminist Literary Criticism', in *Modern Literary Theory*, (ed.) Ann Jefferson and David Robey (London, 1986), pp. 204–21.)

Summary

The title of 'Feminist, Female, Feminine' alludes silently to the three categories of nineteenth-century women's writing identified in Elaine Showalter's *A Literature of Their Own*. Moi redefines the terms and then uses them as the basis of a (mild) critique of Showalter's own theoretical position.

In the extract reprinted here it is argued that 'feminist' is a political term, 'female' a biological one, and 'feminine' a cultural definition. The essay calls into question the belief that female experience is the basis of feminism, or in other words that politics is a direct effect of biology. Meanwhile, if 'feminine' specifies a cultural rather than a biological difference, to oppose 'feminine' to 'masculine' in an absolute binary opposition is ultimately to reaffirm an essentialist and patriarchal distinction. It follows that to privilege 'feminine writing' (the *écriture féminine* of French feminism) is to be in perpetual danger of falling into yet another form of biological essentialism.

The essay goes on to develop the argument that 'the feminine' is not an essence but a culturally produced position of marginality in relation to patriarchal society. As a relational position rather than a fact of nature, it is a place from which to conduct a feminist politics committed to change.

Notes

1. Kate Millett, *Sexual Politics* (London, 1971), p. 25.
2. Dale Spender, *Women of Ideas and What Men Have Done to Them* (London, 1982).
3. Sandra M. Gilbert and Susan Gubar, *The Madwoman in the Attic: the Woman Writer and the Nineteenth-Century Literary Imagination* (New Haven, 1979).

4. Rosalind Coward, 'Are Women's Novels Feminist Novels?', *The New Feminist Criticism*, (ed.) Elaine Showalter (London, 1986), p. 230.

5. For a discussion of such political differences within American feminism, see Hester Eisenstein, *Contemporary Feminist Thought* (London, 1984).

6. Coward, 'Are Women's Novels Feminist Novels?', p. 237.

7. Mary Ellmann, *Thinking About Women* (New York, 1968); Penny Boumelha, *Thomas Hardy and Women: Sexual Ideology and Narrative Form* (Brighton, 1982).

8. Hélène Cixous and Catherine Clément, *The Newly Born Woman*, trans. Betsy Wing (Minneapolis and Manchester, 1986), p. 64.

9. Verena Andermatt Conley, in her book on Cixous, would certainly disagree: see *Hélène Cixous: Writing the Feminine* (Lincoln, Neb. and London, 1984). For a discussion of some of her views, see also Toril Moi, *Sexual/Textual Politics: Feminist Literary Theory* (London, 1985), pp. 123–6.

10. Meaning in Derrida's theory is always plural, unfixed, in 'play'.

11. Julia Kristeva, *Revolution in Poetic Language* (New York, 1984). For Lacan and the symbolic order, see Elizabeth Wright, *Psychoanalytic Criticism: Theory in Practice* (London, 1984); Moi, *Sexual/Textual Politics*; and Terry Eagleton, *Literary Theory: An Introduction* (Oxford, 1983); as well as Anika Lemaire, *Jacques Lacan* (London, 1977), which for me remains the most serious and wide-ranging introduction to Lacan. (See also the Glossary. Eds.)

12. For a necessary critique of the political implications of Kristeva's theories at this point, see Moi, *Sexual/Textual Politics*, pp. 150–73.

13. Elaine Showalter, *A Literature of Their Own: British Women Novelists from Brontë to Lessing* (Princeton, 1977).

9   Shoshana Felman, 'Woman and Madness: the Critical Phallacy'
(From *Diacritics*, 5 (1975), pp. 2–10.)

Summary

Felman's essay was originally written as a review of three books, *Women and Madness* by Phyllis Chesler, Luce Irigaray's *Speculum de l'autre femme* and a new edition of Balzac's short story, *Adieu*. Chesler treats women's madness as either an effect or a refusal of the role allotted to women in our culture. Chesler's book reproduces the voices of women. Irigaray is also critical of the place of silence allocated to women, but she undertakes to speak *for* women in her own voice, and so casts doubt on her own undertaking. Chesler, without a theory, leaves women in the position of victims: Irigaray, on the other hand, offers a theoretical analysis, but fails to analyse the position from which she herself speaks. *Adieu*, meanwhile, is a story about a woman, madness and silence. Just as the institution of literary criticism systematically omits women from its concerns, silences them, so the modern commentators on *Adieu* excise the role of the woman in the story. Balzac's 'realism' is thus seen to concern itself with men and with reason: women and madness are located outside or beyond the 'real' world. Felman goes on to offer an alternative, feminist reading of *Adieu*. For the heroine reason and 'femininity' prove to be synonymous, in that what constitutes sanity is the recognition of man, of her lover, giving him back his identity, his own reflection, his interpretation of the world. But the restoration of her reason brings about the death of both the woman and her lover, and the end of the story. The fiction thus both depicts and aligns itself with a realm beyond 'realism', beyond both reason and masculinity, and beyond the limits of representation.

Notes

1. Phyllis Chesler, *Women and Madness* (New York, 1973), p. xxii.

2. Ibid., pp. 68–9.

3. Ibid., p. 138.

4. Ibid., p. 56.

5. Ibid., p. xxiii.

6. Luce Irigaray, *Speculum de l'autre femme* (Paris, 1974).

7. Freud has thus pronounced his famous verdict on women: 'Anatomy is destiny'. But this is precisely the focus of the feminist contestation.

8. Honoré de Balzac, *Adieu [Colonel Chabert, suivi de El Verdugo, Adieu, et du Requisitionnaire]*. Edited and annotated by Philippe Berthier. Preface by Pierre Gascan (Paris, 1974).

9. Balzac, *Adieu*, p. 9. Quotations from the *Préface*, the 'Notice' and from Balzac's text are my translations; in all quoted passages, italics mine unless otherwise indicated.

10. Ibid., pp. 10–11.

11. Ibid., p. 12.

12. Ibid., p. 266.

13. Ibid., p. 265.

14. Ibid., pp. 11–12.

15. Ibid., pp. 14–17.

16. Ibid., p. 17.

17. Ibid., p. 16.

18. Louis Althusser, *Lire le Capital*, 1 (Paris, 1968), pp. 26–8 (translation mine; Althusser's italics).

19. Balzac, *Adieu*, pp. 148, 156, 159, 164.

20. Ibid., p. 164.

21. Ibid., p. 196.

22. Ibid., p. 150.

23. Ibid., pp. 208–9.

24. Ibid., pp. 147, 151.

25. Ibid., p. 157.

26. Ibid., p. 202.

27. Ibid., p. 208.

28. Ibid., p. 159.

29. Ibid., p. 180.

30. Ibid., p. 197.

31. Michel Foucault, *Histoire de la folie à l'âge classique* (Paris, 1972), p. 540 (translation mine).

32. Balzac, *Adieu*, pp. 200–1.

33. Ibid., p. 201.

34. Ibid., p. 207.

35. Ibid., p. 163.

36. Ibid., p. 200.

37. Ibid., pp. 209–10.

38. This suicidal murder is, in fact, a repetition, not only of Philippe's military logic and his attitude throughout the war scene, but also of a specific previous moment in his relationship with Stéphanie. Well before the story's end, Philippe had already been on the point of killing Stéphanie, and himself with her, having, in a moment of despair, given up the hope of her ever recognising him. The doctor, seeing through Philippe's intentions, had then saved his niece with a perspicacious lie, playing precisely on the specular illusion of her proper name: ' "You do not know then," went on the doctor coldly, hiding his horror, "that last night in her sleep she said, 'Philippe!' ". "She named me," cried the baron, letting his pistols drop' (Balzac, *Adieu*, p. 206).

39. Here again, the ambiguous logic of the 'saviour,' in its tragic and heroic narcissism, is prefigured by the war scene. Convinced of his good reason, Philippe, characteristically, *imposes* it, by force, on others, so as to 'save' them; but ironically and paradoxically, he always saves them *in spite of* themselves: ' "Let us save her in spite of herself!" cried Philippe, sweeping up the countess' (Balzac, *Adieu*, p. 182).

40. Balzac, *Adieu*, p. 8.

10   Jane Moore, 'Promises, Promises: The Fictional Philosophy in Mary Wollstonecraft's *Vindication of the Rights of Woman*' (First given at the Cardiff Critical Theory Seminar, November 1987.)

Summary

Do contemporary theories of language and subjectivity help or hinder the feminist reader of past texts? That is, does reading from the inescapable perspective of the twentieth century necessarily impose present-day theoretical presuppositions on to a different past, thereby eliminating historical difference? In the light of these questions the essay explores the consequences of using a deconstructive methodology to analyse Mary Wollstonecraft's *Vindication of the Rights of Woman*.

The essay locates oppositions of genre and, correspondingly, of gender at work in the *Vindication*: the literary is associated with the feminine, while reason and a plain-speaking philosophical prose is aligned with masculinity. Deconstruction, it is argued, enables the reader to undo these oppositions and to reveal their radical instability. On the other hand the essay suggests that if the radical edge of the *Vindication*'s project to persuade women to speak a 'male' language of reason is to be brought fully into view, then the twentieth-century deconstructive reader needs to employ simultaneously another focus: this is history.

To situate an eighteenth-century taxonomy of genre and gender in its difference from twentieth-century conceptions of the relationship between sex and text, the essay suggests, is not to fix past meanings and past oppositions, which would reinvest them with the authority that deconstruction usefully denies; nor is it to give way to the indefinite sliding of meanings beyond all historical and cultural limits, as deconstruction proposes. Rather, it is to expose the historical instability and cultural constitution of genre and gender categories, without simultaneously collapsing past and present. It is in consequence to reveal the past and the present as moments in a continuous history of change.

Notes

1. Gillian Beer, 'Representing Women: Re-presenting the Past', pp. 63–80 above.

2. Ibid., p. 67 above.

3. Colin MacCabe, 'Foreword' to Gayatri Chakravorty Spivak, *In Other Worlds: Essays in Cultural Politics* (New York and London, 1987), p. xi; Christopher Norris, *Deconstruction: Theory and Practice* (London and New York, 1982), p. 92.

4. Norris, *Deconstruction*, p. 98.

5. Hélène Cixous, 'Sorties: Out and Out: Attacks/Ways Out/Forays', p. 101 above; Sandra M. Gilbert and Susan Gubar, 'Sexual Linguistics: Gender, Language, Sexuality', p. 81 above.

6. Cixous, 'Sorties', p. 101 above. Cixous not only identifies the binarism structuring Western patriarchal thought: she actively challenges it. 'Sorties' argues that the movement which makes oppositions possible also undoes them: 'the movement whereby each opposition is set up to make sense is the movement through which the couple is destroyed. A universal battlefield. Each time, a war is let loose. Death is always at work', p. 102 above. What Cixous locates here is the textual movement of differance. That is, differance as distinct from difference: unlike difference, differance invokes both difference and deferral. As such it introduces the possibility that meanings are not static, their binarism is not fixed. Rather, each term belonging to an opposition ceaselessly invades the other so that the moment in which the different meanings of words is made possible is also the moment in which that difference is unmade: difference slides into differance.

Cixous's work at this point is much influenced by Jacques Derrida's critique of the static logic of binary thought, as well as by his argument that meanings are produced not in the field of difference but on the textual battleground of differance. The implications that the notion of differance has for how we understand the production of genre difference are discussed in Derrida's essay 'The Law of Genre', *Glyph* 7 (1980), pp. 202–232. This essay argues that the system of generic classification, like all seemingly self-evident closed systems, is opened out by the impossibility of the classifying mark that makes generic taxonomy possible. On another level the problem of the impossibility of generic taxonomy becomes one of metaphor, or more precisely, one of metaphor in philosophy. This problematic is addressed by Derrida's essay 'The White Mythology', in *Margins of Philosophy*, trans. Alan Bass (Brighton, 1982), pp. 207–29. Here it is argued, as Michael Ryan puts it, that 'because all language is metaphoric (a sign substituted for a thing), no metametaphoric description of language is possible that escapes infinite regress.' (*Marxism and Deconstruction: A Critical Articulation* (Baltimore and London, 1982), p. 20). One of the implications of the infinite regress of metaphor is that it is no longer possible to believe in the separate existence of literary and philosophical modes of language. In Cixous's 'Sorties', however, this deconstructive line of thought is not maintained. Philosophical and literary modes are not collapsed; on the contrary their difference is maintained in a metaphor of sexual difference: each discursive mode is associated respectively with masculine and feminine forms of writing.

7. Hélène Cixous, *The Newly Born Woman*, p. 65 above.

8. Cixous, 'Sorties', p. 111 above.

9. Mary Wollstonecraft, *Vindication of the Rights of Woman* (London, 1792); Miriam Brody (ed.), Harmondsworth, 1986. Parenthetical notation refers to page numbers in this edition.

10. Mary Jacobus, 'The Difference of View', p. 54 above.

11. John Locke, *Essay Concerning Human Understanding* (London, 1690; reprinted London and New York, 1961), pp. 105–6. Cited in Paul de Man, 'The Epistemology of Metaphor', *Critical Inquiry*, 5 (1978), 13–30, p. 15.

12. Jean-Jacques Rousseau; cited in Wollstonecraft's *Vindication*, p. 183.

13. For more information about male and female reformers of women's education during the eighteenth century see Alice Browne, *The Eighteenth Century Feminist Mind* (Brighton, 1987); especially pp. 102–21.

14. John Bennett, *Letters to a Young Lady*, 2nd edn, 2 vols. (London, 1795), vol. 1, pp. 168–9. Cited in Browne, *The Eighteenth Century Feminist Mind*, pp. 123–4.

15. See Browne, *The Eighteenth Century Feminist Mind*, p. 105.

16. Sarah Scott, *Millenium Hall* (London, 1762; reprinted London, 1986).

17. Mary Hays, *Memoirs of Emma Courtney* (London, 1796; reprinted London, 1987); Mrs Opie, *Adeline Mowbray: or, The Mother and Daughter* (London, 1804; reprinted London, 1986).

18. I have drawn here on an observation made by Kelvin Everest in his reading of William Godwin's *Enquiry Concerning Political Justice*. See Kelvin Everest and Gavin Edwards, 'William Godwin's "*Caleb Williams*": Truth and "*Things As They Are*"', in *1789: Reading Writing Revolution: Proceedings of the Essex Conference on the Sociology of Literature* (ed.) Francis Barker et al., Colchester, 1982, 129–59, p. 134.

19. Miriam Brody, 'Introduction' to Wollstonecraft's *Vindication*, p. 41.

20. I have placed the terms 'philosophy' and 'literature' within cautionary brackets and inverted commas in order to draw attention to the impossibility of fixing their meanings. I wish to stress that, like all categories of knowledge which pretend to be self-enclosed, they cannot avoid the deconstructive operations of differance; but I want also to demarcate philosophy from literature so as to retain the historical specificity of their (separate) meanings.

I do not continue the practice of framing the terms philosophy and literature in inverted commas, except where it seems me that it may be useful to (re)emphasise that these terms are always under erasure, although, of course, not fully erased.

21. Kelvin Everest has argued that late eighteenth-century radicals invoked the notion of 'truth' from the perspective of becoming, rather than of being: thus the emphasis is not on what is, but on what might be. See Everest and Edwards, 'William Godwin's *"Caleb Williams"*: Truth and *"Things As They Are"*', pp. 134–5. In the light of Everest's observations it should be remarked that it may well be possible to produce a non-contradictory reading of the *Vindication*'s inscription of reason-as-truth in the future tense.

22. Quoted in Mary Wilson Carpenter, 'Sibylline Apocalyptics: Mary Wollstonecraft's *Vindication of the Rights of Woman* and Job's Mother's Womb', *Literature and History*, 12 (1986), 215–28, p. 227, n. 9.

23. Miriam Brody, 'Introduction' to Wollstonecraft's *Vindication*, p. 41. For counter-readings of the *Vindication* which, unlike Brody's and Wardle's, do not suggest that a rationalist philosophy is that text's only discourse, see Mary Wilson Carpenter, 'Sibylline Apocalyptics'. This essay focuses on the *Vindication*'s 'prophetic' discourses and suggests that the text's (re)inscription of the *Book of Job* invokes a 'suppressed female plot of origin', p. 22. See also Cora Kaplan, 'Wild Nights: Pleasure/Sexuality/Feminism', in *Sea Changes: Essays on Culture and Feminism* (London, 1986), pp. 31–56. Kaplan suggests that rather than silencing female sexuality, as it aims to do, the *Vindication* is suffused with and proliferates the sexual. Finally, it is another woman, Mary Poovey, who has noted that the language of the *Vindication* becomes increasingly obscure, even 'purposefully vague', when Wollstonecraft confronts women's sexuality. See Poovey, *The Proper Lady and the Woman Writer: Ideology as Style in the Works of Mary Wollstonecraft, Mary Shelley, and Jane Austen* (Chicago, 1984), pp. 77–80.

24. Mary Wollstonecraft, *The Wrongs of Woman: or, Maria* (London, 1789); reprinted together with *Mary, A Fiction* (ed.) Gary Kelly, Oxford, 1984. All references are to page numbers in this edition.

Another edition of *The Wrongs of Woman* which is commonly cited is *Maria: or, The Wrongs of Woman* (ed.) Moira Ferguson (New York, 1975). It is interesting to note that the American and British editions have differently ordered titles. The insertion of 'Maria' in front of 'The Wrongs of Woman' in the title of the American edition could, perhaps, be seen to bear out an American concern for the politics of the individual over those of the collective. Furthermore, it might be said that privileging the individual 'Maria' over the 'Wrongs' that women suffer correspondingly prioritises the text's 'literary' content, and thus subordinates its 'philosophical' concerns. All of these reversals contradict what the text itself stresses: namely, that 'Woman' refers to the female sex in general: '. . . the history ought rather to be considered, as of woman, than of an individual', 'Author's Preface', p. 73.

25. Wollstonecraft, *The Wrongs of Woman*, p. 73.

26. Ryan, *Marxism and Deconstruction*, p. 83.

27. 'Negative affirmation': the phrase is Michael Ryan's.

28. Marilyn Butler, *Romantics, Rebels and Reactionaries: English Literature and its Background 1760–1830* (Oxford, 1981), p. 55.

29. Mary Robinson, *The False Friend*, 4 vols. (London, 1799), vol. 2, p. 77. Quoted in Alice Browne, *The Eighteenth Century Feminist Mind*, p. 154.

30. Horace Walpole is said to have called Mary Wollstonecraft 'a hyena in petticoats'. This compound metaphor, signifying animality, sexuality and femininity, constructs Wollstonecraft not as a rational being, who has the power to name animals, but as the animal who is named; this is interesting not least because it seems to correspond to Romanticism's desire to fix a tamed and sensuous, rather than sensual, meaning of femininity.

31. Maria Edgeworth, *Belinda* (London, 1801; reprinted London, 1986).

32. This is the argument of Everest's essay, 'William Godwin's "*Caleb Williams*": Truth and "*Things As They Are*"'.

11   Gayatri Chakravorty Spivak, 'Three Women's Texts and a Critique of Imperialism' (From *Critical Inquiry*, 12 (1985), pp. 243–7, 247– 51, 252–61.)

Summary

'Three Women's Texts' raises questions concerning the politics of interpreting nineteenth-century British literature from the perspective of the twentieth century. What has been the impact of feminism on twentieth-century readings of *Jane Eyre*? And is it possible, through attending to the imperialist values in circulation at the moment of textual production, to produce an alternative to previous feminist interpretations of that text – a reading which shows British Imperialism as the price paid for nineteenth-century female individualism? The essay suggests that it is and proposes that only by being historically specific is it possible to recognise the full extent to which nineteenth-century British literature is caught within the history of imperialism, as well as the impossibility in these texts of a fully realised cultural identity for subjects from the Third World.

Notes

1. My notion of the 'wording of a world' upon what must be assumed to be uninscribed earth is a vulgarisation of Martin Heidegger's idea; see 'The Origin of the Work of Art', in *Poetry, Language, Thought*, trans. Albert Hofstadter (New York, 1977), pp. 17–87.

2. See Charlotte Brontë, *Jane Eyre* (New York, 1960); all further references to this work, abbreviated JE, will be included in the text.

3. See Jean Rhys, *Wide Sargasso Sea* (Harmondsworth, 1966); all further references to this work, abbreviated WSS, will be included in the text. And see Mary Shelley, *Frankenstein; or, The Modern Prometheus* (New York, 1965); all further references to this work, abbreviated F, will be included in the text.

4. I have tried to do this in my essay 'Unmaking and Making in *To the Lighthouse*', in Gayatri Chakravorty Spivak, *In Other Worlds: Essays in Cultural Politics* (New York and London, 1987), pp 30–45.

5. As always, I take my formula from Louis Althusser, 'Ideology and Ideological State Apparatuses (Notes towards an Investigation)', in *'Lenin and Philosophy' and Other Essays*, trans. Ben Brewster (New York, 1971), pp. 127–86. For an acute differentiation between the individual and individualism, see V. N. Vološinov, *Marxism and the Philosophy of Language*, trans. Ladislav Matejka and I. R. Titunik, Studies in Language, 1 (New York, 1973), pp. 93–4, 152–3. For a 'straight' analysis of the roots and ramifications of English 'individualism', see C. B. MacPherson, *The Political Theory of Possessive Individualism: Hobbes to Locke* (Oxford, 1962). I am grateful to Jonathan Rée for bringing this book to my attention and for giving a careful reading of all but the very end of the present essay.

6. I am constructing an analogy with Homi Bhabha's powerful notion of 'not-quite/not-white' in his 'Of Mimicry and Man: The Ambiguity of Colonial Discourse', *October*, 28 (Spring 1984), p. 132. I should also add that I use the word 'native' here in reaction to the term 'Third World Woman'. It cannot, of course, apply with equal historical justice to both the West Indian and the Indian contexts nor to contexts of imperialism by transportation.

7. See Roberto Fernández Retamar, 'Caliban: Notes towards a Discussion of Culture in Our America', trans. Lynn Garafola, David Arthur McMurray, and Robert Márquez, *Massachusetts Review*, 15 (Winter–Spring 1974), pp. 7–72; all further references to this work, abbreviated 'C', will be included in the text.

8. See José Enrique Rodó, *Ariel* (ed.) Gordon Brotherston (Cambridge, 1967).

9. For an elaboration of 'an inaccessible blankness circumscribed by an interpretable text', see my 'Can the Subaltern Speak?', in Cary Nelson and Lawrence Grossberg (eds), *Marxism and the Interpretation of Culture*, Urbana, Ill., 1988, pp. 271–313.

10. See Elizabeth Fox-Genovese, 'Placing Women's History in History', *New Left Review*, 133 (May–June 1982), pp. 5–29.

11. Rudolph Ackermann, *The Repository of Arts, Literature, Commerce, Manufactures, Fashions, and Politics* (London, 1823), p. 310.

12. See Terry Eagleton, *Myths of Power: A Marxist Study of the Brontës* (London, 1975); this is one of the general presuppositions of his book.

13. See Sandra M. Gilbert and Susan Gubar, *The Madwoman in the Attic: The Woman Writer and the Nineteenth-Century Literary Imagination* (New Haven, Conn., 1979), pp. 360–2.

14. Immanuel Kant, *Critique of Practical Reason*, in *The Critique of Pure Reason, The Critique of Practical Reason and Other Ethical Treatises, The Critique of Judgement*, trans. J. M. D. Meiklejohn et al. (Chicago, 1952), pp. 326, 328.

15. I have tried to justify the reduction of sociohistorical problems to formulas or propositions in my essay 'Can the Subaltern Speak?' The 'travesty' I speak of does not befall the Kantian ethic in its purity as an

accident but rather exists within its lineaments as a possible supplement. On the register of the human being as child rather than heathen, my formula can be found, for example, in 'What is Enlightenment?' in Kant, *Foundations of the Metaphysics of Morals, What is Englightenment? and a Passage from The Metaphysics of Morals*, trans. and (ed.) Lewis White Beck (Chicago, 1950). I have profited from discussing Kant with Jonathan Rée.

16. Jean Rhys, in an interview with Elizabeth Vreeland, quoted in Nancy Harrison, *An Introduction to the Writing Practice of Jean Rhys: The Novel as Women's Text* (Rutherford, N.J., forthcoming). This is an excellent study of Rhys.

17. See Louise Vinge, *The Narcissus Theme in Western European Literature up to the Early Nineteenth Century*, trans. Robert Dewsnap et al. (Lund, 1967), chapter 5.

18. For a detailed study of this text, see John Brenkman, 'Narcissus in the Text', *Georgia Review*, 30 (Summer 1976), pp. 293–327.

19. This is the main argument of my 'Can the Subaltern Speak?'.

20. See Barbara Johnson, 'My Monster/My Self', *Diacritics*, 12 (Summer 1982), pp. 2–10.

21. See George Levine, *The Realistic Imagination: English Fiction from Frankenstein to Lady Chatterly* (Chicago, 1981), pp. 23–35.

22. Consult the publications of the Feminist International Network for the best overview of the current debate on reproductive technology.

23. For the male fetish, see Sigmund Freud, 'Fetishism', *The Standard Edition of the Complete Psychological Works of Sigmund Freud* (ed.) and trans. James Strachey et al., 24 vols. (London, 1953–74), 21, pp. 152–7. For a more 'serious' Freudian study of *Frankenstein*, see Mary Jacobus, 'Is There a Woman in This Text?', *New Literary History*, 14 (Autumn 1982), pp. 117–41. My 'fantasy' would of course be disproved by the 'fact' that it is more difficult for a woman to assume the position of fetishist than for a man; see Mary Ann Doane, 'Film and the Masquerade: Theorising the Female Spectator', *Screen*, 23 (1982), 3–4, pp. 74–87.

24. Kant, *Critique of Judgement*, trans. J. H. Bernard (New York, 1951), p. 39.

25. See [Constantin François de Volney], *The Ruins: or, Meditations on the Revolution of Empires* (trans. pub., London, 1811). Johannes Fabian has shown us the manipulation of time in 'new' secular histories of a similar kind; see *Time and the Other: How Anthropology Makes Its Object* (New York, 1983). See also Eric R. Wolf, *Europe and the People without History* (Berkeley and Los Angeles, 1982), and Peter Worsley, *The Third World*, 2nd edn. (Chicago, 1973); I am grateful to Dennis Dworkin for bringing the latter book to my attention. The most striking ignoring of the monster's education through Volney is in Gilbert's otherwise brilliant 'Horror's Twin: Mary Shelley's Monstrous Eve', *Feminist Studies*, 4 (June 1980), pp. 48–73. Gilbert's essay reflects the absence of race-determinations in a certain sort of feminism. Her present work has most convincingly filled in this gap; see, for example, her recent piece on H. Rider Haggard's *She* ('Rider Haggard's Heart of Darkness', *Partisan Review*, 50 (1983), pp. 444–53.

26. 'A letter is always and a priori intercepted, . . . the "subjects" are

neither the senders nor the receivers of messages . . . The letter is constituted
. . . by its interception' (Jacques Derrida, 'Discussion', after Claude Rabant,
'Il n'a aucune chance de l'entendre', in René Major (ed.), *Affranchissement:
Du transfert et de la lettre* (Paris, 1981), p. 106; my translation). Margaret
Saville is not made to appropriate the reader's 'subject' into the signature
of her own 'individuality'.

27. The most striking 'internal evidence' is the admission in the 'Author's
Introduction' that, after dreaming of the yet-unnamed Victor Frankenstein
figure and being terrified (through, yet not quite through, him) by the
monster in a scene that she later reproduced in Frankenstein's story, Shelley
began her tale 'on the morrow . . . with the words "It was on a dreary
night of November"' (F, p. xi). Those are the opening words of chapter 5
of the finished book, where Frankenstein begins to recount the actual
making of his monster (see F, p. 56).

12 Julia Kristeva, 'Women's Time' (Extract from 'Women's Time', *Signs*, 7 (1981), pp. 13–35, trans. Alice Jardine and Harry Blake.)

Summary

'Women's Time' begins by arguing that people can be thought of as
belonging to national units on the one hand, or to transnational or
international groupings on the other (young people, for instance, or women).
These distinct ways of classifying people correspond to two ways of thinking
about time, one historical and linear, and the other cyclical (repetitive,
according to the rhythms of nature) or monumental (eternal, time-less,
mythic). The second of these ways of thinking, the cyclical or monumental,
has been associated specifically with women, but this association, common
to many cultures and especially to mystical ones, is not fundamentally
incompatible with masculine values.

The extract reprinted here begins by differentiating between the traditional form of feminism, which seeks a place and rights for women within
the nation and linear history, and a more recent phase which locates the
feminist struggle primarily within sexual relations. This second phase
emphasises the difference between men and women, and draws on psychoanalysis as the main existing theory of sexual difference. But Kristeva's own
version of Freud is profoundly modified by Lacan, so that the fear of
castration is precisely symbolic – the fear of the loss of presence, totality,
pleasure, which is consequent upon the acquisition of language as separation
from nature. This separation, the entry into the symbolic order, a world of
difference and so of power and meaning, is the sociosymbolic contract which
is the basis of identity, and it is common to both women and men.

But its implications have been different for each. The place in the symbolic
order allotted to women has been an unequal, frustrating one, their task
merely to perpetuate the contract by transmitting it to the next generation.
One reaction to this is the construction of a revolutionary countersociety,
but the essay draws attention to the dangers which ensue when power

changes hands without changing its nature. Another reaction has been the quest for creativity through the idealisation of the experience of motherhood, or through the production of a specifically women's writing, *écriture féminine*. The essay identifies both these reactions as 'religious', a mythologising of Woman. In their place it proposes a third phase for feminism: instead of stressing the single difference between men and women, we might affirm the sociosymbolic internalisation of difference itself as the foundation of identity. The affirmation of difference as the basis of subjectivity would release at once the individuality and the multiplicity of each person's possible identities.

Notes

1. See D. Desanti, 'L'Autre Sexe des bolcheviks,' *Tel quel* 76 (1978); Julia Kristeva, *On Chinese Women*, trans. Anita Barrows (New York, 1977).

2. See Arthur Hertzberg, *The French Enlightenment and the Jews* (New York, 1968); B. Blumenkranz and A. Seboul (eds), *Les Juifs et la révolution française* (Paris, 1976).

3. In a section of the article which precedes the extract reprinted here Kristeva says, 'I think that the apparent coherence which the term "woman" assumes in contemporary ideology, apart from its "mass" or "shock" effect for activist purposes, essentially has the negative effect of effacing the differences among the diverse functions or structures which operate beneath this word.' (*Signs*, 7 (1981), p. 18.).

4. This work is periodically published in various academic women's journals, one of the most prestigious being *Signs: Journal of Women in Culture and Society*, University of Chicago Press. Also of note are the special issues: 'Ecriture, féminité, féminisme,' *La Revue des sciences humaines*, Lille III (1977), 4; and 'Les Femmes et la philosophie,' *Le Doctrinal de sapience*, Editions Solin 3 (1977).

5. See linguistic research on 'female language': Robin Lakoff, *Language and Women's Place* (New York, 1974); Mary R. Key, *Male/Female Language* (Metuchen, N.J., 1973); A. M. Houdebine, 'Les Femmes et la langue', *Tel quel*, 74 (1977), pp. 84–95. The contrast between these 'empirical' investigations of women's 'speech acts' and much of the research in France on the conceptual bases for a 'female language' must be emphasised here. It is somewhat helpful, if ultimately inaccurate, to think of the former as an 'external' study of language and the latter as an 'internal' exploration of the process of signification. For further contrast, see e.g. 'Part II: Contemporary Feminist Thought in France: Translating Difference' in *The Future of Difference*, (eds) Hester Eissenstein and Alice Jardine (Boston, 1980); the 'Introductions' to *New French Feminisms*, (eds) Elaine Marks and Isabelle de Courtivron (Brighton, 1981); and for a very helpful overview of the problem of 'difference and language' in France, see Stephen Heath, 'Difference', *Screen*, 19 (1978), 3, pp. 51–112. – AJ.

6. This is one of the more explicit references to the mass marketing of '*écriture féminine*' in Paris over the last ten years. – AJ.

7. The expression *à leur corps défendant* translates as 'against their will,'

but here the emphasis is on women's bodies: literally, 'against their bodies.' I have retained the former expression in English, partly because of its obvious intertextuality with Susan Brownmiller's *Against Our Will* (New York, 1975). Women are increasingly describing their experience of the violence of the symbolic contract as a form of rape. – AJ.

8. See *On Chinese Women*.

9. See M. A. Macciocchi, *Elements pour une analyse du fascisme* (Paris, 1976); Michèle Mattelart, 'Le Coup d'état au féminin', *Les Temps modernes* (January 1975).

10. See Jacques Lacan, 'Dieu et la jouissance de la femme' in *Encore*, Paris (1975), pp. 61–71, especially p. 68. This seminar has remained a primary critical and polemical focus for multiple tendencies in the French women's movement. For a brief discussion of the seminar in English, see Heath, 'Difference'. – AJ.

11. Again a reference to *écriture féminine* as generically labelled in France over the past few years and not to women's writing in general. – AJ.

Glossary

Note: Words or phrases given in italics are also defined in their alphabetical place in the Glossary.

Althusser, Louis   French structuralist Marxist whose work on *ideology* challenges the humanist assumption that the *individual* is the *author* and guarantor of his or her meanings. A seminal essay is his 'Ideology and Ideological State Apparatuses (Notes towards an Investigation)', in *Lenin and Philosophy and Other Essays*, trans. Ben Brewster (London, 1971), pp. 127–86. For a critical, accessible introduction to his work in the light of subsequent theories of ideology and *discourse* see Diane Macdonell, *Theories of Discourse: An Introduction* (Oxford, 1986).

author   See *individual*

binary opposition(s)   A binary opposition comprises two terms which are classified hierarchically so that the second term is assumed to be derivative from and exterior to the first. For example, nature/culture, logos/pathos, man/woman.

bisexuality   The 'bi' of bisexuality invokes the binary numerology of two. Correspondingly, an oppositional mode of sexual difference is produced. This has the effect of fixing a polarised structure of sexual difference in which the sexes are always-already and forever locked in antithesis.

deconstruction   The uncovering of the trace of otherness within what seems single and self-identical. Deconstruction undoes the hierarchic *binary oppositions* which are no more than an effect of linguistic *difference*.

Derrida, Jacques   Influential French philosopher whose work challenges the basis of the Western philosophical tradition. Derrida's account of language is available in relatively accessible form in *Positions*, trans. Alan Bass (London, 1987). For an introduction to his work see

Christopher Norris, *Derrida* (London, 1987).

desire   See *lack*.

differance   The term differance is a development by *Jacques Derrida* of *Ferdinand de Saussure*'s account of language as a structure of difference. Spelt with an 'a' to distinguish it from *difference*, differance signifies not only 'difference' but also 'deferral'. The idea of deferral resists the closure of meanings which might appear to be the effect of difference, for it involves the belief that signification always delays or displaces pure intelligibility. Differences of meaning are therefore not anchored in concepts: rather those differences slide constantly within the infinite *displacement* and deferral of meaning. In other words, meaning is constructed only by the process of referring to other (absent) meanings, with the consequence that the relatively stable structure of difference slides into and is destabilised by differance.

difference   *Ferdinand de Saussure* proposed that words have no inherent meaning but take on meaning from their difference from other words.

discourse   In the work of *Michel Foucault* a discourse is a knowledge (physics, psychoanalysis, for example) inscribed in a specific vocabulary and sometimes a specific syntax. A particular discourse may be identified by the institution and interests it serves as well as by the *subject* positions it constructs.

displacement   Cited by Freud and later *Lacan* with reference to the potentially unknowable structure of the unconscious, displacement is a term, like *supplement* and *differance*, deployed as a means of preventing the conceptual closure of meaning and fixing of *binary oppositions*.

'*Dora*'   From the feminist point of view, *Dora* is perhaps the most famous of Freud's case histories. In 1900, when she was eighteen, Dora was treated by Freud for hysteria. She left before he had completed his analysis. Her rebellious refusal to continue treatment and the diagnosis of hysteria have been of more than passing interest to recent feminist theory, especially French feminism.

écriture féminine   Feminine (female) writing. French has only one adjective from *femme* (woman), and that is *féminin*.

Consequently, in French the distinction between female (a matter of nature) and feminine (an effect of cultural construction) is a difficult one to make. *Ecriture féminine* is written by/from the (female) body.

Foucault, Michel   French philosopher and historian of ideas. Foucault's recurrent concern is the relation between knowledge and power. See for example *Discipline and Punish: the Birth of the Prison*, trans. Alan Sheridan (London, 1977) and *The History of Sexuality*, vol. 1, trans. Robert Hurley (London, 1979).

ideology   Ideologies are the beliefs, meanings and practices which shape our thoughts and actions. In the work of *Althusser*, from which most of the essays in this volume derive their use of the term, ideology not only defines our understanding of the world, and our position in it, but is the condition of our experience. Althusser's treatment of ideology differs from the common association of ideology with a set of external doctrines that *individuals* knowingly choose or reject, such as a 'Thatcherite' ideology; instead, it is central to his thesis that all *subjects* are *interpellated* by ideology: there is no escaping ideological subjection. Unlike classical Marxism, which approaches ideology as an expression of the determining economic base, thereby suggesting that ideologies are formulated as abstract ideas in the individual's consciousness or mind, Althusser asserts that ideology has a material existence in the State apparatuses (the Church, the family, educational institutions, etc.). These apparatuses constitute the social formation and have ideological effects. Althusser stresses that all ideologies are produced out of struggle. Thus, a dominant ideology, though it may present its beliefs as self-evident, natural and true, is always the result of a struggle with antagonistic ideologies.

imaginary   In the work of *Jacques Lacan* the imaginary is a condition of illusory unity, mastery and plenitude. It is beyond *difference*, and therefore outside (differentiated from) the *symbolic order*.

individual   The concept of the individual (woman, man, child) derives from humanist, commonsense assumptions that the source and guarantor of meaning is the autonomous mind of an individual. In this context the belief that individuals are the authors of meaning, thus consciously controlling and authorising the meanings they produce, has been challenged by poststructuralism, which has called into question the concepts of 'origin', 'truth' and 'individuality'. Roland Barthes, in particular, has proclaimed the death of the author. See 'The Death of the Author', in *Image, Music, Text*, trans. Stephen Heath (London, 1977), pp. 142–8.

interpellation   Interpellation by *ideology* is the universal mechanism by which *individuals* recognise themselves and are recognised as *subjects*. In his 'ISA's' essay *Althusser* argues that it is only in ideology that individuals are constituted as subjects: the process of interpellation by ideology addresses individuals as unique subjects, conferring on them an identity which appears 'obvious'. But this 'obviousness' is itself an ideological effect, 'the elementary ideological effect'. The result is that individuals accept their subject position in the social formation as 'freely chosen', so that they 'work by themselves'.

jouissance   Ecstasy (sexual); coming. Also enjoyment (of rights, property, etc.).

Lacan, Jacques   French psychoanalyst and theorist who reread Freud in the light of *Saussure*'s theory of language. Jane Gallop, *Reading Lacan* (Ithaca, New York, 1985), is excellent but is not addressed to beginners. For an introduction to Lacanian theory see Malcolm Bowie, 'Jacques Lacan', in *Structuralism and Since: From Levi-Strauss to Derrida*, John Sturrock (ed.) (Oxford, 1979), pp. 116–53.

lack   The *subject*, which comes into existence only with the entry into the *symbolic order*, can never be the origin of meaning, but only its (unstable) effect. Its own consequent otherness, its exclusion from the *imaginary*, is the cause of the lack in the subject which initiates desire.

Law of the Father (*nom du père*)   For *Lacan* the primary Other is the symbolic father, whose name guarantees and makes possible the process of signification within the *symbolic order*.

logocentrism   According to *Jacques Derrida*, logocentrism gives independent existence to concepts, which are no more than an effect of linguistic *difference*. Logocentrism makes meaning the origin of language, and finds the guarantee of the truth of an idea outside language – in the mind of God or, more recently, in the subjectivity of the *individual*.

metaphysics From the point of view of *Jacques Derrida*, any claim to truth which resides outside or beyond language is metaphysical. The effort to fix meaning, to arrest its play, depends on the metaphysics of presence, a faith in an essential truth made present in the sign.

other The *subject* is constituted in its encounter with the other: it is in the subject's address to others, and its address by others, that the subject's identity is conferred and confirmed. The relationship between subject and other is characterised by desire and *lack*.

phallocentrism The order of the masculine and the *symbolic*, where masculine sexuality is both privileged and reproduced by a belief in the phallus as primary signifier. Thus, the feminine is subordinated to a masculine order, and woman is placed on the side of negativity and *lack* (of a penis).

phallogocentrism This term brings together the notions of *phallocentrism* and *logocentrism*. Both these terms have been associated, especially by French feminism, with the organisation of sexual difference and language in Western patriarchal cultures.

power In the work of *Michel Foucault* power is defined as a relation. Power is exercised in *discourses* and institutions; it structures the relations of *difference* (of control, or lack of it) between competing discourses and the *subjects* constituted by them. For a useful and accessible analysis of discourse, power and resistance from the perspective of feminist poststructuralism see Chris Weedon, *Feminist Practice and Poststructuralist Theory* (Oxford, 1987); especially chapter 5, pp. 107–35.

problematic Theoretical framework, complete with its own set of problems (and solutions).

real The real in Lacanian theory is part of the triad '*imaginary/symbolic/real*'. The real both breaks the dualism of the *imaginary* and the *symbolic* and introduces the notion of a world of objects and things whose existence precedes and exceeds the *subject*. The only way for the subject to realise this world is from its position in the symbolic order, which gives it the means of naming (of creating the world of things in words). But this task can never be completed, precisely because the real can be known only in language, which always defers it (see *differance*).

Saussure, Ferdinand de Swiss linguist who developed the science of signs in his pioneering *Course in General Linguistics*, published in 1916. Saussure's theory of language is revolutionary in its insistence that language is not a way of labelling things which already exist outside language, but a system of differences with no positive terms, out of which meaning arises.

selfsame In Betsy Wing's translation of Hélène Cixous's 'Sorties', the selfsame is taken from the French word '*propre*' which corresponds to 'ownself'. This suggests property and appropriation as well as proper, appropriate and clean.

semiotic In Julia Kristeva's writing the semiotic is a domain which precedes the *subject*'s entry into the *symbolic order*. It is pre-oedipal, pre-*imaginary*, and characterised by a rhythmic babble, that is, a language which is unformulated in terms of the rules of the symbolic. Although the semiotic is cited as the place of a repressed femininity, it is not inherently female: it is also present in, and challenges, the symbolic. This is evident in moments when language becomes unstable and meanings are ruptured.

sociosymbolic See *symbolic order*.

subject That which acts and speaks, which says 'I'. Because the subject is not the origin but the effect of the meanings it speaks, it can never be fully present to itself in its own utterance. It is thus inevitably split, unfixed, in process.

supplement A supplement is something 'added on', seemingly self-consciously, to a prior term in order to make good an omission within it. Thus, the supplement appears to be exterior and secondary to the primary term it supplements. *Jacques Derrida*, however, has argued against the *metaphysical* logic which fixes the supplement in a subordinate position to a prior term: he suggests that if the supplement is necessary to compensate for the absence it reveals in a prior term, then it is not so much an external extra as a necessary constituent of the term it supplements. See, for example, Derrida's critique of Rousseau's insistence that writing is inferior to and at the same time the supplement of speech, in *Of Grammatology*, trans. Gayatri Chakravorty Spivak (Baltimore, 1976), pp. 141–64, 165–268.

symbolic order   The order of language and culture. It is also the location of *difference*. In *Jacques Lacan*'s reading of Freud, the fear of castration is parallel to the recognition of difference, as the child enters the symbolic order.

Suggestions for Further Reading

Accessible

Beauvoir, Simone de, *The Second Sex* (1949), trans. H. M. Parshley (London, 1972). Influential account of the social construction of woman.

Belsey, Catherine, *The Subject of Tragedy: Identity and Difference in Renaissance Drama* (London and New York, 1985). Poststructuralist analysis of the construction of the gendered subject in fictional and non-fictional texts of the sixteenth and seventeenth centuries.

Bowlby, Rachel, *Just Looking: Consumer Culture in Dreiser, Gissing and Zola* (New York and London, 1985). Looks at department stores as one of the sites for the construction of female desire in the late nineteenth century.

Coward, Rosalind, *Female Desire: Women's Sexuality Today* (London, 1984). Sharp analysis of women in popular culture. Wears its theoretical sophistication lightly.

Doane, Janice and Devon Hodges, *Nostalgia and Sexual Difference: the Resistance to Contemporary Feminism* (New York and London, 1987). The patriarchal use of the past in current anti-feminist writing.

Ellmann, Mary, *Thinking About Women* (1968, London, 1979). Sophisticated and witty exposé of some patriarchal myths.

Jacobus, Mary (ed.), *Women Writing and Writing about Women* (London, 1979). Excellent collection of essays in feminist criticism by Gillian Beer, Elaine Showalter, Cora Kaplan and others.

Kaplan, Cora, *Sea Changes: Essays on Culture and Feminism* (London, 1986). Very readable Marxist and psychoanalytic exploration of the construction of femininity in texts as diverse as Wollstonecraft's *Vindication of the Rights of Woman* and McCullough's *The Thorn Birds*.

Moi, Toril, *Sexual/Textual Politics: Feminist Literary Theory* (London and New York, 1985). Critical account of the state of feminist criticism.

Newton, Judith and Deborah Rosenfelt (eds), *Feminist Criticism and Social Change: Sex, Class and Race in Literature and Criticism* (New York and London, 1985). Collection of essays by British and American Women. The emphasis is on appropriating recent deconstructionist and French feminist theories for a materialist–feminist criticism.

Robinson, Lillian S., *Sex, Class and Culture* (Bloomington, Indiana, 1978 and New York, 1986). Pioneering analysis of a range of cultural signifying practices.

Spender, Dale, *Man Made Language* (London, 1980). How patriarchy silences women.

Weedon, Chris, *Feminist Practice and Poststructuralist Theory* (Oxford, 1987). Clever and convincing case for the feminist appropriation of recent theory.

Woolf, Virginia, *A Room of One's Own* (1929, London, 1977). Still full of critical insights.

More Difficult, but Worth It

Cixous, Hélène and Catherine Clément, *The Newly Born Woman*, trans. Betsy Wing (Minneapolis and Manchester, 1986). Together and separately, Cixous and Clément pose the question of a specifically feminine language.

Conley, Verena Andermatt and William V. Spanos (eds), 'On Feminine Writing: a *Boundary 2* Symposium', *Boundary 2*, xii (1984), 2. Contains fictional and non-fictional work by Cixous, as well as an interview with Derrida about the (non)place of woman.

De Lauretis, Teresa, *Alice Doesn't: Feminism, Semiotics, Cinema* (Bloomington, Indiana, 1984). Sophisticated and elegant poststructuralist analysis.

Gallop, Jane, *Feminism and Psychoanalysis: the Daughter's Seduction* (London, 1982). Lacanian discussion of sexual difference, desire and language.

Jacobus, Mary, *Reading Woman: Essays in Feminist Criticism* (London and New York, 1986). Literary criticism which brings the insights of psychoanalysis to bear in a feminist context, while at the same time bringing a feminist critique to bear on psychoanalysis.

Jardine, Alice, *Gynesis: Configurations of Woman and Modernity* (Ithaca, New York, 1985). Challenging and thought-provoking analysis of the relationship between (French) feminism and (American) postmodernism.

Jardine, Alice and Paul Smith (eds), *Men in Feminism* (New York and London, 1987). Addresses the current controversy over men's increasing involvement with feminist criticism.

Marks, Elaine and Isabelle de Courtivron (eds), *New French Feminisms: An Anthology* (Brighton, 1981). Invaluable. Contains work by over twenty French feminists.

Moi, Toril (ed.), *French Feminist Thought: a Reader* (Oxford, 1987). Valuable collection of essays by Julia Kristeva, Luce Irigaray, Michèle Montrelay and others.

Moi, Toril (ed.), *The Kristeva Reader* (Oxford, 1986). Indispensable for students of Julia Kristeva.

Rose, Jacqueline, *Sexuality in the Field of Vision* (London, 1986). The case for psychoanalysis in theory and critical practice.

Spivak, Gayatri Chakravorty, *In Other Worlds: Essays in Cultural Politics* (New York and London, 1987). Skilled, precise, convincing analyses of literature and cultural difference from a perspective that admits Marxist, feminist, deconstructionist and psychoanalytic theories.

Notes on Contributors

Gillian Beer is Reader in Literature and Narrative at the University of Cambridge and a Fellow of Girton College. Her most recent books are *Darwin's Plots* (London, 1983) and *George Eliot* (Key Women Writers, Brighton, 1986). This study relates George Eliot to the Victorian women's movement.

Catherine Belsey lectures in English at University College Cardiff. She is author of *Critical Practice* (London and New York, 1980); *The Subject of Tragedy: Identity and Difference in Renaissance Drama* (London and New York, 1985); and *John Milton: Language, Gender, Power* (Oxford and New York, 1988).

Hélène Cixous is Professor of English at the University of Paris VIII. Her publications include her doctoral thesis, *The Exile of James Joyce or the Art of Replacement* (New York, 1972), her novel *Angst* (London, 1986) and *The Newly Born Woman* (with Catherine Clément; Minneapolis and Manchester, 1986).

Rosalind Coward teaches Media Studies at Reading University. She is author of *Language and Materialism* (with John Ellis; London, 1977); *Patriarchal Precedents: Sexuality and Social Relations* (London, 1983); and *Female Desire: Women's Sexuality Today* (London, 1984).

Shoshana Felman is Professor of French and Comparative Literature at Yale University. She is the editor of *Literature and Psychoanalysis: the Question of Reading: Otherwise* (Baltimore and London, 1982) and author of *The Literary Speech Act: Don Juan with Austin, or Seduction in Two Languages* (Ithaca, N.Y., 1983); *Writing and Madness: Literature/ Philosophy/Psychoanalysis* (Ithaca, N.Y., 1985); and *Jacques Lacan and the Adventure of Insight: Psychoanalysis in Contemporary Culture* (Cambridge, Mass., 1987).

Sandra M. Gilbert is Professor of English at Princeton University. With Susan Gubar, she has written *The Madwoman in the Attic: the Woman Writer and the Nineteenth-Century Literary Imagination* (New Haven and London, 1979), and edited *Shakespeare's Sisters: Feminist Essays on Women Poets* (Bloomington, Indiana, 1979) and *The Norton Anthology of Literature by Women: the Tradition in English* (New York, 1985).

Susan Gubar is Professor of English at Indiana University. With Sandra M. Gilbert, she is author of *The Madwoman in the Attic* and editor of *Shakespeare's Sisters* and *The Norton Anthology of Literature by Women.*

Mary Jacobus is Professor of English and Women's Studies at Cornell University. She is author of a study of Wordsworth, *Reading Woman: Essays in Feminist Criticism* (New York and London, 1986) and *Romanticism, Writing and Sexual Difference: Essays on The Prelude* (forthcoming), as well as editor of *Women Writing and Writing About Women* (London, 1979).

Julia Kristeva teaches at the University of Paris VII. She is also a practising psychoanalyst. Her books include *About Chinese Women* (London, 1977); *Desire in Language: a Semiotic Approach to Literature and Art* (Oxford and New York, 1980); *Powers of Horror* (New York, 1982); and *Revolution in Poetic Language* (New York, 1984).

Toril Moi is the author of *Sexual/Textual Politics* (London, 1985), and editor of *The Kristeva Reader* (Oxford, 1986) and *French Feminist Thought* (Oxford, 1987). She lives in Oxford.

Jane Moore is the Mima Morgan Scholar at University College Cardiff. She has taught courses in feminist literary criticism, and is currently working on the politics of genre and gender in the late eighteenth century.

Dale Spender divides her time between London and Sydney. Her publications include *Man Made Language* (London 1980 and 1985); *Women of Ideas and What Men Have Done to Them* (London, 1982); *Feminist Theorists* (London and New York, 1983); *There's Always Been a Women's Movement* (London, 1985); *Mothers of the Novel* (London, 1986); and *Writing a New World: Two Centuries of Australian Women Writers* (London, 1988).

Gayatri Chakravorty Spivak is Professor of English at the University of Pittsburgh. She translated and introduced Derrida's *Of Grammatology* (Baltimore and London, 1976). She is author of a study of Yeats and of *In Other Worlds: Essays in Cultural Politics* (New York and London, 1987).

Index